INTRODUCTION

Examination courses in Physical Education and Sport Studies have now become established within the post-16 curriculum and are a very popular and successful part of school, college or higher education.

This new edition has been written to address the change in content and style of the AQA AS Physical Education syllabus which commenced in September 2008.

This Physical Education course is multidisciplinary in nature, covering anatomy and physiology, a small amount of biomechanics, skill acquisition, and contemporary studies including a small amount of comparative studies and historical studies. These subject areas have generated a substantial quantity of specialist literature each with its own specific language. At times you may be overwhelmed by the amount of material covered in such a one year examination course. 'AS Revise PE for AQA' addresses the problem of dealing with copious notes by summarising the content of the subject matter and attempting to explain in simple language what are sometimes complicated concepts or issues. Sample questions are provided at the end of each syllabus section, with answers at the end of the book. The answers will amplify the subject matter and provide clues as to how the exam itself should be approached. A new feature this time is the requirement that the final exam questions on each section of the syllabus shall include an essay type answer. This allows students to express their ability and knowledge in the context of properly written language (prose) with attention to grammar and punctuation.

Materials are presented in a concise and visual approach for effective and efficient revision. Modern terminology, nomenclature and units have been used wherever possible. At the end of the book there is a comprehensive index available for easy reference.

HOW TO USE THIS REVISION GUIDE

The ideal use of this Revision Guide would be to purchase it at the start of the course and relate each of the summary pages to the specific areas of the syllabus as an aide memoire. The inclusion of specific questions and full answers provide a means of self-testing. Don't be tempted to find out the answers before attempting a question.

In reality, whole examination questions contain a much broader content than those given in this guide. Examiners will attempt to examine more than one small area of the syllabus within the context of one full question and therefore it is important that you revise all aspects of your syllabus.

The main use of the Revision Guide should be during the final revision period leading up to your examinations, as it should help you to understand and apply concepts i.e. link summary content with examination question.

The aim of this Student Guide is to provide an aid that enhances syllabus analysis, and to raise your level of success in examinations.

THE QUALITY OF AUTHORS

We are an expert team of writers, who have considerable experience in teaching 'A' Level Physical Education, who have written past and current examination syllabuses, who have set and marked examination questions within this subject area and taught at revision workshops throughout the UK. Much of the material within this book has been thoroughly student tested.

We hope that this Revision Guide will prove useful to staff and students. Jan Roscoe Publications will welcome any comments you would wish to make about the book's utility or layout. Thank you for using our work.

Dennis Roscoe
Bob Davis
Jan Roscoe

CREDITS

ACKNOWLEDGMENTS

We would like to thank Bob Davis for his co-operation and adherence to our demanding deadlines, and John Norris of Macprodesign for his patience in setting out the book and creating equanimity among the graphics and text. We thank Poplar Services for their patience in linking our work to their computers, and JRP staff member Linda Underwood for working hard in the background while I put this book together. We thank Helen Roscoe for her contribution as cover designer and photographer and Lois Cresswell for her patience as photographic model. We thank members of the Belgian Olympic Athletics Squad for permission to use their images. Lynn Goodkin and Lauren Hunt have been also been patient enough to proof read the text.

Dennis Roscoe
Editor

ACKNOWLEDGMENTS FOR GRAPHICS

Figure A.16	istockphoto Yuri Maryunin
Figure C.1	istockphoto johnny scriv
Figure C.7	istockphoto Robert Churchill
Figure C.15	istockphoto Richard Hobson
Figure C.16	istockphoto Lisa F. Young
Figure C.21	istockphoto Joseph Justice
Figure C.24	istockphoto webphotographeer
Figure C.27	istockphoto Joe Gough
Figure C.51	istockphoto Toby Creamer
Figure C.52	with kind thanks to PGL Ltd
Figure C.53	istockphoto Purdue9394
Figure C.65	istockphoto Michael Krinke
Figure 2A.3	istockphoto Birgitte Magnus
Figure 2B.8	istockphoto Rich Legg
Figure 2B.9	istockphoto bradleym

All other graphics are by Helen Roscoe, Jan Roscoe and Dennis Roscoe.

HIGH QUALITY PHOTOS

ROSCOE et al
A2 Revise PE for AQA
ISBN 978-1-901424-57-7

A2
Revise
PE
for
AQA

Dennis Roscoe
Bob Davis
Jan Roscoe

Jan Roscoe Publications

REVISION SUMMARY NOTES

Fiedler's Contingency Model (1967)

According to **Fiedler**, the **effectiveness** of a leader is dependent on 2 factors:
- **The personality coach**.
- **The situation**.

The personality of the leader is **measured** using **The Least Preferred Co-worker Scale (LPC)**. The test records whether a leader is **task-orientated** (concerned with achievement) or **person-orientated** (concerned with the members of the group).

The **type of situation** is said to determine which type of leader will be most successful.

According to Fiedler:
- A **task-orientated** leader is most successful in the most favourable and least favourable situations.
- A **person-orientated** leader is most successful in the most favourable and least favourable situations.

QUALITY GRAPHS

REVISION SUMMARY CHARTS

PRACTICE QUESTIONS & ANSWERS

6) How has modern technical developments influenced performance in sport today?   5 marks
Answer
- *Equipment such as the javelin allows it to be thrown farther.*
- *All-weather surfaces allow games to be played when grass would not and improves performance.*
- *Athletic tracks are faster today producing higher standards.*
- *The timing of races is now more accurate improving confidence.*
- *Better media communications have stimulated interest.*
- *In car racing, modern cars are faster, but safer.*
- *Specialised footwear for athletics and climbing.*
- *Research into swimming and water resistance.*
- *TV evidence used in cricket and rugby.*
- *Fitness suites for improving strength and mobility.*

This new Revise Series covers all aspects of the examinable A2 PE AQA syllabus that commenced in September 2008. The book consists of student notes, full colour illustrations, photographs, exam questions and full answers. Key concepts are clearly defined with examples that can be used in answers to exam questions, thus enabling the student to self-text. This student revision guide supports a comprehensive revision plan and will enhance student grades.

HOW TO ORDER

tel **+44(0)151 420 4446**
(open every day 9am-5pm)

fax **+44(0)151 495 2622**
(open 24 hours a day)

email **sales@jroscoe.co.uk**

by post to: **JRP Publications, 'Holyrood', 23 Stockswell Road, Widnes, Cheshire WA8 4PJ, United Kingdom**

For **full listings** see the **JRP Catalogue** or visit **www.jroscoe.co.uk**

Jan Roscoe Publications
Sport and PE curriculum resources

- Purchasing Helpline
- Competitive Discounts
- Website
- Product Database
- Exhibitions on Request
- Book Jacket Service
- Prop Promotions
- Website Ordering
- Online Catalogue
- Next Day Delivery
- Exclusive Offers
- Visit our Warehouse

www.jroscoe.co.uk   **CATALOGUE 2009**

CONTENTS

AS Revise PE for AQA

AS UNIT 1 PHED1: Opportunities for and the effects of leading a healthy and active lifestyle

SECTION A – UNIT 1

APPLIED EXERCISE PHYSIOLOGY

SECTION A – UNIT 2

APPLIED EXERCISE PHYSIOLOGY IN PRACTICAL SITUATIONS

SECTION B – UNIT 1

SKILL ACQUISITION

CONTENTS

SECTION B – UNIT 2

SKILL ACQUISITION IN PRACTICAL SITUATIONS

SECTION C – UNIT 1

OPPORTUNITIES FOR PATICIPATION

APPLIED EXERCISE PHYSIOLOGY

UNIT 1

HEALTH EXERCISE AND FITNESS

NUTRITION

PULMONARY FUNCTION

CARDIAC & VASCULAR FUNCTION

ANALYSIS OF MOVEMENT

LEVERS

UNIT 2

APPLIED EXERCISE PHYSIOLOGY
IN PRACTICAL SITUATIONS

HEALTH, EXERCISE AND FITNESS

This section focuses on how understanding the body and its systems can help lead to a healthy and active lifestyle. **Health, exercise and fitness** will help you understand those aspects of fitness that are important to good health and physical performance.

Definitions of health and fitness

Health is defined as '**a state of complete physical, social and mental well-being, free from mental and physical disease**'.

Good **physical** state results from regular exercise, proper diet and nutrition, and proper rest for physical recovery. An athlete may be physically fit but emotionally unstable and therefore unhealthy.

Fitness can mean different things to different people (figure A.1) and has been defined as '**the ability to carry out our daily tasks without undue fatigue**', or '**the successful adaptation to the stressors of one's lifestyle**' Dick (1989).

- When we examine these definitions we need to ask ourselves 'what does the person need to be fit for?' Dick's definition suggests that fitness is how well our bodies cope with and adapt to the stressors of daily life.

- Both definitions universally define fitness for all ages, gender and lifestyles. For example, fitness for an old age pensioner could be measured by his / her ability to walk the dog on a daily basis. In the case of global superstar Paula Radcliffe, her concept of fitness may be measured by her physical state of fitness to win her next marathon race.

- Fitness is also **highly specific** when you consider the anaerobic fitness requirements for a 100m sprint and the aerobic fitness requirements for long distance running.

- From this starting point we are able to build up a picture of the fitness requirements of an individual in relation to his / her required performance.

Components of health-related fitness

Physical Fitness consists of (see figure A.2):

- **Health-related physical components** – which are anatomically and physiologically based, and so assess a person's physical performance capacities. They include stamina, muscular endurance, strength, speed, power, flexibility and body composition.

- **Skill-related motor components** – consist of neuro-muscular components of fitness which are skill-related and include the capacity to repeat a particular exercise. These include reaction time, agility, co-ordination, speed and balance.

Some of the standardised tests aimed at measuring these fitness components are mentioned below and are briefly described on page 78. For fuller descriptions of standardised tests refer to your class textbook.

figure A.1 – what is fitness?

physical well-being · tasks without fatigue · **WHAT IS FITNESS?** · highly specific · successful adaptation to stressors

figure A.2 – physical fitness

agility · co-ordination · balance · **skill-related fitness** · reaction time · strength · **PHYSICAL FITNESS** · muscular endurance · flexibility · **health-related fitness** · speed · stamina · body composition · power

Health-related physical components

Stamina

Stamina is also known as **cardio-respiratory endurance** and can be defined as '**the ability to provide and sustain vigorous total body activity aerobically**'.

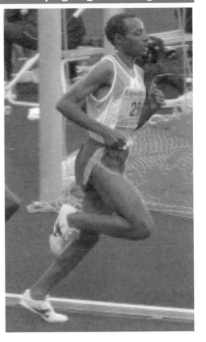

- Stamina involves the ability of the cardiovascular and respiratory systems to take in and transport oxygen to large muscle groups working dynamically.
- Stamina (figure A.3) enables moderate to high intensity exercise to be undertaken for prolonged periods of time as in the case of marathon running.
- A key component of stamina is aerobic power or **maximum oxygen uptake** ($\dot{V}O_{2max}$).
- A $\dot{V}O_{2max}$ test assesses the maximum amount of oxygen that a person can consume per minute during a progressive exercise test to exhaustion and is assessed directly when using closed-circuit spirometry.
- Simple **predicted** $\dot{V}O_{2max}$ tests are used as indicators of aerobic fitness or stamina, and include the Physical Work Capacity test (PWC170 – see page 78), the Cooper's Run / Walk test, the Multi-stage Shuttle Run test, and the Queen's College Step test (see page 78).
- Elite marathon athletes run at optimal percentages of their $\dot{V}O_{2max}$ in order to achieve world class performances.
- Percentage of **slow twitch fibres**, and **mitochondria** and **myoglobin** concentrations are some of the factors that affect stamina.

Muscular endurance

Muscular endurance can be defined as '**the ability of a muscle or muscle groups to sustain repeated contractions over time sufficient enough to cause muscular fatigue**'.

- Muscular endurance relies on the ability of the body to produce energy under aerobic and anaerobic conditions.
- This type of exercise stresses slow twitch fibres and fast twitch fibres type IIa – both muscle fibre types are fatigue resistant.
- Simple tests that evaluate local muscular endurance include the Multi-Stage Abdominal test and Maximum Chin test i.e. the total number of chin-ups completed to exhaustion or within one minute.

Strength

Strength is defined as '**the maximum force exerted by a specific muscle or muscle groups during a single maximal muscle contraction (1RM)**'.

- **Static strength** is exerted without change of muscle length, for example holding a weight at arms length, or pushing hard in a stationary rugby scrum thus creating an **isometric muscle contraction**.
- **Dynamic** or **explosive strength** is the maximal strength exerted during a movement or exercise in which muscle length changes. Most sports use this type of maximal strength. This is the sort of strength weight lifters use in competition when performing an Olympic lift (figure A.4), and is the most usual in sports situations such as throwing and sprinting. Most games or activities require flat out movements such as sprinting and therefore require dynamic strength.
  A sub-category of dynamic strength is **elastic / plyometric strength** or the ability to apply as large a force as possible using an **eccentric** contraction (in which the active muscles get longer) **followed** by a **concentric** contraction (in which the active muscles get shorter). For example, rebound jumping and high jump take-off.
- Strength can be assessed with the use of **dynamometers**.
- Strength exercises stress **fast twitch fibres type IIb** which are able to generate high forces rapidly. Long-term, this type of exercise results in **muscle hypertrophy** (enlargement of individual muscle fibres).

Speed

Speed is defined as '**the maximum rate at which a person is able to move his / her body**'.

- In physical terms, speed is the **distance moved per second**.
- In physical performance it refers to the **speed of co-ordinated joint actions** and whole-body movements and is the ultimate test in a 30m sprint.
- Speedy movements stress **fast twitch fibres type IIb** which are able to generate high forces rapidly and which long-term will result in muscle hypertrophy.

Power

Power is defined as '**the ability to use strength quickly (strength x speed)**'.

- Measured in joules per second or **watts**.
- Power is visible in activities that require **explosive strength** such as throwing a heavy object such as a shot, or a long jumper during take-off.
- Standard tests include the **Vertical Jump test** (also known as the Sergeant Jump – see table 27, page 78) and Standing Broad Jump test.
- Power exercises stress **fast twitch fibres type IIb** which are able to generate high forces rapidly, and long-term results in muscle hypertrophy.

Flexibility

Flexibility is defined as '**the ability to move a joint through its complete range of movement**'.

- Flexibility concerns the **stretching** of muscles and tissues such as ligaments and tendons around skeletal joints (figure A.5).
- The degree of movement is determined by the **joint type** referred to on page 53.
- The way in which the joint moves relative to the body's axes and planes is also relevant to the sports situation. See page 54 for further explanation of this.
- A standardised test is the Sit and Reach trunk flexion test.
- A gymnast needs great flexibility to achieve desired movement patterns.

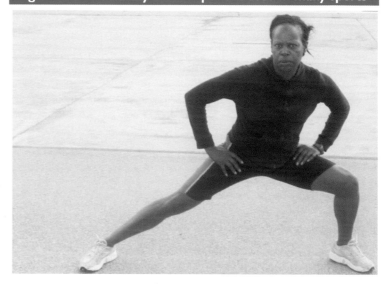

figure A.5 – flexibility is a component used in many sports

Body composition

Body composition is a concept describing '**the relative percentage of muscle, fat and bone**'.

- Body composition analysis is a suitable tool for the assessment of a person's state of fitness. See the section on percentage of body fat on page 25.

Components of skill-related / motor fitness

Reaction time

Reaction time is defined as '**the time taken to initiate a response to a given stimulus**'.

- The stimulus may be **visual**, for example a batsman responding to the release of the ball from the bowler.
- Or **aural** as in the reaction time between the starter firing the gun and the athlete moving out of the starting blocks.
- The response time taken represents the amount of time it takes a person to move once he / she realises the need to act.
- Reaction time can be assessed using computer software or the Stick Drop test.
- See page 96 onwards for a further explanation of reaction time.

Agility

Agility is defined as ' **the physical ability that enables a person to quickly change body position in a precise manner**'.

- Agility is a combination of balance, co-ordination, speed and flexibility.
- Rugby players need great agility as they weave in and out and around opposition.
- How quickly can you complete the Illinois Agility Run – a standardised test that assesses speed and agility?

Co-ordination

Co-ordination is defined as '**the ability to perform smooth and accurate motor tasks, often involving the use of senses**'.

- Good co-ordination is observed in elite gymnasts (figure A.6) such as those performances associated with world champion Beth Tweddle.
- Assess your own co-ordination skills by trying to juggle with 3 tennis balls.

Balance

Balance is defined as '**the ability to retain the centre of mass of a sportsperson's body above the base of support**'.

- It is the awareness of the body's position in space and depends upon the **co-ordination** between the inner ear, brain, skeleton and muscles.
- Balance can be **static** where a position is held as in a handstand.
- Or **dynamic** - the ability to maintain balance under changing conditions of body movement, shape and orientation. For example, the changing balance required during a pole vault performance.
- Balance can be assessed by using the Standard Stork test.

Effects of lifestyle choices on health and fitness

Lifestyle choices are all about choices made which affect daily life and their direct impact on health and fitness. Figure A.7 outlines choices which may affect your quality of life, and the following discussion explains the ways in which your choices will affect your chances of an active and long life.

Smoking – the facts

- Chemicals in tobacco adversely affect nearly every organ and system in the body.
- 40% of male smokers die before reaching retirement age.
- Pregnant women smokers increase the risk of harming the unborn child.
- Children born to smokers are on average smaller and take longer to reach maturity than children born to non-smokers.
- Such children tend to be later learning to read and tend to have disorders such as attention deficit disorder.
- Risk of cancer.
- Women smokers increase the risk of cervical cancer.
- Once lung cancer or emphysema is diagnosed, death will be sooner rather than later.
- Respiratory problems (refer to figure A.8).
- Smoking worsens respiratory conditions such as colds / bronchitis.
- Passive smoking has all the same risks as first hand smoking.

figure A.6 – a gymnast uses agility, co-ordination and balance

figure A.7 – lifestyle choices

- diet
- exercise
- stress
- LIFESTYLE CHOICES
- alcohol
- smoking
- recreational drugs

figure A.8 – smoking

- increased risk of lung (and airway) cancer
- tar deposits in alveoli
- exercise reduces risks
- SMOKING
- reduced lung surface area for intake of oxygen
- tired and out of breath
- carbon monoxide attaches to haemoglobin
- reduced oxygen carrying capacity of red blood cells

Recreational drugs – the facts

What are we talking about? See figure A.9 for examples of some of the substances taken by people under this heading.

Effects of drug taking:

- Drugs harm essential organs of life.
- Drugs destroy family and social life.
- Drugs drive the users toward criminal behaviour to fund the habit.
- Drugs destroy self-esteem / self-respect through reliance on drug.

Be smart - don't start!

figure A.9 – recreational drugs

Alcohol – the facts

- Alcohol intake guidelines:

    males: 3 to 4 units per day.

    females: 2 to 3 units per day.

- 14% of children who drink alcohol are alcohol dependent.
- 20,000 adults in the UK die each year from alcohol-related diseases.

Associated risks with heavy drinking

- **Mouth** / throat / oesophagus damage - cancer - damage to ciliated lining.
- **Liver** - cirrhosis / alcohol hepatitis / enlarged fatty liver.
- **Muscles** - atrophy / pain / spasms.
- **Vascular** - vasodilation within skin / hypertension.
- **Stomach** - ulcers / cancer.
- **Nervous system** - destroys brain cells / slurred speech / taste and smell deficiency.
- **Heart** - weakens / enlarges heart muscle / increased risk of heart attack.
- **Bones** – osteoporosis.
- **Reproductive organs** - erectile dysfunction / harms foetal development.
- **Lungs** – cancer.
- **Psychiatric disorders** - alcoholism / depression / link to suicide.

The effect of **smoking**, over-consumption of **alcohol** and the use of recreational **drugs** severely limit healthy lifestyle choices.

Diet

A **balanced diet** contains proportions of carbohydrates, fats, proteins, minerals, vitamins, water and roughage (fibre) needed to maintain good health (see page 21 onwards for the details about diet).

- A **balanced diet** will depend on gender, growth stage, age, amounts and type of physical activity.
- **Malnutrition** means a bad diet, which can cause health problems and includes obesity and anorexia nervosa.

Overweight is defined as '**a body weight that exceeds the norm or standard weight for a particular, height, frame size and gender**'.

Obesity is defined as '**a surplus of adipose tissue resulting from excessive energy intake relative to energy expenditure**'.

- Obese **males** - body fat greater than 25%.
- Obese **females** - body fat greater than 35%.

The main cause of obesity is that energy intake (eating carbohydrate and fat) is far greater that energy output.

This concept is known as a **positive energy balance** and can be expressed as:

ENERGY INTAKE > ENERGY OUTPUT

The over-consumption of fatty foods, the use of convenience food and drinks, and ready-made meals, containing excess amounts of sugar and salt, lead to increased levels of obesity.

Obesity and health disorders – the facts

- Over 30,000 deaths a year are caused by obesity - in England.
- 22% of the British adult population are obese.
- 75% of the British adult population are overweight.
- Child obesity has increased 3-fold in the last 20 years.

Obesity can lead to many health problems such as:
- **Arthritis** – a disease in which joints become inflamed.
- **Heart** and **vascular** diseases such as **coronary heart attack** and **angina**, and **atherosclerosis** caused by lipid deposits accumulating in the inner lining of the arteries.
- **Diabetes** – a condition which occurs when a person's body cannot regulate glucose levels. Obesity and overweight conditions are major risk factors for type 2 diabetes.

Stress

Stress (refer to figure A.10) is a response of the body to a demanding situation and is manifested by:
- **Physiological** symptoms such as increased heart rate and sweating.
- **Psychological** symptoms such as feeling out of control.
- **Behavioural** symptoms such as nail biting and trembling.

Stressors are the causes of stress and include:
- **Physical stressors** are conditions of the body and surroundings that affect an individual's well-being. For example, thirst, hunger, lack of sleep, pollution.
- **Emotional stressors** include worry, depression, fear and grief and can strongly affect physical and emotional well-being.
- **Social stressors** arise from an individual's relationship with other people.

Not all stressful experiences are harmful:

figure A.10 – stress and stressors

Eustress

- The term **eustress** is a type of stress with a positive effect whereby the performer actively seeks the thrill of the danger and enjoys the excitement and feeling of satisfaction when it is over. For example, bungy jumping and free rock climbing.
- Eustress helps make life more enjoyable by helping the individual to meet challenges and do his / her best.

Distress

- Unpleasant situations also cause stress. This negative stress is also known as distress.
- Distress can have a negative effect on a person's total health and fitness.

Effective ways to manage stress

- Rest in a quiet place.
- Reduce breathing rate, mental activity and muscle tension.
- Identify the stressors, take action, manage time effectively, and think positively.
- Keeping the body physically fit and in good health can help the individual manage stress and work towards living a healthy lifestyle.

Work-life balance

It is important to have a balance between the demands of work, exercise, social life and sleep. A lifestyle dominated by work and issues connected with work can lead to many of the sedentary lifestyle issues mentioned above.

Effects of exercise on health

Cardiovascular

- Exercise slows down degenerative diseases (CHD).
- Exercise increases high density lipoproteins (HDL) and decreases low density lipoproteins (LDL are responsible for depositing cholesterol and narrowing lumen of arteries).
- Hence blood pressure remains stable thus preventing hypertension.

Respiratory

- Exercise slows down decline in $\dot{V}O_{2max}$ and hence aerobic capacity remains higher than it otherwise would be.
- Hence the capability for long duration low intensity work remains higher.

figure A.11 – effects of exercise on health

respiratory

cardiovascular

psychological

EXERCISE IMPROVES WELL-BEING

neuromuscular

body composition

Body composition

- Exercise reduces obesity by burning off excess fat during and after activity when the body's metabolic rate remains elevated.
- Cardiac workload (hence risk of CHD) is less with lower body mass.
- Capability to move around (walk, run and climb) therefore is better with a lower body mass.
- Exercise relieves symptoms of osteoarthritis.
- Exercise prevents osteoporosis.

Neuromuscular

- Exercise sustains strength and co-ordination levels.
- Exercise enhances tensile strength and flexibility of tendons and ligaments thus allowing for a fuller range of joint movement.

Psychological

- Immediately following activity a person experiences a feeling of well-being, reduction in anxiety.
- Long-term increase in work performance, hence a more positive attitude to work.
- Improved self-esteem and self-efficacy.
- Benefits of social interaction.

Informed individuals are able to make decisions about lifestyle choices that ultimately will affect the quality of health and fitness (see figure A.12).

figure A.12 – aerobics as fun for health

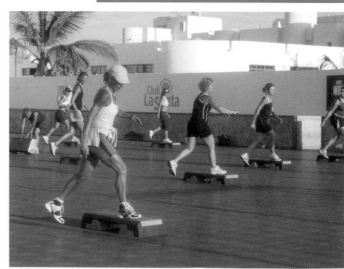

It is possible to gain fun and fulfilment from involvement in sport as an official, spectator, coach or volunteer. The Beijing Olympics would not have happened without its 1.2 million volunteers (figure A.13)!

figure A.13 – volunteers have fun

NUTRITION

The seven classes of food and their exercise-related function

A **balanced diet** is (figures A.14 and A.15) the combination and proportions of carbohydrates (CHO), fats, proteins, roughage, water and essential minerals and vitamins which best provide for a sportsperson's nutritional requirements.

Metabolism
The term metabolism describes the way in which energy is used and the rate of energy usage by the human body.

figure A.14 – a balanced diet?

figure A.15 – balanced diet

protein

vitamins

fat

minerals

BALANCED DIET

carbohydrate (CHO)

dietary fibre

water

NUTRITION

Table I – **summary of dietary content**

type of food / sources	function as a food fuel - how is it used	energy content kJ g⁻¹	percentage in a balanced diet
carbohydrate (CHO) sugars, rice potatoes, pasta	**Main energy supply**. Absorbed as glucose in small intestine. Transported around body as blood glucose. Available for immediate energy. Excess stored as muscle and liver glycogen and as fat.	17	60 %
fats butter, oil, pastry, fried food	**Secondary energy supply**. Absorbed as fatty acids and glycerol in the small intestine. Stored as triglycerides in adipose tissue. Triglycerides conveyed to the liver via the circulatory system. In the liver they are converted to glucose. Available as delayed (20 minutes delay) energy source for long duration low intensity aerobic exercise.	39	20-25 %
proteins meat, eggs, milk, cheese, nuts	Absorbed as amino acids in the small intestine. Used for growth and repair by all tissues. Used as an energy source when the body is depleted of CHO and fat. Excess protein, not needed for tissue repair, is broken down and used as an energy supply.		10-15 %
vitamins	Organic substances needed for crucial functions in almost all bodily functions. Regulate metabolism and facilitate energy release. Have important functions in bone formation and tissue synthesis.		small amounts essential
minerals	Calcium provides structure in bones and teeth. Iron needed for red blood cell production. Other minerals also assist in synthesising glycogen, fat and protein.		small amounts essential
dietary fibre wholegrain cereals, vegetables	Non-starch, structural polysaccharide including cellulose. Only available from plants sources. Gives bulk to food residues in the intestines. Aids gastrointestinal functioning.	20 to 40 grams per day	large amounts necessary
water	Constitutes 72% of muscle weight and around 50% of adipose tissue. Provides the body's transport and reactive medium. Transports nutrients and leaves the body in urine and faeces. Lubricates joints, keeping bony surfaces from grinding against each other. Provides structure and form to the body. Some sports drinks designed to meet both energy and fluid needs of athlete.	up to 5 litres per day	large amounts necessary

The need for a balanced diet

Energy balance

When energy input is equal to energy output a **neutral energy balance** is achieved, as a result of which a person's weight remains constant. This concept can be expressed as:

ENERGY INPUT = ENERGY OUTPUT

Table 2 - **a comparison of daily energy intake for athletes**

activity	daily energy intake kJ - females	daily energy intake kJ – males
Tour de France		25000
triathlon		20000
rowing	12600	14700
swimming	8400	15500
hockey	9200	13400
soccer		14700
running	9200	13000
gymnastics	6000	
body building	5900	14500

Table 2 shows the variation in energy expended during competition and training, (measured in kJ per day) in elite male and female endurance (figure A.16), strength and team sport athletes. Except for high-energy intake of athletes at extremes of performance and training, the daily energy intake does not exceed 17000 kJ for men and 12500 kJ for women. Note that the difference between males and females can be accounted for by size difference. Values per kg of body mass would be similar.

figure A.16 – endurance cyclists consume huge amounts of energy

The performer's use of nutritional information

Diets for endurance athletes and power athletes

Within rather broad bands, a balanced diet from a regular food intake provides the nutrient requirements for all sports people. However, for the elite sports performer, dietary intake varies depending on the intensity and duration of the exercise.

Carbohydrate requirements

Glycogen is the most important and the most valuable fuel for any type of exercise, hence a **high CHO diet** significantly improves performance. Post-exercise, a sports-type carbohydrate supplement will start the reloading of depleted muscle glycogen stores. For rapid carbohydrate replenishment after training, food with a **high glycemic index** (GI) is recommended – for example, bananas, brown rice, raisins or wholemeal bread should be eaten with two hours of completing the physical activity. This is because eating these foods will be more efficient in increasing blood glucose concentrations and the greater insulin release needed to convert glucose into glycogen. Optimal glycogen replenishment will benefit individuals involved in regular intense training and in tournaments that span over a period of days.

Carbo-loading

Carbo-loading is a process where extra carbohydrate is taken in after a short period of carbohydrate starvation. The extra carbohydrate available causes stored muscle glycogen content to overcompensate, and so the available muscle glycogen levels are greater than normal. Carbo-loading can augment endurance performance in events lasting longer than 90 minutes by increasing muscle glycogen stores above normal levels. This dietary technique requires increased fluid intake because water is needed to store additional glycogen.

Fat

Fat intake should be restricted for both endurance and power athletes since muscle tissue is more powerful than fat tissue. However, in power events such as sumo wrestling, it would be impossible to acquire a very large body mass without fat gain. Hence sumo wrestlers will need a higher percentage of dietary fat to increase their body mass.

Protein requirements

For an endurance athlete the recommended protein intake is 1.2-1.4 grams per kg body mass per day. Strength and power athletes need additional protein when compared with endurance athletes, with recommended protein intake at 1.4-1.8 grams per kg body mass per day. This need for a difference in protein intake is because after heavy resistance training the rate of protein breakdown and resynthesis is greater (muscle hypertrophy).

Vitamins / minerals / supplements and water needs

- Regular and intense exercise increases the requirements for vitamins, minerals and dietary fibre.
- **Glutamine** (a constituent of skeletal muscle and also needed by the body's immune system) as a supplement increases the chance of recovery from infections. This is because intense exercise stresses the muscular system, which then requires dietary glutamine as an amino acid for recovery. At the same time, the immune system requires dietary glutamine to cope with ambient infections.
- **Creatine** supplementation has been shown to increase muscle creatine levels and so increase performance in anaerobic sports such as sprinting.
- Most elite sportspeople take **nutritional supplements** such as amino acid and CHO supplementation, often taken in liquid form following intense training sessions.
- **Exercise is thirsty work**. Fluid loss during exercise depends on the intensity and duration of the exercise, temperature and humidity, body size and fitness levels. The longer and more intense the exercise period, for example in a long distance race, the more the need to drink before, during and after the race.

When and what should you eat before a competition?

- Food should be eaten between 3-4 hours prior to the competition so that it is well digested and absorbed into the bloodstream.
- The meal needs to be high in carbohydrates, low in fat and moderate in fibre to aid the digestive process.
- An example meal could be pasta bake with spinach, a banana and a still flavoured drink.

Definition of obesity

figure A.17 – obesity

The terms overweight and obesity (figure A.17) are interchangeable in common language, but have slightly different definitions. **Overweight** is defined as '**a body weight that exceeds the norm or standard weight for a particular person based on height and frame size**'. These weight values were based on population averages, so it is possible for a person to be overweight and yet have a lower than normal body fat content.

Obesity is defined as '**a surplus of adipose tissue resulting from excessive energy intake relative to energy expenditure**'. Hence obesity is the term which is relevant to people who take part in sport.

The definition of obesity implies that the actual amount of body fat or its percentage of total weight can be estimated. The problem is that exact standards for allowable fat percentages have not been established. However, men with more than 25% body fat and women with more than 35% should be considered obese. This definition highlights the major cause of obesity, namely an obese person would have energy intake far greater than energy output, which would be the result of inactivity and which would create a **positive energy balance**. This relationship is expressed as:

ENERGY INTAKE > ENERGY OUTPUT

Excess carbohydrate (CHO) is stored as glycogen. When glycogen stores are filled, CHO together with excess fat intake are converted to fatty acids and glycerol, and then is stored as triglycerides or fat in adipose tissue. This is situated around major organs such as the heart and stomach, underneath the skin, and in skeletal muscle. Upper body obesity poses a significantly greater risk to disease.

Excessive weight gain is associated with certain health conditions such as coronary heart disease and hypertension with an increased risk of mortality and morbidity.

Controlling Obesity

The only method of controlling obesity is to shift the energy relationship so that energy output exceeds energy intake – known as a **negative energy balance** and expressed as:

ENERGY OUTPUT > ENERGY INTAKE

A negative energy balance can be achieved with the help of a **Weight Loss Plan** (figure A.18) that should be developed from four main principles:

figure A.18 – weight loss plan

- **Personal** so that the individual truly wishes to lose weight.
- **Specific** in defining what the individual wants to achieve i.e. goal.
- **Realistic** in the weight loss goal is attainable for body shape and lifestyle.
- **Measurable** in that the individual will know when they have reached their goal.
- Keeping a **food diary** and **activity log** will help to monitor progress.

Percentage body fat and BMI

Clinical methods used to assess levels of obesity

Body composition

Body composition is a concept describing the relative percentage of muscle, fat and bone, and percentage body fat can be estimated using a **skinfold fat thickness** measurements. Fat is stored beneath the skin and so by pinching the skin between thumb and index finger you can assess skinfold thickness. If you can pinch more than 1.5 cm you are probably too fat. The standard test involves measuring skinfold fat thickness at a minimum of 3 sites on the body, then added together by using the **Jackson and Pollock equation** which will give an estimate of percentage body fat. Further devices estimate body fat percentage by measuring the conductivity of the body, then comparing this with standardised tables according to gender, body mass, and height.

Body mass index (BMI)

Body mass index is now the most widely used clinical standard to estimate obesity. To determine a person's BMI, body weight in kilograms is divided by the square of the body height in metres. For example, a person weighs 104 kg and is 1.83 m tall would have a BMI $= \dfrac{104}{1.83^2} = \dfrac{104\,\text{kg}}{3.35\,\text{m}^2} = 31\,\text{kg/m}^2$

BMI values are divided into five categories: underweight, normal weight, overweight, obesity and extreme obesity.

What is a good level of fat?

An **essential** (minimum requirement which would allow full body functions) body fat percentage for men is between 2% and 3% and for women between 8% and 12%. Normally **only** healthy elite athletes attain these percentages.

How is a person's body fatness related to good health?

Relative body fat is a major concern of athletes. Achieving a desired weight goal can lead to clinical eating disorders such as anorexia nervosa, which has occurred in some female endurance-based athletes. A person restricting food intake to levels well below energy expenditure causes anorexia nervosa.

Establishing weight standards should be based on using established standards of relative body fat for each sport.
Hence it is important to have a diet that maintains appropriate weight and body composition to maximise physical performance.

Practice questions

1) Name and define **two** main components of health-related fitness required by an elite swimmer. Explain how these components are used in this sport.   4 marks

2) a) What is meant by the term specific fitness?   2 marks
   b) Compare the fitness components essential for an elite sprinter with those required by an elite marathon runner.
   4 marks

3) a) Using a sport of your choice, identify **two** main components of health-related fitness required and explain their importance.   4 marks
   b) Power is a major fitness component required by high jumpers. Define what is meant by power.   2 marks
   c) Describe a recognised specific test for measuring the power output of a high jumper.   3 marks
   d) Identify **two** skill-related / motor fitness components that are considered important for high jumpers.   2 marks

4) Briefly describe an outline for a week's exercise programme that would be suitable for overweight and ageing adult. In your answer identify the major fitness components to be stressed.   8 marks

5) There is overwhelming medical evidence that supports the direct relationship between smoking and reduced oxygen transportation. Explain how smoking interferes with oxygen transportation.   4 marks

6) Lifestyle choices can have a negative effect upon our health and fitness.
   a) Identify **three** lifestyle choices that have adverse effects on our future health and fitness.   3 marks
   b) Choose **one** of your answers given in part a) and discuss how you could influence an individual to change to healthy lifestyle choices.   3 marks

7) What are the purposes of the three main groups of food?   3 marks

8) a) Discuss how a balanced diet could be manipulated to increase an athlete's glucose reserves prior to a marathon race.
   6 marks
   b) Carbohydrates are used as an energy source during both aerobic and anaerobic conditions. It is therefore beneficial that an elite athlete's stores of carbohydrate are at a maximum before competition day. Discuss the advantages and disadvantages of glycogen loading.   4 marks
   c) How can an athlete's diet aid the recovery process?   2 marks

9) You have been asked to provide some nutritional strategies for an elite swimmer competing in seven races in the Regional Championships in a week's time. What can you recommend?   3 marks

10) Provide recommendations for carbohydrate, fat and protein intake for a cross-country skier and a ski jumper. Give reasons for your recommendations.   6 marks

11) What are the effects of obesity on health and what are its causes based on energy considerations?   4 marks

12) Describe the most effective way of reducing body weight.   4 marks

13) What is body mass index? What is its significance?   3 marks

PULMONARY FUNCTION AND TRANSPORT OF BLOOD GASES

Introductory anatomy of the respiratory system

 STUDENT NOTE Prior knowledge of the structure and function of the respiratory and cardiovascular systems is assumed, however we include elements of these systems throughout this unit.

Lung structure

From figure A.19 you can see that the air pathway as the air is breathed in, is through the **nasal cavity** to **pharynx** to **larynx** to **trachea** to **bronchi** to **bronchioles** to **respiratory bronchioles** to **alveolar ducts** to **alveoli**.

The **trachea** consists of an incomplete ring of cartilage that keeps the airway open and allows swallowing. The nasal cavity, pharynx, larynx, trachea and bronchi have ciliated linings and **mucous glands** to provide a cleaning and filtering mechanism for incoming air.

The **pulmonary pleura** is a self-enclosed serous membrane covering the lungs, and lining the thoracic cavity, middle wall of the thorax and diaphragm. This membrane secretes pleural fluid into the pleural cavity thereby reducing friction between lung tissue and ribs, and aiding inspiration as pleural pressure reduces, and expiration as pleural pressure increases.

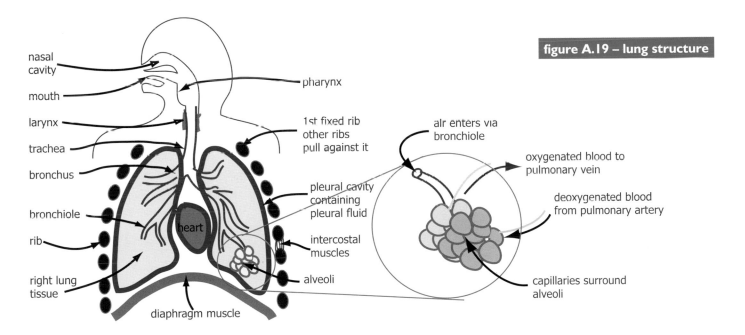

figure A.19 – lung structure

nasal cavity
mouth
larynx
trachea
bronchus
bronchiole
rib
right lung tissue
diaphragm muscle

pharynx
1st fixed rib other ribs pull against it
pleural cavity containing pleural fluid
intercostal muscles
alveoli
heart

air enters via bronchiole
oxygenated blood to pulmonary vein
deoxygenated blood from pulmonary artery
capillaries surround alveoli

Lung tissue

Alveoli (see figure A.19) are elastic, moist, and permeable (a single layer of epithelial cells) and are surrounded by a network of capillaries. These are adapted for gaseous exchange as oxygen travels through the capillary walls **from** the lung space **into** the blood within the capillaries, and carbon dioxide travels in the opposite direction through the capillary walls.

Pulmonary ventilation is '**the process by which we move air into and out of the lungs**'.

Mechanics of breathing

The actual mechanism of breathing is brought about by changes in air pressure (intrapulmonary pressure) in the lungs relative to atmospheric pressure, as a result of the muscular actions of the 11 pairs of intercostal muscles and the diaphragm. For a summary view of the mechanism of breathing, see figure A.20 for inspiration and figure A.21 for expiration.

Table 3 – **inspiration and expiration at rest and during exercise**

inspiration	expiration
at rest	**at rest**
external intercostal muscles contract	external intercostal muscles relax - a passive process
diaphragm contracts - becomes flatter	diaphragm relaxes - domes upward into chest cavity - a passive process
internal intercostal muscles relax	
ribs and sternum move upwards and outwards	ribs and sternum move downwards and inwards
increase in chest cavity volume	decrease in chest cavity volume
pressure between pleural membranes is reduced	pressure between pleural membranes is increased
allows elastic pulmonary tissue to expand	compressing elastic pulmonary tissue
lung volume increases	lung volume decreases
pulmonary air pressure falls below atmospheric pressure (outside the body)	pulmonary air pressure is driven above atmospheric pressure (outside the body)
hence atmospheric air is forced into the lungs	hence atmospheric air is forced out of the lungs via the respiratory passages
until lung pressure equals the pressure outside again	until lung pressure equals the pressure outside again
during exercise	**during exercise**
additional muscles in the chest and torso contract (scalenes, sternocleidomastoid, pectoralis major / minor)	internal intercostal muscles and abdominal muscles contract powerfully, acting on ribs and body cavity
chest cavity volume further increased	chest cavity volume is further reduced
more air forced into the lungs	more pulmonary air is forced out of the lungs

STUDENT NOTE See page 57 below for an introductory description of the location of the various muscles listed above. More detail can be found in specialist books or charts on the human anatomy or the skeleto-muscular system.

figure A.20 – inspiration

figure A.21 – expiration

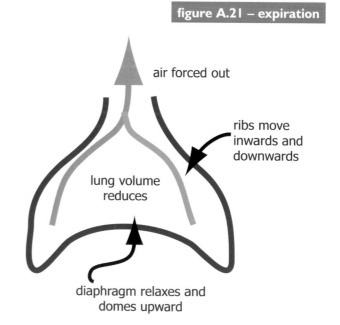

air rushes in

ribs move upwards and outwards

lung volume increases

diaphragm contracts (flattens)

air forced out

ribs move inwards and downwards

lung volume reduces

diaphragm relaxes and domes upward

Lung volumes and capacities

Interpretations from spirometer readings

A **spirometer** is a device that is used to measure pulmonary volumes. Figure A.22 presents a typical lung volume trace resulting from a person breathing into a calibrated spirometer, at rest and during exercise. Note that during the exercise period tidal volume increases considerably because of the encroachment on inspiratory reserve volume (IRV) and expiratory reserve volume (ERV), but more noticeable on the IRV.

Definitions for pulmonary volumes and average values for male and females are shown in table 4 below.

Lung **volumes** vary with age, gender, body size and stature, and are defined and explained in table 4.

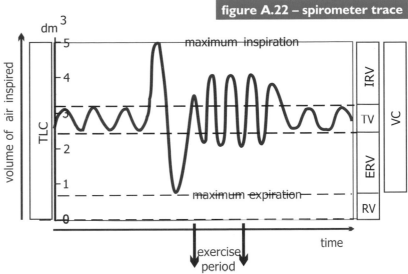

figure A.22 – spirometer trace

Table 4 – **lung volumes and definitions**

lung volumes		definitions	average values (ml)		change during exercise
			male	female	
TLC	total lung capacity	total volume of air in the lungs following maximum inspiration.	6000	4200	slight decrease
VC	vital capacity	maximum volume of air that can be forcibly expired following maximum inspiration.	4800	3200	slight decrease
TV	tidal volume	volume of air inspired **or** expired per breath.	600	500	increase
IRV	inspiratory reserve volume	volume of air that can be forcibly inspired above resting tidal volume.	3000	1900	decrease
ERV	expiratory reserve volume	volume of air that can be forcibly expired above resting tidal volume.	1200	800	decrease
RV	residual volume	volume of air remaining in the lungs after maximal expiration.	1200	1000	stays same
$\dot{V}E = TV \times f$	minute ventilation	volume of air inspired **or** expired in one minute.	7200	6000	dramatic increase

Lung **capacities** are made up of combinations of lung volumes. The following list uses as examples the average **male** values from table 4 above.

Inspiratory capacity (IC)	= TV + IRV	(3600 ml).
Expiratory capacity (EC)	= TV + ERV	(1800 ml).
Vital capacity (VC)	= TV + IRV + ERV	(4800 ml).
Functional residual capacity (FRC)	= RV + ERV	(2400 ml).
Total lung capacity (TLC)	= VC + RV	(6000 ml).

Minute ventilation

Minute ventilation ($\dot{V}E$) is defined as '**the volume of air that is inspired or expired in one minute**'. Minute ventilation can be calculated by multiplying tidal volume (**TV**) by the number of breaths (**f**) taken in one minute (see the last row of table 4 on page 29). Below are examples of minute ventilation values you would expect at rest and during differing intensities of exercise. A normal male resting breathing frequency is about 12 breaths per minute, and this is the value of **f** in the first row of the list below. This would increase to about 25 (breaths per minute) for submaximal exercise, and rapid breathing of about 55 breaths per minute during maximal exercise.

(dm³)	$\dot{V}E$	=	TV	x	f	
at rest	7.2	=	0.6	x	12	= 7.2 litres per minute or 7,200 ml per minute – since 1 dm³ is 1 litre or 1000 ml.
submax	60	=	2.4	x	25	= 60 litres per minute or 60,000 ml per minute.
max	121	=	2.2	x	55	= 121 litres per minute or 121,000 ml per minute.

Hence from submaximal to maximal exercise breathing rate or respiratory frequency doubles (this dramatic increase often corresponds with the onset of anaerobic metabolism or the onset of blood lactate accumulation or **OBLA**) at the expense of a decreasing tidal volume. What actually is happening is a regulation of minute ventilation in response to **increased carbon dioxide** production and the need to get rid of carbon dioxide during expiration. Tidal volume decreases slightly because it is not physically possible to inspire the maximum possible volume of air during maximal exercise at a high breathing rate. This regulatory response is discussed further on page 34.

Figure A.23 compares the changes in minute ventilation with time during low intensity and high intensity exercise.

> **STUDENT NOTE** You will be required to sketch and interpret these patterns in your exam.

Ventilation – response to exercise

During the short period before exercise begins, during the exercise period, and during the recovery period immediately after exercise (see graph in figure A.23), the following describes the reasons for the changes in rate of minute ventilation.

figure A.23 – ventilation during exercise and recovery

- The **anticipatory rise** in $\dot{V}E$, is due to the hormonal action of **adrenaline** and **noradrenaline** on the respiratory centre in the brain. This rise is caused by the excitement in anticipation of exercise beginning.

- The **rapid rise** of $\dot{V}E$ at the start of the exercise period, is due to **proprioceptor** sensory **stimulation**, and also due to continued release of hormones. During this period, exercise is anaerobic in nature and does not require oxygen from the respiratory system. However, an oxygen debt is building up, and this will need to be dealt with later.

- During **submaximal** exercise, a **levelling off** of $\dot{V}E$ occurs as a **steady state** is developed between oxygen required and provided by the respiratory system. Some recovery of O_2 debt (aerobic) occurs.

- As exercise ends, there is a **rapid decline** in $\dot{V}E$ due to cessation of proprioceptive stimuli, then a levelling out to pre-exercise values.

- During **maximal** workloads there is a continued **slower increase** in $\dot{V}E$ as anaerobic systems continue to be stressed. This produces lactic acid + CO_2 + K^+, which stimulate chemoreceptors at a maximal level. The main stimulant for increased rates of ventilation is the presence of carbon dioxide in the blood flowing past chemoreceptors (chemoreceptors detect decrease in blood oxygen, decrease in carbon dioxide, or decrease in pH). See section on page 35 below for details of the location and function of these receptors which stimulate the respiratory centre in the brain.

- The **rapid decline** in $\dot{V}E$, as recovery begins, is due to cessation of proprioceptive stimuli and the withdrawal of hormones.

- Later, there is a **much slower decrease** in $\dot{V}E$ due to the clearance of metabolites such as **lactic acid** and **carbon dioxide** as bodily systems return to normal resting values.

Principles of diffusion and partial pressures

Diffusion

The exchange of gases between lungs and blood and their movement at tissue level takes place passively by **diffusion**.

This is the movement of molecules through space by random collision with other molecules.

This process would eventually result in random mixing of all the molecules present in a space. Molecules move using this process through gases and liquids, and can migrate through membranes (like tissue boundaries such as cell walls).

A diffusion gradient is a situation where the concentration of molecules of a particular substance (say oxygen for example), is greater on one side of a space than on the other side of the same space. Hence a steep diffusion gradient will cause molecules to move across a space or through a membrane **by random** mixing.

Steep **diffusion gradients** are maintained by the factors shown in figure A.24.

Gases diffuse from high to low pressure, and so the rate of exchange (either at lungs or tissue site) depends on the **partial pressure** of each gas (in blood or tissue site or alveolar air), **gas solubility** (in blood or tissue cell fluids), and **temperature**.

Partial pressure

Partial pressure (p) is defined as '**the pressure a gas exerts within a mixture of gases**', so pO_2 and pCO_2 are the partial pressures exerted by oxygen and carbon dioxide respectively within a mixture of these and other gases (for example nitrogen) present in the air or the tissues. Partial pressure of a substance depends on the number of molecules of that substance in a space, so the greater the partial pressure, the greater the number of molecules present, or the greater the concentration of molecules of the substance.

figure A.24 – factors affecting gaseous exchange

pO_2 · gas solubility · pCO_2 · temperature · **GASEOUS EXCHANGE** · good lung ventilation · moist alveolar lining · **maximise diffusion gradient** · vast surface area of alveoli · large amount of muscle myoglobin · short distance between alveolar lining and blood · large amount of red corpuscles

Gas exchange systems

Gaseous exchange is '**the process whereby oxygen from the air in the lungs is transferred by diffusion to the blood flowing through the alveoli**' (see figure A.25). At the same time, carbon dioxide is transferred from the blood arriving at the lungs, into the air in the lungs which is subsequently breathed out. The gases travel **through** the capillary / alveolar walls, with oxygen diffusing **into** the blood, and carbon dioxide diffusing **out of** the blood.

figure A.25 – oxygenation of haemoglobin

from pulmonary artery · pulmonary ventilation · to pulmonary vein · capillary · plasma · red cell · capillary wall · diffusion of O_2 · diffusion of CO_2 · O_2 enters red cell · film of moisture · alveolar wall

figure A.26 – tissue respiration

diffusion of CO_2 · capillary · plasma · tissue fluid · diffusion of O_2 · tissue cell

The reverse process happens at the **tissue site** (for example, active muscle tissue – see figure A.26). Here, oxygen is transported by the blood **into** the tissue and there it diffuses into tissue cells. At the same time, carbon dioxide diffuses **out of** tissue cells into the blood (which then flows back through the venous system and the heart and back to the lungs).

How gaseous exchange is achieved in the alveoli

The first step in oxygen transport involves the diffusion of oxygen **from** the alveoli **into** the blood.

In venous blood (arriving at the lungs from tissues) the partial pressure of oxygen (pO_2) = 5.3 kPa. However, the partial pressure of oxygen in alveolar air is 13.3 kPa, so the oxygen travels through the alveolar and capillary walls **from** the air in the lung space **into** the blood where it combines with haemoglobin in the red corpuscles using the formula:

$$Hb + 4O_2 \rightarrow Hb(O_2)_4$$

One of the short-term effects of physical activity is to cause a **small increase** in **pulmonary blood pressure**, which distorts red blood corpuscles within the alveolar capillary system, and this enables **10 times as much oxygen** to be picked up as at rest.

The role of haemoglobin

The **oxyhaemoglobin dissociation curve** (see figure A.27) describes the percentage of haemoglobin saturated with oxygen at a given pO_2. At 13.3 kPa pO_2, oxygen will combine with Hb at 98% of the **maximum possible** (see the red vertical line labelled **A** on figure A.27, this is at 13.3 kPa and intersects the graph line at almost 100%). So this means that haemoglobin leaving the lungs is almost completely saturated with oxygen. (Note that 3% of oxygen dissolves in blood plasma).

Blood carrying this oxygen then travels out of the lungs to the heart via the pulmonary vein, then out to the body through the aorta and main arteries. At altitude, the pO_2 is less, which means that haemoglobin cannot carry as much oxygen as at sea level, therefore reducing the ability to perform physical work. This is called **hypoxia** (lowered pO_2).

At the same time, carbon dioxide is transferred in **the opposite direction**, from the blood into the alveolar air.
The concentration of carbon dioxide in atmospheric air is about 0.049% (very small), and therefore pCO_2 in venous blood arriving (via the heart) from the body tissues is higher than in the alveoli air (breathed into the lungs). Therefore carbon dioxide diffuses through the alveolar membrane (from blood to air in the lung) and is expired. Between 3% and 6% of air breathed out is CO_2 as shown in table 5.

figure A.27 – oxyhaemoglobin dissociation curve

Table 5 – **differences between inhaled and exhaled air**

differences between inhaled and exhaled air			
	inhaled(%)	exhaled air at rest (%)	exhaled air during exercise (%)
O_2	21	17	15
CO_2	0.049	3	6

How gaseous exchange is achieved at the tissue cell site

The second step in oxygen transport involves the transfer of oxygen from the blood into tissue cells.

The role of myoglobin

Myoglobin is a substance somewhat similar to haemoglobin in that it attracts and binds to molecular oxygen. Myoglobin has a greater affinity for oxygen than haemoglobin and is located within cells, where its role is to enable oxygen to be carried across a cell to the **mitochondria** where the oxygen is consumed and energy transfer takes place (which for example enables muscle tissue to contract). Arriving (arterial) blood has an oxygen partial pressure ($pO_2 = 13.3$ kPa). This is greater than tissue pO_2 since the oxygen is being used up in the cells during the energy creating process. Because **myoglobin** in the tissue cells has a greater affinity for oxygen than does haemoglobin, oxygen diffuses **through** the capillary and cell walls **from** the blood **into** the tissue cells. Myoglobin then facilitates oxygen transfer to the mitochondria, notably at the start of exercise and during intense exercise when cellular pO_2 decreases considerably.

Oxygen transfer at rest

At a pO_2 of 5.5 kPa, which is the normal pO_2 in resting tissue capillaries, haemoglobin is about 70% saturated (this corresponds to red vertical line **B** in figure A.27). This means that approximately 30% of the oxygen bound to haemoglobin is released into the blood and can diffuse into the tissue spaces.

Oxygen transfer during vigorous exercise

During **vigorous exercise** the pO_2 in tissue spaces may decline to levels as low as 2.5 kPa. Therefore, looking at line **C** in figure A.27, only about 25% of the haemoglobin remains saturated, and hence 75% of the oxygen bound to haemoglobin is released into the blood and can diffuse through the capillary walls into the active tissue spaces. The absorption and utilisation of oxygen from the blood leads to a difference in the oxygen content of arterial and venous blood known as the **arterio-venous oxygen difference** or **a-$\bar{\text{v}}$O$_{2diff}$**.

Differences in oxygen and carbon dioxide – arterio-venous oxygen difference (a-$\bar{v}$O$_{2diff}$)

At rest, as blood moves from arteries to veins, its oxygen content varies from 20 ml of oxygen per 100 ml of arterial blood to 15 ml of oxygen per 100 ml of venous blood. In figure A.28 you can see the difference between these two values (20 ml − 15 ml = 5 ml. This value represents the **arterio-venous oxygen difference (a-$\bar{\text{v}}$O$_{2diff}$**). Note that the bar over the v in a-$\bar{\text{v}}$O$_{2diff}$ refers to an average based on calculations for mixed venous return. This value represents the extent to which oxygen has been removed from the blood as it passes through the body. This means that, **at rest**, about 75% of the blood's original oxygen load remains bonded to the haemoglobin. This is called the **oxygen reserve**, which is immediately available for exercise as it begins.

During exercise the a-$\bar{\text{v}}$O$_{2diff}$ value triples leaving only 25% of the blood's original oxygen load remaining bonded to the haemoglobin as illustrated in figure A.29.

A **long-term effect** of aerobic training is to increase the a-$\bar{\text{v}}$O$_{2diff}$ because trained athletes can extract more oxygen from the blood. This increase in a-$\bar{\text{v}}$O$_{2diff}$ is also attributed to a more effective distribution of arterial blood from inactive tissue to the active tissue and increased capillarisation and utilisation of capillaries around and through active tissues.

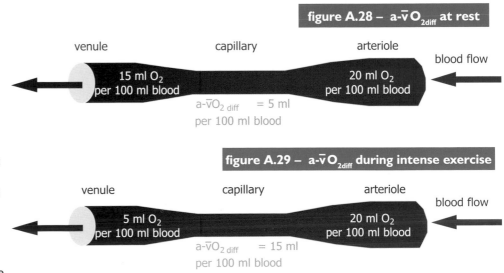

figure A.28 – a-$\bar{\text{v}}$O$_{2diff}$ at rest

venule capillary arteriole

blood flow

15 ml O$_2$ per 100 ml blood

20 ml O$_2$ per 100 ml blood

a-$\bar{\text{v}}$O$_2$ diff = 5 ml per 100 ml blood

figure A.29 – a-$\bar{\text{v}}$O$_{2diff}$ during intense exercise

venule capillary arteriole

blood flow

5 ml O$_2$ per 100 ml blood

20 ml O$_2$ per 100 ml blood

a-$\bar{\text{v}}$O$_2$ diff = 15 ml per 100 ml blood

The effect of blood acidity, partial pressure of carbon dioxide and temperature on oxygen release – the Böhr effect

Other factors influence the degree to which oxygen binds to haemoglobin. **During exercise**, tissue cell and blood **temperature** increases, **pCO_2** increases due to the greater need for energy, and **pH** decreases due to the greater presence of H^+ ions from lactic acid or creation of H^+ ions from carbonic acid by the released carbon dioxide. All these conditions cause reduction in the affinity of haemoglobin for oxygen. This means that more oxygen is released (that would not be the case if no exercise were being taken), and hence more oxygen is then available to active tissue sites which are working harder. **So the harder the tissue is working, the more oxygen is released.**

The effect of increases in acidity, pCO_2 and temperature is to cause the oxyhaemoglobin dissociation curve to shift downward and to the right (enhanced unloading). This phenomenon is called the '**Böhr effect**'.

Carbon dioxide transport

Carbon dioxide is produced in the cells as an end product of tissue cell respiration (production of energy from combination of fuel with oxygen). Hence, the fluid within cells has a higher pCO_2 than in the blood, so CO_2 diffuses back though cell and capillary walls in the **opposite** direction (from tissue to departing blood) as oxygen (refer back to figure A.26, page 31).

Carbon dioxide is **transported** in venous blood as shown in figure A.30. In the lung capillaries, the carbon dioxide is released. It diffuses from the blood into the alveoli and is expired out of the lungs (refer back to figure A.25, page 31).

figure A.30 – carbon dioxide transport

- carbaminohaemoglobin (23%)
- **CARBON DIOXIDE TRANSPORT**
- carbonic acid (dissociated into H^+ and HCO_3^-) (70%)
- dissolved in plasma (7%)

Neural regulation of pulmonary ventilation (breathing)

The **respiratory control centre** (**RCC** – see figure A.31) is located within the medulla oblongata of the brain, and regulates pulmonary ventilation. Rate of breathing (also called the **frequency** of breathing (f) and defined as '**the number of breaths taken in one minute**') and **depth of breathing** (**TV**) are controlled by neurones within the medulla. Although the medullary neurones establish a basic rhythm of breathing, their activities can be influenced by input from other parts of the brain and by input from peripherally located receptors summarised in figure A.32 below.

figure A.31 – respiratory control in the brain

- inspiratory centre
- expiratory centre
- respiratory control centre
- **THE BRAIN**
- apneustic centre
- pneumotaxic centre

figure A.32 – primary factors affecting control of ventilation

- temperature
- stretch receptors in lung tissue (proprioceptors)
- proprioceptors in joints and muscles
- central chemoreceptors
- peripheral chemoreceptors
- higher centres of the brain
- irritant receptors
- to ventilatory muscles
- **RESPIRATORY CONTROL CENTRE IN THE MEDULLA**

The **RCC** consists of two parts:

- The **inspiratory centre** is responsible for the basic rhythm of ventilation. At rest impulses are sent via the **phrenic** and **intercostal nerves** to the external intercostal muscles and diaphragm causing these muscles to contract to bring about inspiration. When stimulation ceases these muscles relax causing expiration.
- The **expiratory centre** is inactive during quiet breathing. However, during forceful breathing such as during exercise, the expiratory centre actively sends impulses to stimulate the muscles of expiration (sternocleidomastoid, scalenes, pectoralis major and minor) to increase the **rate of breathing** (refer to table 3 on page 28, to remind yourself of the mechanics of breathing).

Two additional brain centres aid the control of breathing:

- The **apneustic center** controls the intensity of breathing. It does this by prolonging the firing of the inspiratory neurones, thereby increasing **TV**.
- The **pneumotaxic centre** antagonises the apneustic center, resulting in the fine-tuning of the breathing rate (**f**).

The role of blood carbon dioxide in changing breathing rate

Chemoreceptors

Chemoreceptors respond to increased concentration of CO_2 in the blood.

- **Central chemoreceptors** (located in the medulla) are the major regulators whose function is to attempt to keep pCO_2 to below 5.3 kPa as well as controlling increased acidity (or decreased pH due to increased numbers of H^+ ions from carbonic acid in the blood plasma).
- **Peripheral chemoreceptors** (in the aortic and carotid bodies) provide an early warning system as they sense the constituents of blood as it passes them.
- Both central and peripheral chemoreceptors respond to **increased** pCO_2 and **decreased** pH and pO_2 (oxygen concentration in the blood).

These receptors send messages to the inspiratory centre which then stimulates respiratory muscles to increase **rate (f)** and **depth of breathing** (**TV**) as described above. For example, lack of oxygen at high altitude stimulates respiration, so that the person will breathe more often and more deeply. This has nothing to do with exercise, but indicates how these receptors work. This chemical control (via the pneumotaxic and apneustic centres of the brain) adjusts ventilation to maintain arterial blood chemistry within narrow limits. This means that these brain centres attempt to keep blood oxygen to a maximum, and blood carbon dioxide to a minimum by causing the person to adjust breathing rate and depth.

Other systems for control of breathing

Refer back to figure A.32.

Proprioceptors in joints and muscles

Proprioceptors (such as working muscle spindles) send signals to the RCC about the tension within and state of contraction of a muscle, and hence whether a muscle is being used intensely or not. During physical activity, increased stimulation will increase rate and depth of breathing via the inspiratory centre as described above.

Lung stretch receptors

A type of **proprioceptor**, these lung receptors are located within the walls of the bronchii and bronchioles. When stimulated, these receptors relay information, via the vagus nerves, to the RCC to inhibit the inspiratory centre, resulting in expiration via the expiratory centre. As expiration proceeds, the stretch receptors are no longer stimulated and the decreased inhibitory effect on the inhibitory centre allows the inspiratory centre to become active again. This effect is known as the **Hering-Brewer Reflex**. Its overriding effect is to prevent over-inflation of the lungs.

Temperature

Thermoreceptors (located in the hypothalamus part of the brain) respond to increases in body / blood temperatures. These receptors directly excite the neurones of the RCC and help control ventilation during prolonged exercise.

Irritant receptors

The activation of touch, thermal and pain receptors can also stimulate the RCC.

Higher centres of the brain

Through the cerebral cortex, it is possible consciously to increase or decrease rate and depth of breathing. Swimmers and sports divers **hyperventilate** and **breath-hold** to improve physical performance. At the start of a swimming race athletes hyperventilate on the starting blocks to prolong breath-hold time during the swim. In short course racing, the breath-hold time can be the whole of the racing time. Snorkel divers hyperventilate to extend the time over which they can hold their breath. During breath-hold time the pO_2 content of the blood can fall to critically low values before arterial pCO_2 increases to stimulate breathing.

Emotions acting through the limbic system can also affect the RCC.

Effect of long-term training on lung function

Intense **aerobic** exercise (figure A.33) has the effect of forcing the person to breathe more deeply and more often (the vital capacity of the lung is fully utilised, and the breathing frequency (**f**) increases). Therefore, as a result of long-term exercise, the following adaptations take place within the body which tend to make the transfer of oxygen from air breathed in to working muscle more efficient.

figure A.33 – effect of exercise on respiratory systems

- respiratory muscles get fitter and stronger
- increase in lung volumes and capacity to breathe air
- improved blood flow to upper lobes of lungs
- smaller oxygen debt
- EFFECT OF EXERCISE ON RESPIRATORY SYSTEMS
- improved utilisation of the alveoli
- improved recovery from exercise
- increase in gaseous exchange

- Improved **strengthening** of respiratory muscles.

- **Increases** in pulmonary blood flow particularly to the upper lobes of the lungs, hence greater utilisation of alveoli for pulmonary diffusion.

- Hence **increased** gaseous exchange and $\dot{V}O_{2max}$ at high intensity aerobic workloads.

- At **submaximal workloads** oxygen requirements will be less because of **greater efficiency** of oxygen uptake and general improvements in lung function such as increases in tidal volume (TV) and vital capacity (VC) at the expense of residual volume (RV).

- At **submaximal workloads** there would be a **slight decrease** in **f** (frequency of breaths).

- During **maximal aerobic workloads** there would be a **big increase** in **f**, hence a large increase in minute ventilation ($\dot{V}E$).

CARDIAC AND VASCULAR FUNCTION

Introductory anatomy of the heart

Heart structure

The heart (figure A.34) is a muscular pump lying deep within the chest cavity and slightly to the left of the sternum.

Heart layers

The **heart** consists of three layers:

figure A.34 – heart structure

- The outer layer, known as the **pericardium,** is a double layered bag surrounding the heart. The fluid between the two layers reduces friction between the heart itself and the surrounding tissue as the heart moves (beats). This layer also maintains the heart's shape.

- The second layer is called the **myocardium** or striped cardiac muscle tissue consisting of united fibres (united because they are all in one mass) joined by intercalated discs. This muscle tissue is activated by the '**all-or-none law**'. The cardiac impulse is transmitted throughout the entire myocardium at the same point in time, and hence this muscle tissue is all activated at once. When there is no cardiac impulse, none of the heart muscle can be activated. Since the heart generates its own impulse it is said to be **myogenic**. The **septum** consists of myocardial tissue (muscle) and divides the heart into two sections, each of which acts as a pump.

- The third layer is an inner glistening membrane called the **endocardium**. Its function is to prevent friction between the heart muscle and flowing blood.

Heart chambers

The heart consists of **four** chambers:
- **Two** are at the top (**atria**). Both the right and left atria have thin walls.
- **Two** are at the bottom (**ventricles**). Both ventricles have thicker walls than the atria. The left ventricle wall is the thickest, since this ventricle pumps blood to the main body mass, whereas the **right ventricle** pumps blood to the **lungs only**.

Heart valves

Heart valves **prevent backflow of blood**, with the (**cuspid**) **mitral** or **bicuspid** valve sited between the left atria and the left ventricle, and the **tricuspid** valve sited between the right atria and the right ventricle. The **semi-lunar** valves prevent back-flow of blood into the heart from the pulmonary artery and aorta, and only allow blood to flow in one direction through the heart. This means that when the heart muscle contracts, it only pumps the blood out to the lungs (pulmonary artery) or body (aorta), and not back the wrong way.

Blood vessels

Blood Vessels attached to the heart are the **vena cavae** and the **pulmonary artery** on the right side, and the **pulmonary vein** and the **aorta** on the left side.

Coronary blood supply

The coronary blood supply consists of arteries (within the cardiac muscle itself) which supply glucose and oxygen (O_2) to myocardial tissue, and coronary veins, which transport carbon dioxide (CO_2) and other wastes from the heart muscle.

How the heart works

The cardiac impulse

- The dynamic action of the heart is that of a dual-action pump in that both sides of the heart contract simultaneously, even though the functions of the two sides are different.

- Cardiac contractions are initiated by an electrical impulse (the **cardiac impulse** – see figure A.35) that originates from the pacemaker or sinoatrial node (**SA node**). Because the heart generates its own impulses it is said to be **myogenic**.

- The electrical impulse travels down the atrial mycardium until it reaches the atrioventricular node (**AV node**) situated in the wall of the atrial septum. This is followed by the atrial walls contracting (atrial systole).

- The AV node conducts the impulse through the **bundle of His** to the branched network of **Purkinje fibres** located within the septum and the ventricular walls (both the bundle of His and the Purkinje fibres are modified cardiac muscle), causing both ventricles to contract (**ventricular systole**).

The heart's conducting system regulates the sequence of events that make up the cardiac cycle.

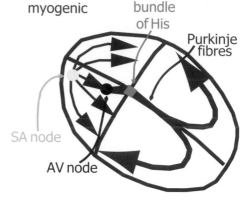

figure A.35 – the cardiac impulse

The cardiac cycle

The cardiac cycle (figure A.36) is a sequence of events that make up one heartbeat and lasts for about 0.8 seconds, thus occurring about 75 times per minute.

The cardiac cycle consists of a period of relaxation of the heart muscle, known as **diastole** (0.5 seconds) followed by a period of contraction of the heart muscle, known as **systole** (0.3 seconds). During systole the electrical impulse is initiated in a set-timed sequence.

figure A.36 – the cardiac cycle

pulse

CARDIAC CYCLE

diastole = 0.5s

systole = 0.3s

atrial systole

ventricular systole

Cardiac diastole

During **diastole** (0.5 seconds), the relaxed heart muscle allows the chambers to fill with blood. This occurs with the cuspid valves open, and the semi-lunar valves closed.

Cardiac systole

During **atrial systole** (0.3 seconds), the SA node impulse causes a wave-like contraction over the atria forcing blood past the cuspid valves into the ventricles. The semi-lunar valves remain closed.

In **ventricular systole**, the impulse reaches the AV node, the cuspid valves close because the fluid pressure (of blood) in the ventricles is greater than in the atria, and rises further as the ventricles contract. The semi-lunar valves open (since now the fluid pressure in the ventricles is greater than in the main arteries) and blood is pushed out into the pulmonary artery (towards the lungs) and the aorta (around the body).

The **pulse** is a wave of pressure produced by the contraction of the left ventricle. This pressure wave transmits itself around the arterial system of the rest of the body. The frequency of the waves represents the number of beats per minute (heart rate).

Cardiac output, stroke volume and heart rate

- See figure A.37.
- **Heart rate** (HR) is defined as '**the number of beats of the heart per minute (bpm)**'.
- The average resting HR for males is 70 bpm, and for females 72 bpm.
- At rest, the HR for a trained athlete = 60 bpm (less than this would be bradycardia) and the HR for an untrained person = 70-90 bpm.
- **Maximum heart rate** can be calculated using the formula: $HR_{max} = 220 - age$.

figure A.37 – cardiac factors

- **Stroke volume (SV)** is defined as 'the volume of blood pumped by the left ventricle of the heart per beat' and is determined by venous return and elasticity and contractility of the myocardium.
- The **SV** for a trained athlete = 110 ml, and the **SV** for an untrained person = 70 ml.
- **Cardiac output ($\dot{Q}$)** is the volume of blood pumped by the left ventricle of the heart in one minute, and is the product of stroke volume and heart rate:

$$\dot{Q} = SV \times HR$$

For an untrained person at rest, $\dot{Q} = 80 \times 70$ = 5.60 l/min (or dm³ min⁻¹).
For an untrained person during maximal exercise, $\dot{Q} = 110 \times 190$ = 19.81 l/min (or dm³ min⁻¹).
For an endurance athlete at rest, $\dot{Q} = 110 \times 51$ = 5.61 l/min (or dm³ min⁻¹).
For an endurance athlete during maximal exercise, $\dot{Q} = 190 \times 200$ = 38 l/min (or dm³ min⁻¹).

Cardiac hypertrophy

Regular aerobic training results in **hypertrophy** of the cardiac muscle, meaning that the muscle becomes larger and stronger. This means that the heart pumps a larger volume of blood out per beat, hence the stroke volume is larger. This is termed **bradycardia** and has the consequence of producing a resting HR below 60 bpm. This in turn affects cardiac output, as illustrated in the equations above.

At rest, a bigger, stronger heart pumps more blood out per beat, even though the body's requirement for oxygenated blood would be approximately the same as for an untrained person. Hence resting heart rate decreases, with the net effect of an unchanged cardiac output. Highly trained sportspeople tend to have resting heart rates of well below 60 bpm.

During **maximum exercise**, an increase in heart rate, coupled with an increase in stroke volume, results in an increase in cardiac output. As expected, cardiac output for the endurance athlete is more than double that of the untrained person due to **cardiac muscle hypertrophy**.

During the **recovery period** following maximal exercise, heart rate will decrease more rapidly, and so will return to its resting level much more quickly for the endurance athlete when compared with an untrained person.

Hence heart rate recovery is used as an **index of cardio-respiratory fitness.**

Heart rate – response to exercise

figure A.38 – heart rate response to exercise

Changes in heart rate during different intensities of physical activity

Referring to the graph in figure A.38:

a = **Anticipatory rise** due to the hormonal action of adrenaline and noradrenaline. This happens because the person tends to get excited **before** the exercise starts, and hence heart rate rises slightly.

b = **Sharp rise** during anaerobic work due to proprioceptor sensory stimulation, and also due to continued release of hormones and action of the skeletal muscle pump (see pages 41 and 44 respectively).

c = **Steady state** and some recovery of O_2 debt (aerobic).

d = **Continued high HR** due to maximal workloads which continue to stress anaerobic systems, producing lactic acid + CO_2 + K^+, which stimulate chemoreceptors. Additionally, intrinsic factors are also stimulated at maximal level (refer to page 42).

e = **Rapid recovery** due to cessation of proprioceptive stimuli, the skeletal muscle pump, and the withdrawal of hormones.

f = **Slow recovery**, clearance of metabolites such as lactic acid, as systems return to normal resting values.

Stroke volume – response to exercise

Referring to the graph in figure A.39:

a = an increase in stroke volume, from a resting value of 60 ml beat^{-1} to 85 ml beat^{-1} to the start of the exercise period, is due to the release of hormones such as adrenaline and noradrenaline. This effect is known as the **anticipatory rise**.

b = an increase in stroke volume as exercise commences. This is primarily due an **increased venous return** and **increased myocardial contraction during ventricular systole** (**Starling's Law of the Heart**) which causes the heart muscle to contract more forcefully from 85 ml beat^{-1} to more than 110 ml beat^{-1} during submaximal work.

- Note that stroke volume increases to maximal values during submaximal work and does not increase further as work increases towards maximal effort. This is because once the heart is expanding and contracting utilising its fullest possible size, it obviously cannot get any bigger even though the energy needs of the body are greater.

- At this increased value, stroke volume is unable to increase any further since the overlap of the actin and myosin fibres during cardiac systole has reached maximum, and therefore stroke volume levels off.

c = as work intensity increases during maximal exercise, there is a slight decline in stroke volume. At this point heart rate will rise rapidly to sustain the continued increase in cardiac output to meet exercise demands.

Cardiac output – response to exercise

Since **cardiac output** is the product of stroke volume and heart rate values ($\dot{Q}$ = SV x HR), it will increase directly in line with exercise intensity.

Starling's law of the heart

This is a simple but important way in which we can look at how blood flows through the heart. Starling's law simply says that '**the same volume of blood must enter the heart as leaves it during a period of time**'. This is because blood is an incompressible fluid which cannot change volume under the pressures to be found in or around the heart. Hence this is a mechanism for return of venous blood to the heart once it has flowed around the body and given up its energy to muscle or the vital organs.

Cardiovascular drift

With **prolonged aerobic exercise**, at a constant exercise intensity such as marathon racing or **aerobic exercising in a hot environment**, stroke volume gradually decreases and **heart rate** increases, and hence cardiac output remains approximately constant as in figure A.40. During this process arterial blood pressure declines. These responses are due to the need to transfer excess heat produced by active tissues from deep in the body (known as the core) to the skin where it has access to the outside environment. This heat is moved by the blood during vasodilation of blood vessels directly underneath the skin. Evaporation is the primary route for heat dissipation and so as fluid or sweat evaporates heat is lost. Loss of fluid results in

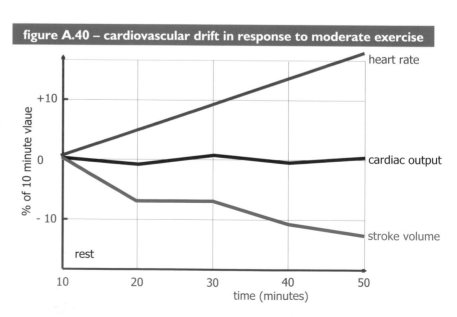

figure A.39 – stroke rate response to exercise

figure A.40 – cardiovascular drift in response to moderate exercise

a reduced plasma volume and subsequent decreased venous return and stroke volume. A **reduced stroke volume** initiates a compensatory **heart rate increase** to maintain a **nearly constant cardiac output** as exercise progresses. All these circulatory responses are collectively referred to as the **cardiovascular drift**.

It is important for athletes to **rehydrate** with sports drinks (water containing a little sodium and glucose) during prolonged exercise periods or whilst performing aerobic exercise in a hot environment to minimise the loss of fluids and thus reduce the effects of the cardiovascular drift.

Regulation of heart rate

The cardiac control centre (**CCC**), in the medulla oblongata in the brain, regulates feedback that results in changes to heart rate from important **neural**, **hormonal** and **intrinsic** factors (see figure A.41 below).

Neural factors

Neural factors are the key controlling regulators of heart activity, and they are:

- **Chemoreceptor reflexes** which involve receptors located in blood vessels such as the aortic arch and carotid sinuses, detect chemical changes such as blood O_2, CO_2, H^+ concentrations, and pH levels. Decrease in O_2 and pH levels, and increase in CO_2 and H^+ concentrations, **all** stimulate increases in heart rate via the cardiac accelerator nerve.
- **Proprioceptor reflexes** found in muscle spindles and Golgi tendons respond to mechanical stimuli such as compression, bending or stretching of cells, and detect changes in movement. Increase in tension within cell structures will increase heart rate via the cardiac accelerator nerve.
- **Baroreceptor reflexes** are receptors located in blood vessels (such as the aortic arch and carotid sinuses). Their role is to detect changes in blood pressure. When blood pressure is too high the parasympathetic nerve releases acetylcholine which decreases heart rate.

Hormonal factors

Hormones are released by the body in response to various stimuli, and those that affect heart rate are:

- **Noradrenaline** and **adrenaline** (the key hormonal regulators) act to accelerate heart rate (tachycardia) and increase the strength of ventricular contraction which increases stroke volume.
- **Acetylcholine** slows the heart (bradycardia) as described below.
- **Thyroid** hormone and **glucagon** increase HR.
- **Increase in glucagon** levels assist in the breakdown of **glycogen to release glucose** into the circulatory system to fuel muscular contractions.

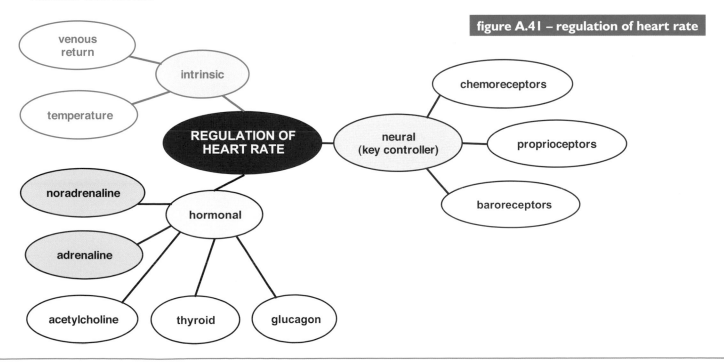

figure A.41 – regulation of heart rate

Intrinsic factors

Intrinsic factors account for changes in venous return:

- **Venous return** is the amount of blood that returns to the heart during each cardiac cycle. This changes as a result of the actions of the skeletal muscle and respiratory pumps, and electrolyte balance (Na^+, K^+) in muscular tissue.
- **Myocardial temperature** also affects venous return, in that the speed of nerve impulse transmission increases with temperature, and this will increase heart rate.
- **Starling's Law of the Heart** states that cardiac output is equal to venous return. An increase in venous return stretches the ventricular walls more and results in an increased strength of contraction and therefore an increase in stroke volume.

Neural control

Neural impulses (resulting from feedback from neural, hormonal and intrinsic control) override the inherent rhythm of the heartbeat. Signals originate in the **cardiac control centre (CCC)** in the medulla and travel via the antagonistic actions of the sympathetic and parasympathetic nervous systems, to the pacemaker or SA node.

Sympathetic influence

- The **sympathetic nervous system**, the **SNS** (via the cardiac accelerator nerve) releases the neurotransmitters adrenaline and noradrenaline onto the SA node to **speed up** heart rate.

Parasympathetic influence

- The **parasympathetic nervous system**, the **PNS** (via the vagus nerve) releases the neurotransmitter **acetylcholine** onto the SA node to **slow down** heart rate.

Endurance training creates an imbalance between these two sets of nerves in favour of parasympathetic dominance. This type of training is also known to decrease the intrinsic firing rate of the SA node. These adaptations account for the significant **bradycardia** observed amongst highly conditioned endurance athletes.

The vascular system

The vascular system consists of blood and blood vessels.

Blood

Blood is composed of:

- **Plasma** is the fluid portion of blood consisting of around 60% of total blood volume. Plasma can decrease by 10% of its normal amount or more with intense exercise at high temperatures.
- **Red blood cells** contain an iron-rich protein called haemoglobin. Haemoglobin combines with oxygen and transports it around the body.
- **White blood cells** fight infection and disease.
- **Platelets** are responsible for blood clotting.

Blood transports gases, nutrients such as oxygen and glucose, waste products such as carbon dioxide, and hormones such as adrenaline.

Transportation of oxygen and carbon dioxide by the vascular system

 STUDENT NOTE Transport of O_2 and CO_2 to and from the lungs and in the context of gaseous exchange within working tissue was discussed above. Most of this information is repeated here in the context of the vascular system.

Oxygen transport

- **97%** of the **oxygen** carried by the blood is transported via **haemoglobin** in the **red corpuscles,** since haemoglobin readily attaches itself to O_2 when exposed to it in the alveoli within lung tissue. The remaining **3%** of the oxygen carried is dissolved in the blood plasma.
- **Exercise** causes a **small increase** in **pulmonary blood pressure, which distorts red blood corpuscles** within the alveolar capillary system, and this enables **10 times as much oxygen** to be picked up as at rest.

- The formula for the oxygenation of **haemoglobin** (Hb) is: **Hb $+4O_2 \rightarrow$ Hb$(O_2)_4$**, where one molecule of Hb combines with 4 molecules of O_2.
- The amount of oxygen transported by the blood is a function of cardiac output and the oxygen **content** of the blood.
- At rest, we use about **25%** of available oxygen. This leaves an unextracted 75% of the available oxygen in blood returned to the heart via venous return. This is called the **oxygen reserve**, which is immediately available for exercise when it begins.

Carbon dioxide transport

Carbon Dioxide (CO_2) is produced by the **respiration** process in tissue cells, the oxidation of fuels in oxygen to produce energy, which in muscle cells enables the person to move / run / jump. CO_2 is transported in venous blood as:

- **Carbonic acid** (most of which dissociates into H^+ and HCO_3^-) (70%).
- **Carbaminohaemoglobin** (23%).
- **Dissolved in blood plasma** (7%).

Carbon dioxide is excreted from the lungs during expiration. This CO_2 has to be removed from the tissue cells since if it stays it forms carbonic acid (dissociated into H^+ and HCO_3^- as mentioned above), which in effect acts as a poison and will reduce a muscle cell to complete inactivity within a few seconds. Further notes on gas transport and exchange are to be found on pages 32 onwards.

Hence it is very important to maintain an efficient blood transport system (carrying oxygen into, and carbon dioxide away from muscle) if a person is to be able to exercise and live healthily.

Pulmonary and systemic circulation

There are two systems circulating blood from the heart as in figure A.42.

The systemic circulatory system

This system consists of all the vessels which carry oxygenated blood away from the heart via the aorta, the arteries and arterioles and on to the capillaries embedded in the working tissues of the body. Then after giving up the oxygen (to the working tissues), the deoxygenated blood returns to the heart via venules, veins and vena cavae.

The pulmonary circulatory system

This system consists of the pulmonary arteries, which carry this de-oxygenated blood from the right atrium of the heart to the lungs, where the blood is re-oxygenated from the air breathed into the lungs. Oxygenated blood is then returned to the heart via the pulmonary veins.

Blood vessel structure

Blood vessels (see table 6 on page 44 and summary in figure A.43) have properties that help circulation and allow blood to perform many of its functions.

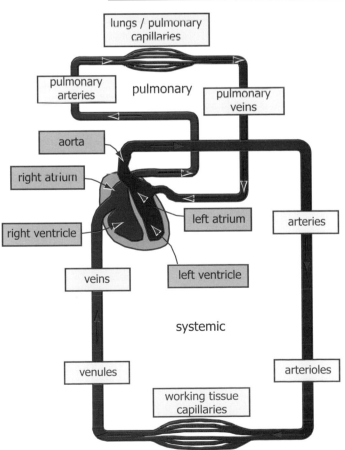

figure A.42 – the circulatory system

lungs / pulmonary capillaries

pulmonary arteries

pulmonary

pulmonary veins

aorta

right atrium

left atrium

arteries

right ventricle

left ventricle

veins

systemic

venules

arterioles

working tissue capillaries

Table 6 – **blood vessel structure and function**

type of blood vessel	vessel structure	vessel function / structure	vessel function	blood pressure in vessels
elastic arteries (aorta)	are thin-walled with large diameters	middle layer (tunica media) contains a high proportion of elastic fibres and little smooth muscle	during ventricular systole, these arteries extend with a rise in left ventricular pressure and recoil (contract) during ventricular diastole	transport blood at high pressure
muscular arteries	thick-walled vessels with small diameters	middle layer (tunica media) consists of some elastic fibres and lots of smooth muscle	smooth muscle controls the shape of the central space or lumen via **vasoconstriction** and **vasodilation**	transport blood at high pressure
arterioles	reduce in size and muscular content as they get closer to the capillary bed	smooth muscle (in the tunica media)	smooth muscle contracts (to reduce blood inflow) and relax (to increase blood inflow) to control inflow to their own capillary bed	blood pressure reduces as vessel diameter reduces but total CSA of all vessels increases
pre-capillary sphincters (contained within arterioles)	placed before capillary bed (within muscle or other tissue)		contract (to reduce blood inflow) and relax (to increase blood inflow) to control inflow to their own capillary bed	
capillaries	tiny blood vessels whose walls are one cell thick, have semi-permeable walls or small spaces in the walls (tunica intima)	walls allow fluids rich in nutrients (O_2 and glucose) to be delivered to tissue cells. Nutrients travel through the capillary walls into the tissue cells	waste products (CO_2 and urea / lactate) are removed by travelling through the capillary walls from the tissue cells into the blood fluids (this is the opposite direction to the nutrients)	very low blood pressure as total vessel area reaches a maximum
venules	walls consist of an inner wall (tunica intima), surrounded by a few smooth muscle cells	positioned where several capillaries unite to collect outflow from a capillary bed at low pressure	as venules approach the veins they develop a thin middle layer coat (tunica media)	blood pressure still very low
muscular veins	thin walled vessels contain less smooth muscle and fewer elastic fibres than arteries of same size	have non-return valves, called pocket valves, positioned within the central space (or lumen) of these vessels	sympathetic nerves causing **venoconstriction** activate the tunica media. The outer wall (tunica externa) is supported by collagen	low blood pressure
veins	low pressure blood reservoirs moving stored blood into general circulation during exercise	blood flows in the veins because of muscular action in the surrounding skeletal muscle - **skeletal muscle pump**	contracting muscle squashes veins forcing blood forwards towards the heart (since blood cannot flow back away from the heart due to the pocket valves within each vein)	low blood pressure
vena cavae	are valveless and contain more smooth muscle in the middle wall	smooth muscle acts to constrict or dilate the vessel (venomotor control)	deliver blood to the right atrium of the heart	low blood pressure

Except for single-walled capillaries and venules, all blood vessels have 3 layers. The thickness and composition of the layers vary with blood vessel type and diameter. Smooth involuntary muscle (within the middle layer of blood vessel walls) regulates the diameter of blood vessels via **vasomotor** and **venomotor control** as described below and at the top of page 47.

The further away from the heart, the bigger the total cross sectional area of all blood vessels carrying blood, hence the speed of flow is lower (as the blood flows into a bigger space) see figure A.43, right.

The venous return mechanism

The **venous return mechanism** (see figure A.44) is the process by which blood returns to the right side of the heart. It depends on:

- **Gravity** that assists the flow of blood from body parts above the heart.
- **Skeletal muscle pump** as described above.
- **Respiratory pump** relies upon the changes in pressure that occurs in the thoracic and abdominal cavities during inspiration and expiration. These pressure changes compress nearby veins and so assist blood flow back to the heart.
- **Valves (pocket valves)** ensure that blood can only flow in one direction back towards the heart.
- **Venomotor control** describes the limited capacity of veins to change their shape and therefore slightly increase venous return, due to **venoconstriction**. For a fuller description of this concept see page 47.

Hence the mechanism by which the bulk of blood returns to the heart during exercise is via the skeletal muscle pump, with the respiratory and cardiac pumps also helping.

figure A.43 – blood vessels

figure A.44 – venous return

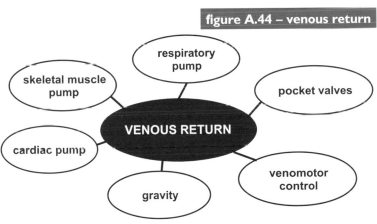

How is blood flow controlled?

Changes in blood vessel diameter depend upon the metabolic needs of body tissues. The vasomotor centre located in the medulla oblongata of the brain, controls blood pressure and blood flow. This is an example of **negative feedback control**, in which an **increase** of blood pressure, as sensed by baroreceptors, causes a **decrease** in the blood pressure by changing blood vessel diameter. As cardiac output increases, sensory receptors such as **baroreceptors** (responding to changes in blood pressure) and **chemoreceptors** (responding to changes in chemical composition of the blood) are stimulated.

Vasomotor control

Vasomotor control is concerned with the ability of muscular **arteries** and **arterioles** to change their shape. **During exercise**, sensory receptors, such as baroreceptors and chemoreceptors, are stimulated. The vasomotor centre receives this sensory information. From here sympathetic nerves carry impulses to the smooth muscle walls of arteries and arterioles.

Non-active tissue

Within non-active tissues, these impulses cause **vasoconstriction** (tightening or narrowing) in these arteries and arterioles, and to the pre-capillary sphincters, located at the openings of capillaries. The effect of this constriction is to **restrict blood flow** into the capillary bed of the non-active tissue.

Active tissue

In contrast, within **active tissue**, sympathetic stimulation to the smooth walls of arteries and arterioles and pre-capillary sphincters **is reduced**, and the muscles in the arterial walls and pre-capillary sphincters relax. Therefore these vessels dilate or open wider (known as **vasodilation**), the pre-capillary sphincters open up, resulting in **additional blood flow** into active muscles.

Hence, **as exercise begins**, as a result of vasomotor control, blood flow is diverted to active skeletal muscle where it is needed. This redirection of blood flow is called the **vascular shunt** (also known as the blood shunting mechanism) and is illustrated in figures A.45 and A.46.

The vasomotor centre works in conjunction with the cardiac

figure A.45 – the vascular shunt mechanism

vascular shunt mechanism during exercise

ORGANS ◄──► MUSCLES

increased sympathetic stimulation | decreased sympathetic stimulation

vasoconstriction of arterioles and pre-capillary sphincters | vasodilation of pre-capillary sphincters and arterioles

decreased blood flow to capillaries of non-essential organs | increased blood flow to capillaries of working muscles

figure A.46 – the vascular shunt

redistribution of blood during exercise

control centre in maintaining blood pressure.

The vascular shunt

Table 7 illustrates the redistribution of blood flow, as exercise begins, away from the major organs of the body towards working muscle.

Table 7 - **comparison of the distribution of cardiac output at rest and during exercise**

| tissue | proportions of blood in various tissues | | | |
| | rest | | maximal exercise | |
	%	ml min^{-1}	%	ml min^{-1}
liver	27	1350	1	300
kidneys	22	1100	1	250
brain	14	700	3	750
heart	4	200	4	1000
muscle	20	1000	88	22000
skin	6	300	2	600
other	7	350	1	100
total	100	5000	100	25000

STUDENT NOTE

Note the five-fold increase in total rate of blood flow at maximal exercise, and the fact that the brain maintains approximately the same blood flow – otherwise if the rate of flow to the brain reduced substantially, the sportsperson would faint and fall to the ground!

Venomotor control

- **Venomotor control** describes the limited capacity of veins to change their shape. This is the result of venomotor tone, whereby the veins muscular coat receives stimulation from the sympathetic nervous system. The effect of limited **venoconstriction** of veins causes a small increase in blood velocity and hence **an increase** in venous return.

Blood pressure and velocity

Blood pressure is defined as '**the force exerted by the blood on the inside walls of blood vessels**' and so represents the driving force that moves blood through the circulatory system. It is the combination of cardiac output and peripheral resistance of blood vessels and is measured using a sphygmomanometer around the upper arm.

Systolic pressure (the highest pressure) is generated by left ventricular contraction (systole) as blood is ejected into the aorta and main arteries.

Diastolic pressure (the lowest pressure) is reached when the heart relaxes (diastole) and the aortic valves close as blood drains from the arteries.
Hence blood pressure is measured using these two pressures:

<u>systolic pressure</u> mmHg
diastolic pressure

Blood velocity

- You will notice from figure A.47 that as the blood flows through the network of blood vessels the blood velocity falls. This is because blood flow encounters vessels which branch repeatedly, with a bigger space to flow into.

- This means that the vessels have a bigger total combined **cross sectional area** (**CSA**) and hence the blood slows down (**blood velocity** falls – see the solid red line in figure A.47). When blood reaches the capillaries, the **CSA** is a maximum (many tiny vessels) and therefore the blood flows very slowly.

- This process reverses as the blood flows back towards the heart, **CSA** reduces (see the green line in figure A.47), blood velocity increases until it almost matches the speed of blood leaving the heart.

- You have to note that the same volume of blood will return to the heart is leaves it (in any given period of time) – this is **Starling's Law of the Heart**.

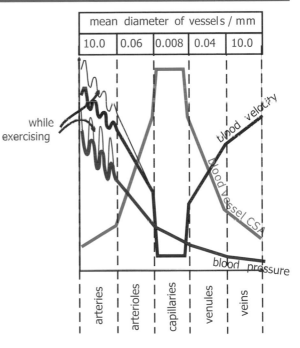

figure A.47 – blood pressure / velocity / CSA of vessels

mean diameter of vessels / mm				
10.0	0.06	0.008	0.04	10.0

while exercising

blood velocity

blood vessel CSA

blood pressure

arteries | arterioles | capillaries | venules | veins

Blood pressure

- Blood pressure forces blood through arteries and arterioles, and as the **CSA** increases, the individual **diameters of blood vessels reduce**. This **increases** the peripheral resistance (the **resistance to flow of a fluid** through a tube), and therefore the blood pressure (black line in figure A.47) falls. Hence, once the blood has flowed through the capillary system the **pressure** forcing the flow onwards is **very low**.

- Therefore in veins, **venous return** is forced by the action of the **skeletal muscle** and **respiratory** pumps, and the action of the **cardiac** pump, which is the action of the heart itself beating as the heart forces blood out into the aorta, and draws blood in from the vena cavae. This follows from Starling's Law of the Heart as mentioned above.

During dynamic rhythmic exercise, the skeletal muscle and respiratory pumps are much bigger, therefore venous return is bigger and **blood flow** is higher. Also, as blood flow is increased, venous return is higher, the heart is stimulated to pump harder and more frequently hence the **systolic blood pressure** is increased – which in turn forces greater blood flow into the arteries - at greater **blood velocity**. Note that diastolic pressure remains relatively unchanged in dynamic exercise as in the values quoted in table 8 (page 48).

Table 8 – **blood pressure at rest and during exercise**

blood pressure in mmHg

	rest	dynamic exercise	static exercise
systolic	120	170	200
diastolic	80	88	120

Looking at table 8, during high resistance exercise such as isometric or static exercise or heavy weight training, there are big increases in both systolic and diastolic values. This is because sustained muscular forces compress peripheral arterioles, considerably increasing resistance to blood flow.

Regular aerobic training

Aerobic training results in a more efficient vascular system as long-term adaptations are produced in both blood and blood vessels.

Effect on blood

- Increases in red blood cell count means **more haemoglobin** is created and is available in blood for oxygen transport and hence an increase in $\dot{V}O_{2max}$.
- Increased blood plasma volume decreases **blood viscosity** and improves circulation and oxygen availability.

Effect on blood vessels

- **Increased** capillarisation, **improved** dilation of capillaries, and **improved** recruitment of existing capillaries in trained muscle, provide a **greater surface area** for gaseous exchange to take place in lungs and at active muscle cell sites.
- **Increased** a-$\bar{v}O_{2diff}$ at active tissue cell sites, because trained athletes can extract more oxygen from the blood. This increase in a-$\bar{v}O_{2diff}$ is also attributed to a more effective distribution of arterial blood from inactive tissue to the active tissue (i.e. improved vascular shunt mechanism) and increased capillarisation and utilisation of capillaries around active tissues.
- **Increased** elasticity and thickness of smooth muscle of arterial walls makes walls tougher and therefore less likely to stretch under pressure, thus maintaining blood pressure forcing blood through capillary network.

Effect on blood pressure

- **Resting blood pressure** (RBP) and BP pressure during submaximal exercise **reduces**.
- But during **maximal exercise** intensity the systolic blood pressure is **increased**.
- Diastolic pressure is decreased compared with pre-training values.

Practice questions

1) a) A hockey player has a match in one hour's time. Describe how inspiration occurs during this resting period.

    4 marks

   b) During the hockey match, the player must increase the volume of gas exchanged in the lungs and muscles. Explain the changes in the mechanics of breathing (inspiration and expiration) which facilitate this increase.

    6 marks

2) a) The diagram in figure A.48 represents the lung volume changes based on a number of spirometer readings during various breathing actions. With reference to the trace, briefly explain resting tidal volume (TV), expiratory reserve volume (ERV), vital capacity (VC), and residual volume (RV).

    4 marks

   b) Using the information in the spirometer trace, state what happens to the following volumes during the exercise period: residual volume, inspiratory volume (IRV), and expiratory volume (ERV).

    3 marks

figure A.48 – spirometer trace

c) Why does tidal volume change by only a small amount during the exercise period?   *3 marks*

d) Identify **two** effects of regular aerobic training on lung volumes and capacities.   *2 marks*

e) A student measured the volume of air that he / she ventilated at rest and during submaximal exercise. The results are shown in table 9 below.

Table 9 – **ventilation at rest and during submaximal exercise**

activity level	inhalation volume	breathing rate	minute ventilation
	(TV)	(f)	volume (V̇E)
at rest	500 ml	one every 6 seconds	A
submaximal exercise	800 ml	one every 2 seconds	B

Define what is meant by the term 'minute ventilation volume' and calculate the values for **A** and **B**, clearly showing the method used.   *4 marks*

3) a) Describe how pulmonary ventilation is regulated during quiet breathing.   *6 marks*

b) Identify the **three** chemical stimuli that control the rate and depth of breathing. How do these chemical stimuli control respiration during exercise?   *6 marks*

4) The breathing characteristics of individuals vary during physical activity. Table 10 shows the proportion of oxygen and carbon dioxide breathed during exercise compared with resting values.

Table 10 - **proportion of O_2 and CO_2 breathed during exercise, compared to at rest**

	inhaled air	exhaled air at rest	exhaled air during exercise
%O_2	21	17	15
%CO_2	0.049	3	6

a) Use the information in table 10 to describe the effects of exercise on gaseous exchange in the lungs. Explain why these changes occur.   *4 marks*

b) How does the blood transport oxygen?   *2 marks*

c) Explain how oxygen is exchanged **between** the blood and active muscle tissues.   *3 marks*

d) Identify the **three** ways CO_2 is transported by the blood.
How does increased CO_2 production stimulate further release of O_2 for tissue cell respiration?   *5 marks*

5) The binding of oxygen to haemoglobin depends on pO_2 in the blood and the affinity of haemoglobin with oxygen. The curves in figure A.49 show how different concentrations of carbon dioxide affect the saturation of haemoglobin at varying partial pressures of oxygen.

a) Explain what is meant by partial pressure of oxygen (pO_2).   *1 mark*

b) What are the values of percentage saturation of haemoglobin on the three curves when the partial pressure of oxygen is 5.0 kPa?   *3 marks*

c) What are the implications of the carbon dioxide values for curves **B** and **C** for an athlete?   *2 marks*

d) Why is the partial pressure of oxygen (pO_2) important to the process of gaseous exchange?   *3 marks*

figure A.49 – oxyhaemoglobin dissociation curve

A — no carbon dioxide present
B — when pCO_2 is 5.3 kPa
C — when pCO_2 is 9.3 kPa

6) Figure A.50 shows a diagrammatic picture of the cardiac impulse. Using the information in this diagram, describe the flow of blood during the specific stages of the cardiac cycle in relation to the cardiac impulse. In your answer explain how the heart valves help control the direction of blood flow. *8 marks*

figure A.50 – the cardiac impulse

myogenic · bundle of His · Purkinje fibres · SA node · AV node

7) $\dot{Q} = SV \times HR$. Explain the meaning of this equation and give typical resting values that you would expect in an endurance-based athlete. *6 marks*

8) A fit 18 year old female student performs a 400m time trial in one minute.

a) Sketch and label a graph to show a typical heart rate response from a point 5 minutes before the start of the run, during the time trial, and over the 20 minute recovery period. *4 marks*

b) Explain why heart rate takes some time to return to its resting value following the exercise period. *2 marks*

c) Identify a hormone that is responsible for heart rate increases prior to and during an exercise period. *1 mark*

d) Heart rate is regulated by neural, hormonal and intrinsic factors. How does the nervous system detect and respond to changes in heart rate during an exercise period? *4 marks*

9) Running a marathon in hot conditions sets up a competition between the active muscles and the skin for limited blood supply. How does the human body respond to meet the needs of supplying oxygen to exercising muscle and how can the athlete control this response? *3 marks*

10) Jodie Swallow is a top class female British Triathlete, and has a resting heart rate of 36 bpm. Give reasons why such an athlete might have a low resting heart rate. *4 marks*

11) Table 11 shows the rate of blood flow (in cm³ per minute) to different parts of the body in a trained male athlete, at rest and while exercising at maximum effort on a cycle ergometer.

Table 11 - **estimated blood flow at rest and during maximum effort**

organ or system	estimated blood flow in cm³ min⁻¹	
	at rest	during max effort
skeletal muscle	1000	26400
coronary vessels	250	1200
skin	500	750
kidneys	1000	300
liver & gut	1250	375
other organs	1000	975

Study the data carefully before answering the following questions.

a) The rate of blood flow to the 'entire body' increases significantly during exercise. Explain briefly how the heart achieves this. *2 marks*

b) What percentage of the total blood flow is directed to the skeletal muscle at rest and during maximum effort? Show your calculations. *3 marks*

c) How is blood flow to various regions of the body controlled? *4 marks*

12) a) What is meant by the concept venous return mechanism? *2 marks*

b) Describe how it is aided during physical activity when a person is exercising in an upright position. *3 marks*

c) Explain the importance of the skeletal muscle pump mechanism during an active cool-down. *2 marks*

d) What effect does enhanced venous return have upon cardiac output and stroke volume? *3 marks*

13) a) How is oxygen transported by the blood? *2 marks*

b) Identify the **main** method whereby carbon dioxide is transported in venous blood. *1 mark*

c) Explain how increased levels of carbon dioxide levels affect performance during physical activity. *3 marks*

14) A simple calculation for the calculation of blood pressure can be written as:

Blood Pressure = Cardiac Output x Resistance to blood flow

a) Identify **one** factor that affects resistance to the flow of blood within systemic blood vessels.   *I mark*
b) Blood pressure is quoted as two numbers. An example would be resting values of 120/80 mmHg. Explain what each of these numbers refer to.   *2 marks*
c) How would these blood pressure values change during a game of football and a rugby scrum lasting 6 seconds? Give a reason for each of your answers.   *3 marks*

15) Table 12 identifies differences in total blood volume, plasma volume, blood cell volume between untrained and highly trained endurance males (same age, height and body mass). Comment on the data that is presented in table 12 and suggest how the trained athlete would benefit from these increased volumes.   *4 marks*

Table 12 – **blood volumes in trained and untrained males**

subjects	total blood volume (dm³)	plasma volume (dm³)	blood cell volume (dm³)
trained male	7	4.2	2.8
untrained male	5.6	3.2	2.4

Introductory anatomy of the skeletal and muscular systems

STUDENT NOTE

A general overview of the skeletal system is meant to be used as an introduction, but will not be directly examined. Your **main** focus for revision is on movement analysis in relation to sporting / activity-based performances.

The skeletal system

- **The appendicular skeletal system** (figure A.51) consists of the shoulder girdle, skull, hip girdle, leg and arm bones.
- **The axial skeleton** (figure A.51) consists of the skull, vertebral column, and ribs and sternum.

The functions of the skeletal system are to act as a lever system, as surface area for attachment of muscle, tendons and ligaments, and to give shape and support to the body. Also, red / white blood cells are manufactured within bone marrow, and bones store fats and minerals.

figure A.51 – the skeleton

short bones / flat bones / long bones / irregular bones / THE SKELETON / axial / appendicular

Types of bones and principal functions

See a summary of these terms in figure A.51.

- **Long bones**, for example, the femur (which acts as a lever).
- **Short bones**, for example, carpals (which have strength and lightness).
- **Flat bones**, for example, the pelvis (which has a large surface area for muscle and tendon attachments), the cranium (has the function of brain protection).
- **Irregular bones**, for example, the vertebrae (which protect the spinal cord), the patella (a sesamoid bone which increases the mechanical advantage of the quadriceps tendon).

STUDENT NOTE

You need to familiarise yourself with the names of bones in figure A.52 that articulate at the ankle, knee, hip, shoulder and elbow, when you answer movement analysis questions.

figure A.52 – the human skeleton

skull, mandible, clavicle, scapula, sternum, ribs, humerus, vertebral column, pelvis, radius, sacrum, ulna, carpals, metacarpals, phalanges, femur, positioning of patella, tibia, fibula, tarsals, metatarsals, phalanges, skull, mandible, ribs, vertebral column, sacrum, ulna, carpals

Bony features

Protrusions and **depressions** act as the places on bones at which ligaments and muscle tendons attach (their shape increases the surface area on the bone available for attachment).

Cartilage

- **Hyaline (articular) cartilage** has a smooth, solid matrix which sits on the ends of bones, and forms the exact surfaces which are in contact and move across one another when a joint is used.
- **White fibro-cartilage** is tough and slightly flexible and exists between vertebrae.
- **Yellow elastic cartilage** is soft and elastic and exists in the ear lobes.

The structure and function of bone tissue

- The **periosteum** is an outer protective covering of bone which provides attachment for muscle tendons and ligaments. The deeper layers of the periosteum are responsible for growth in bone width.
- The **epiphyseal disc** or growth plate is the segment of a bone in which an increase in bone length takes place.
- **Compact bone** consists of solid bone tissue, located down the shaft of a long bone and the outer layers of short, flat and irregular bones. Its dense structure gives strength and support.
- **Cancellous bone** has a lattice-like / spongy appearance. It is light-weight and is located at the ends of a long bone, in addition to providing the internal bone tissue in short, flat and irregular bones.

Types of joints and articulating bones

Articulation is defined 'as a place where two or more bones meet to form a joint'.

Joint types

Joint types (figure A.53) are:

- **Fibrous or immovable** – for example, between bones of the cranium.
- **Cartilaginous or slightly moveable** – for example, vertebral discs.
- **Synovial or freely moveable** (classified in table 13 on page 55).

figure A.53 – joint types

Synovial joint

See figure A.54 for the locations of the elements of a synovial joint.

- **Synovial fluid** reduces joint friction by lubrication, and maintains joint stability.
- **Synovial membrane** encloses fluid and secretes fluid.
- **Joint capsule** is a sleeve of tough, fibrous tissue surrounding the joint.
- A **ligament** is an extension of the joint capsule consisting of strong, fibrous connective tissue that provides stability by joining bone to bone.
- **Articular cartilage** prevents friction between bones, and cushions the ends of bones.
- **Bursae** prevent friction and wear.
- **Pads of fat** cushion the joint.
- **Menisci** help bones fit together and improve stabilisation of the joint.

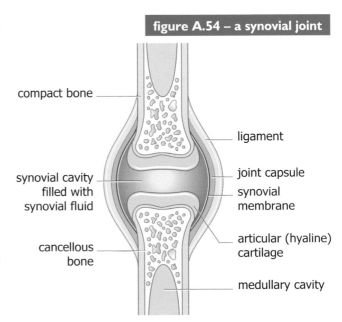

figure A.54 – a synovial joint

Terms used in movement analysis

Terms of movement consist of three main sections:

- Planes of the body.
- Axes of the body.
- Movement patterns.

To help analyse movement, it is possible to imagine a series of lines and surfaces that divide the body into sections – the lines are called **axes** and the surfaces called **planes**.

Planes of the body

The term **body plane** is defined as '**an imaginary flat surface running through the centre of gravity of the body**', and is used to assist in the understanding of movement of body segments with respect to one another. Within each plane an axis can be identified in association with a particular joint about which the movement takes place.

Three imaginary planes

Refer to figure A.55.

- **Frontal (coronal) plane**
  - A vertical plane that divides body into **front and back** sections.
  - Movements in this plane are abduction and adduction, as for example in a cartwheel.
  - And spinal lateral flexion, as for example in side flexion trunk bends.

- **Sagittal (median) plane**
  - A vertical plane that divides the body into **left and right** sides.
  - Movements in this plane include flexion and extension, as for example in somersaults, biceps curl, pole vault take-off, sprinting, dorsiflexion, and plantarflexion.

- **Transverse (horizontal) plane**
  - A horizontal plane that divides the body into upper and lower section.
  - Movements are rotational movement patterns such as supination, pronation, and spinal rotation.
  - Example movements would be twisting / turning, the spinning skater / discus / hammer / ski turns.

Axes of rotation

An axis of rotation is defined as '**an imaginary line about which the body rotates or spins, at right angles to the plane**' – look at figure A.55 axes labelled A, B and C.

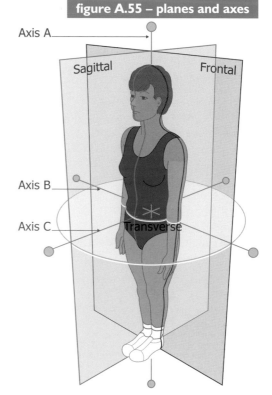

figure A.55 – planes and axes

Axis A

Sagittal   Frontal

Axis B

Axis C   Transverse

Three imaginary axes

- **Longitudinal axis**
  - Axis A on figure A.55.
  - This axis runs vertically from the top of the head to a point between the feet.
  - Movements in the transverse plane about the longitudinal axis are rotational movements.
  - Examples of sporting movements would be the spinning skater and the hammer throw.

- **Transverse axis**
  - Axis B on figure A.55. This axis runs horizontally from side to side across the body between opposite hips at right angles to the sagittal plane.
  - Movements within the sagittal plane about the transverse axis are flexion, extension, hyperextension, dorsiflexion and plantarflexion.
  - Sports movements about this axis include sit ups, and the high jump Fosbury Flop flight phase.

- **Frontal axis**
  - Axis C on figure A.55.
  - This axis runs horizontally from front to back between belly button and lumbar spine.
  - Movements in the frontal plane about the frontal axis include abduction, adduction and spinal lateral flexion.
  - Examples of sports movements about this axis are a cartwheel, and the bowling action in cricket.

Joint actions

In Table 13 the movement ranges of synovial joints are classified according to their axes of movement. This means that joints that allow only one plane of movement are identified as a one-axis joint, a two-axes joint has movement within any two planes, whereas a three-axes joint has movement in all three planes.

Table 13 - **summary of synovial joint types and movement ranges**

synovial joint types	movement range	example body place: articulating bones
ball and socket	3 axes, flexion / extension, abduction / adduction, rotation, circumduction	**hip**: femur, acetabulum of pelvis. **shoulder**: scapula, humerus.
hinge	1 axis, flexion / extension	**knee**: femur, tibia. **elbow**: humerus, radius, ulna.
pivot	1 axis, rotation	**spine**: **atlas**: odontoid process of axis (turns head side to side). **elbow**: proximal ends of radius and ulna.
condyloid (modified ball and socket)	2 axes, flexion / extension, abduction / adduction = circumduction	**knuckles**: joint of fingers: metacarpals, phalanges. **wrist**: radius, carpals.
saddle	2 axes, flexion / extension, abduction / adduction = circumduction	**joint at base of thumb**: carpal, metacarpal.
gliding	a little movement in all directions	**centre of chest**: clavicle, sternum. **spine**: articulating surfaces. **wrist**: carpals. **ankle**: tarsals.

Movement patterns at joints - terminology

The possible ranges of movements within a synovial joint (figure A.56) vary according to the shape of the articular surfaces and therefore according to the joint type. These movement patterns have been categorised according to the relevant body planes.

Movement patterns in the saggital (median) plane:
Flexion means to bend, resulting in a decreased angle around the joint – for example, bending of the knee.

Extension means to straighten, resulting in an increased angle around the joint – for example, straightening of the knee from a bent-legged to straight-legged position.

Hyperextension is the forced extension of a joint beyond its normal range of motion – for example, the arched spine that is created in the flight phase of Fosbury Flop high jump technique.

Plantarflexion involves extending the toes thereby increasing the angle at the ankle – for example, standing on tip-toes.

Dorsiflexion describes movement of the foot towards the shin – for example, walking on one's heels.

Movement patterns in the frontal (coronal) plane:
Abduction means to take away and so is characterised by movement away from the midline – for example, a cartwheel in gymnastics.

Adduction means to bring together and so is characterised by movement towards the midline – for example, bringing the lower legs back together from the inverted cartwheel.

Lateral flexion is sideways bending.

Eversion is the joint action at the ankle characterised by the turning of the sole of the foot laterally outwards – for example, the kick action in breaststroke.

Inversion is the joint action at the ankle characterised by the turning of the sole of the foot medially inwards – for example, a football player inverts the foot to pass the ball with the outside of his / her boot.

Depression describes movement of the shoulders downwards – for example, the preparation for a dead lift, gripping the bar.

Elevation describes movement of the shoulders upwards – for example, a shoulder shrug.

Movement patterns in the transverse (horizontal) plane:
Horizontal abduction and adduction
Start off with your arm stretched out in front of you parallel to the ground, whilst your shoulder is flexed. Now move your arm away and to the side of the body. This is called horizontal abduction (also known as horizontal extension). If you return back to your starting position you will have performed horizontal adduction (also known as horizontal flexion). A discus thrower during the preparatory swing (horizontal abduction) and release of a discus (horizontal adduction) performs these movement patterns.

Pronation is characterised by the rotation of the forearm medially so that the hand faces downwards – for example, a top-spin forehand in tennis.

Supination is characterised by the rotation of the forearm laterally so that the hand faces upwards – for example, the right hand action in a hockey flick.

figure A.56 – movement patterns

MOVEMENT PATTERNS: horizontal abduction, horizontal adduction, pronation, supination, rotation, elevation, depression, inversion, eversion, lateral flexion, adduction, abduction, dorsi flexion, plantar flexion, hyper extension, extension, flexion, circumduction

figure A.57 – major joints – movement patterns

wrist joint (flexion / extension, abduction / adduction)

elbow joint (flexion / extension)

hip joint (flexion / extension, abduction / adduction = circumduction + medial / lateral rotation)

ankle joint (dorsiflexion / plantarflexion, inversion / eversion)

radio-ulnar joint (pronation / supination)

shoulder joint (flexion / extension, abduction / adduction = circumduction + horizontal adduction / abduction medial / lateral rotation)

vertebral column (flexion / extension, lateral flexion, rotation)

knee joint (flexion / extension)

Rotation is the turning of a structure around its long axis. Rotation can be inwards, hence **medial rotation** of the humerus with the forearm flexed brings the hand towards the body – for example, in the breaststroke the humerus rotates medially as the hands enter the water.
Rotation can be outwards, hence **lateral rotation** of the humerus describes a movement whereby the hand moves away from the body – for example, the humerus rotates laterally in preparation for the forehand stroke in tennis.

Circumduction is a combination of flexion, extension, abduction and adduction – for example, when the upper arm moves (arm circling) so that it describes a cone with the shoulder joint at the apex. Circumduction is a combination of two planes – **sagittal** and **frontal** planes.

Most movements that occur in physical activities are combinations of movements explained in figure A.57.

Introductory anatomy of the muscular system

Body muscles

figure A.58 – superficial anterior muscles

facial muscles
sternocleidomastoid
trapezius
anterior deltoid
pectoralis major
biceps brachii
serratus anterior
rectus abdominus
flexors of wrist and fingers
brachoradialis
external abdominal oblique
tensor fascia latae
adductors of thigh:
pectineus
adductor longus
gracilis
vastus lateralis
rectus femoris
vastus medialis
quadriceps group
sartorius
patella
patella ligament
gastrocnemius
tibialis anterior
extensor digitorum longus
soleus
lateral leg muscles

figure A.59 – superficial posterior muscles

sternocleidomastoid
trapezius
posterior deltoid
infraspinatus
teres minor
teres major
triceps brachii
latissimus dorsi
extensors of wrist and fingers
external abdominal oblique
gluteus maximus
gracilis
hamstring group
semitendinosus
biceps femoris
semimembranosus
gastrocnemius
soleus
calcaneal tendon (achilles tendon)

STUDENT NOTE

In your movement analysis you will need to identify major skeletal muscles of the human body (figures A.58 and A.59 above) in relation to joint activity and muscle analysis in tables 14, 15 and 16 below. The muscles identified in these tables give you plenty of choice to select from. However if you refer to your exam syllabus you may wish to focus on the muscles that your exam board has specified.

Table 14 – **wrist, elbow and shoulder movements and muscles**

body part / joint	movement pattern	active (agonist) muscles	movement examples
wrist	extension	**extensor carpi ulnaris,** extensor digitorum	follow through in an over-arm throw
	flexion	**flexor carpi radialis,** flexi carpi ulnaris	dumbbell wrist curls
arm / elbow	flexion	**biceps brachii,** brachialis	bicep curls
	extension	**triceps brachii,** anconeus (forearm)	follow through over-arm throw, bench press, triceps dips
forearm / radio-ulnar (pivot)	supination	**supinator,** biceps brachii	catching the bar during a clean
	pronation	**pronator teres,** pronator quadratus	putting top spin on a tennis ball
shoulder joint	adduction	**latissimus dorsi,** anterior deltoid, teres major / minor	recovery phase in overarm throw, triceps dips
	abduction	**medial deltoid,** supraspinatus	preparation phase shoulder pass
4 rotator cuff muscles stabilise shoulder joint	flexion	**pectoralis major,** anterior deltoid, coracobrachialis	release phase in overarm throw, triceps dips
	extension	**posterior deltoid,** latissimus dorsi, teres major	shoulder position during javelin approach run
	medial rotation	**latissimus dorsi,** posterior deltoid, pectoralis major, teres major, subscapularis	forehand stroke / follow through at table tennis
	horizontal adduction	**pectoralis major,** anterior deltoid	arm swing into the release phase of a discus throw
	horizontal abduction	**posterior deltoid,** trapezius, latissimus dorsi	preparatory swing (backward) of the arm in the discus
	lateral rotators	**teres minor,** infraspinatus	backhand stroke / follow through at table tennis
shoulder or pectoral girdle (scapula + clavicle)	elevation	**upper fibres of trapezius,** levator scapulae, rhomboids	a dumbbell shoulder shrug
	depression	**latissimus dorsi,** lower fibres of trapezius, pectoralis minor, serratus anterior (lower fibres)	preparation for dead lift when gripping the bar
	protraction	serratus anterior	recovery phase during breaststroke
	retraction	rhomboids, trapezuis	pull phase during breaststroke
	upward rotation	**upper fibres of trapezius,** serratus anterior	arm recovery phase during butterfly stroke
	downward rotation	**lower fibres of trapezius,** rhomboids	arm pull phase during butterfly stroke

STUDENT NOTE

The main agonist muscle for each movement is in **red bold** font type in tables 14, 15 and 16.

Table 15 – **trunk and spine movements and muscles**

body part / joint	movement pattern	active (agonist) muscles	movement examples
trunk / spine	flexion	**rectus abdominus**, internal / external obliques, transversus abdominus	sit ups
core stability muscles	extension / hyperextension supports lower back	**erector spinae group** - sacrospinalis / multifidus (deep lumbar portion)	extension - trunk position during netball shot at goal, hyperextension - flight phase of fosbury flop
	rotation	**external obliques**, rectus abdominus, erector spinae	hammer throw swings, barani in trampolining / gymnastics
	lateral flexion	**internal obliques**, rectus abdominus, erector spinae, quadratus lumborum, sacrospinalis	side bends, twisting trunk / abdominal curls

Table 16 – **hip, knee and ankle movements and muscles**

body part / joint	movement pattern	active muscles (main agonist)	movement examples
hip	flexion	**iliopsoas**, rectus femoris, pectineus, sartorius, tensor fascia latae, adductor longus and brevis	squat start (low) position, high knee lift during sprinting, moving the knees up into a tuck position
	extension	**gluteus maximus**, hamstring group, adductor magnus	high jump take-off, rear leg drive during sprinting
	adduction	**adductor longus / magnus / brevis**, pectineus, gracilis	cross over phase during javelin run-up, side footing a football
	abduction	**gluteus medius / minimus**, sartorius, tensor fascia latae, piriformis	movement into the inverted phase of a cartwheel
	medial rotation	**gluteus medius / minimus**, tensor fascia latae, iliopsoas, gracilis	hip movement across circle during travel phase of a discus turn
	lateral rotation	**gluteus maximus**, psoas major, adductors, piriformis, sartorious	movement into a yoga stork position
knee	extension	**quadriceps group** - rectus femoris / vastus medialis / vastus intermedius / vastus lateralis	high jump take-off, rear leg drive during sprinting
	flexion	**hamstring group** - biceps femoris / semimembranosus / semitendinosus, sartorius, gracilis, gastrocnemius	squat start (low) position, high knee lift during sprinting, moving the knees up into a tuck position
ankle	plantarflexion	**gastrocnemius**, soleus, tibialis posterior, peroneus, flexor digitorum longus	take-off phase during jumping
	dorsiflexion	**tibialis anterior**, extensor digitorum longus	landing phase from jump

Agonists and antagonists

Musculo-skeletal attachments

Ligaments attach bone to bone to limit the range of movement of joints.

Tendons attach muscle to bone across joints to transmit the muscle force. They are strong and mainly inelastic – for example the Achilles tendon attaches the gastrocnemius muscle to the periosteal bone tissue of calcaneus or the heel bone.

Origins and insertion of muscles

The tendon at the static end of the muscle is called the **origin** and the tendon at the end of the muscle closest to the joint that moves is called the **insertion** of that muscle.

Antagonistic muscle action

This term describes the fact that muscles work in pairs (see the summary in figure A.60, and the details in figure A.61).

figure A.60 – muscle function

- The **agonist** is the active muscle, the muscle under tension or doing work and functioning as the **prime mover** of a joint during the desired movement.

- The **antagonist** relaxes to allow the agonist to work as movement occurs.

- For example, curling a bar, the agonist = **biceps brachii muscle**, and the antagonist = **triceps brachii muscle.**

A **synergist muscle** holds the body in position so that an agonist muscle can operate, thus preventing any unwanted movements that might occur as the prime mover contracts. For example, the trapezius muscle holds the shoulder in place during the bar curling exercise.

A **fixator muscle** by definition is a synergist muscle, but is more specifically referred to as a **fixator** or **stabiliser** when it immobilises the bone of the prime mover's origin, thus providing a stable base for the action of the prime mover. For example, the deltoid muscle stabilises the scapula during a bar curl.

figure A.61 – muscle function – curling a bar

agonist (biceps)   antagonist (triceps)   synergist (trapezius)   fixator (deltoid)

Types of muscular contraction

During muscular contraction, a muscle may shorten, lengthen or stay the same. When a muscle changes its length, the contraction is classified as **dynamic**. When the muscle remains the same length, a **static** contraction occurs.

Static contractions – isometric muscle contraction

In **isometric contractions** (figure A.62) the length of the muscle does not change, but the amount of tension does increase during the contraction process.

In a training situation isometric work is done by exerting the maximum possible force in a fixed position for sets of 10 seconds, with 60 seconds recovery. Isometric contractions are responsible for the constant length of postural muscles in the body and hence stabilise the trunk in many dynamic activities such as in sprinting.

Dynamic muscle contraction – concentric and eccentric contraction

Concentric muscle contraction

This type of contraction involves a muscle shortening under tension (figure A.63) and is a form of **isotonic muscle contraction**. For example, in the driving upwards phase in a jump or squat, the quadriceps muscle group performs a concentric contraction as it shortens to produce extension of the knee joint.

Eccentric muscle contraction

This type of contraction involves a muscle lengthening under tension and is a form of **isotonic** muscle contraction. When a muscle contracts eccentrically it is acting as a brake, thus controlling the movement. For example, during the downward moving part of a jump or squat, the quadriceps muscle group is lengthening under tension and so the work is labelled **eccentric** or **negative**. Eccentric muscle contraction produces the biggest overload in a muscle, thereby enhancing its development as far as strength is concerned. The chief practical use of eccentric muscle contraction is in **plyometric** or **elastic / explosive** strength work (figure A.64).

For eccentric contractions, the **agonist** muscle is the active muscle, which in this case is lengthening. In the case of the landing from a jump or controlled downward movement in a squat, the quadriceps muscle group lengthens under tension, and is therefore the **agonist**. To be the **agonist** in this situation, the muscle **must** be under tension. The **antagonist muscle** during the example of a downward squatting movement would be the hamstring muscle group, which gets shorter and which relaxes or acts as a fixator for the hip joints.

Many muscle contractions involve a combination of dynamic and static work in which the muscles shorten by some amount, and the degree of tension increases.

figure A.62 – isometric holds

figure A.63 – concentric contraction

concentric muscle contraction (quadriceps)

figure A.64 – eccentric contraction

eccentric muscle contraction (quadriceps)

Analysis of movement

figure A.65 – high jump take-off and flight

Table 17 – **the high jump**

After a continually accelerated run-up with a long penultimate stride, the jumper (figure A.65) has a very fast last take-off stride.

figure b

figure a

physical activity	joint used	articulating bones	movement produced	agonist muscles	type of muscular contraction (isotonic)
high jump at take-off - figure A.65a	ankle - take-off leg	talus, tibia, fibula	plantarflexion	**gastrocnemius**, soleus, tibialis posterior, peroneus, flexor digitorum longus	concentric
	knee - take-off leg	tibia, femur	extension	**quadriceps group:** rectus femoris, vastus medialis, vastus intermedius, vastus lateralis	concentric
	shoulder girdle	clavicle, scapula	elevation	**upper fibres of trapezius**, rhomboids, levator scapulae	concentric
high jump in flight - figure A.65b	hips	femur, acetabulum of pelvis	extension	**gluteus maximus**, assisted by: **hamstring group:** biceps femoris, semimembranosus, semitendinosus	concentric
	spine	vertebrae	extension / hyperextension	**erector spinae group**	concentric

Table 18 – **sprinting leg action**

Note that the lever system at the ankle joint (see figure A.66) is a second class lever with the fulcrum (pivot) under the ball of her foot. See the section on page 68 later for details of lever action at joints.

figure a   figure b   figure c

physical activity	joint type	movement produced	agonist muscles	antagonist muscles	type of muscular contraction
leg action in sprinting – figure A.66a left leg	ankle / hinge	plantarflexion	**gastrocnemius,** flexor digitorum longus	tibialis anterior, entensor digitorum longus	concentric
	knee / hinge	extension	**quadriceps group**	hamstring group	concentric
action of hip joint - figure A.66b - left leg	hip / ball and socket	flexion	**iliopsoas,** rectus femoris, adductor longus / brevis	gluteus maximus, biceps femoris, adductor magnus	concentric
action of the trunk - figure A.66c	spine / cartilaginous	extension	**erector spinae group**	rectus abdominus	isometric

STUDENT NOTE

The main agonist muscle for each movement is in **red bold** font type. The main antagonist muscle for each movement is in **blue bold** font type in table 18 above.

You must list **all muscles** in the quadriceps and hamstring groups when you analyse the actions of the knee and hips during physical activity in table 18 above.

figure A.67 – over arm throw

Table 19 – **the arm action in an over arm throw – sequence analysis**

Note that the lever system operating at the elbow during this movement is a first class lever, with fulcrum (pivot) within the elbow joint, the effort through the triceps muscle, and the load at the hand as force is applied to the ball.

STUDENT NOTE

The main agonist muscle for each movement is in **red bold** font type in tables 19 and 20 below.

figure a   figure b   figure c

physical activity	joint used	articulating bones	movement produced	agonist muscles	type of muscular contraction (isotonic)
arm action in over arm throw - figure A.67 a-c	elbow	humerus, radius, ulna	elbow joint extends as movement progresses	**triceps brachii**, anconeus	concentric
	shoulder girdle	scapula, clavicle	elevation, upward rotation	**elevation: trapezius** upper fibres, levator scapulae. **upward rotation: trapezius** upper fibres, serratus anterior	concentric
	hand joints	carpals, radius, ulna	supination to pronation	**pronator teres**, pronator quadratus	concentric

Table 20 – **the full action of the squat - down then up**

figure A.68 – squat – down then up

figure a   b   c   d   e

physical activity	joint used	articulating bones	movement produced	agonist muscles	plane of movement	movement axis	type of muscular contraction (isotonic)
leg action in squat - figure A.68	knee – figures a to c	tibia, femur	extension to flexion	**quadriceps group**	sagittal	transverse	eccentric
	hip – figures c to e	femur, acetabulum of pelvis	flexion to extension	**gluteus maximus**, hamstring group	sagittal	transverse	concentric
	ankle – figure c	tibia, fibula, talus	dorsiflexion	**tibialis anterior**	sagittal	transverse	concentric

Table 21 – the full action of the push-up - down then up

STUDENT NOTE

Note that during a very controlled downward / eccentric phase in figures A.69 a-c the **agonist** muscle is the **triceps brachii** muscle. This is because the triceps brachii muscle is under extreme tension by defying gravity, and so acts as a brake to control the downward phase of the push-up. The same reasoning applies to the anconeus muscle.

The push-up (d-e), at the elbow joint, takes place within the sagittal plane and around the transverse axis.

During the push-up (d-e), at the shoulder joint (horizontal adduction), takes place within the transverse plane and around the longitudinal axis.

figure a

b

c

d

e

physical activity	joint type	movement produced	agonist muscles	antagonist muscles	type of muscular contraction (isotonic)
arm action in push-up – down movement figure A.69 a to c	elbow / hinge	flexion	**triceps brachii**, anconeus	**biceps brachii**, brachialis	eccentric
up movement figure A.69 c to e	shoulder / ball and socket	horizontal adduction	**pectoralis major**, anterior deltoid	**trapezius**, posterior deltoid	concentric

STUDENT NOTE

The main agonist muscle for each movement is in **red bold** font type. The main antagonist muscle for each movement is in **blue bold** font type in table 21 above.

STUDENT NOTE

The main agonist muscle for each movement is in **red bold** font type in table 22 below.

As the ankle plantarflexes, during the foot strike of the ball, the tibialis anterior lengthens and is under extreme tension. Then as the ball leaves the foot this muscle will shorten (contract) and the foot will dorsiflex.

Table 22 – **this sequence covers the strike phase only for the kick**

physical activity	joint type	movement produced	agonist muscles	body plane	body axis	type of muscular contraction (isotonic)
leg action in kicking (right leg) – figure A.70	ankle / hinge	plantarflexion	**tibialis anterior**	sagittal	transverse	eccentric
	knee / hinge	extension	**quadriceps group**	sagittal	transverse	concentric
	hip / ball and socket	flexion	**iliopsoas**, rectus femoris, adductor longus / brevis	sagittal	transverse	concentric

Practice questions

Warm-up question 1)
Hockey involves movement at many joints in the body. Identify which bones articulate at each of the following joints: shoulder, elbow, radio-ulnar, hip, knee, and ankle.

6 marks

Warm-up question 2)
Complete the missing gaps in table 23 naming the **main** agonist and antagonist muscles, body plane and body axis for each of the actions identified.

Table 23 - **action at joints**

action	main agonist	main antagonist	body plane	body axis
elevating the shoulders				
extending the elbow joint				
flexing the hip joint				
flexing the knee joint				
dorsiflexing the ankle joint				
flexing the trunk				

Warm up question 3)
Describe the following movement terminology, and give a physical activity for each movement: abduction, circumduction, rotation and plantarflexion. In which plane(s) does each movement pattern occur?   *12 marks*

4) Figures A.71 a to c shows the final stride, take-off and flight phase of a long jump.
   Use these three pictures to help you complete the following joint analysis.

a) Name the type of muscle contraction occurring in the leg whose foot is in contact with the ground in figure A.71a, name the **main** agonist muscle responsible for this muscle contraction and explain why you have selected this muscle.
   3 marks

b) Complete the following joint analysis below in table 25 for figure A.71b: *9 marks*

figure A.71 – long jump take-off and flight

figure c

figure b   a

Table 24 – **joint table**

joint	joint type	articulating bones	main agonist muscle
left ankle			
left knee			
left hip			

c) Describe the changes in movement patterns in the left ankle, knee, hip and trunk from figures A.71 b to c.   *4 marks*
d) Suggest **two** factors that affect the range of movement at the hip joint.   *2 marks*

5) Figure A.72 shows a tennis player completing a forehand drive. Use this figure to help you complete the following joint analysis.

a) For the shoulder joint during horizontal adduction, identify the type of joint, the articulating bones, the **main** agonist muscle and the type of muscle contraction.
   4 marks
b) Using the muscles that create elbow flexion during the forehand drive, explain what is meant by antagonistic muscle action.   *4 marks*
c) The movement pattern produced on the right hand side of the trunk and the **main** agonist creating this movement.   *2 marks*
d) In which body plane and around which axis does the tennis forehand occur at the flexed right elbow position show in figure A.72?   *2 marks*

6) The athlete in figure A.73 is holding a plank bridge position. Use the photograph to help you complete the following joint analysis.

a) Identify the joint type, articulating bones, the **main** agonist (prime mover) and type of muscle contraction at the hip joint.   *4 marks*
b) Explain why the muscle contraction is of this type.   *1 mark*
c) Explain the role of the core muscles in relation to the plank bridge position.   *2 marks*

figure A.72 – tennis forehand

d) There are four rotator cuff muscles that are inserted around the cuff or cap over the proximal humerus. Name **one** of these muscles and explain how these muscles provide range of movement and yet collectively protect the shoulder joint.
   2 marks

figure A.73 – athlete holding a plank position

7) Figures A.74 a to c shows an elite sprinter completing a full running stride.

a) Analyse the action of the hip joint from the strike position of the left leg to the completion of a full running stride.
3 marks

b) Identify the **main** agonist muscles responsible for these movement patterns in figures a and b only. *2 marks*

c) At the completion of the full stride focus on the left foot plant, identify the bones that form the ankle joint, the joint action and the **main** agonist responsible for this movement pattern. *4 marks*

d) Figure c shows the right knee in a recovery position. Identify the joint type, **main** agonist muscle group, its antagonist muscle group and the type of muscle contraction occurring at this joint. *4 marks*

e) Explain the term 'body plane'. *2 marks*

f) In what plane and around which axis does the sprint leg action occur? *2 marks*

figure A.74 – sprint – a full stride

figure a figure b figure c

8) Differentiate and give examples of concentric, static and eccentric work. *6 marks*

LEVERS

The term **internal forces** describes the forces acting (figure A.75) when a muscle pulls on its **origin O** and **insertion I**. The force on the origin **H** is equal in size but opposite in direction to the force on the insertion **U**. This changes the **shape** of the person.

Levers

A lever is a **means of applying force at a distance** from the source of the force and has a **fulcrum (pivot)**, **effort** and **load**. In the human body, usually a **joint** and the **attached limbs** or bones act as a lever. **Force** is applied as **effort** by a **muscle** or group of muscles. The **load** is the **force applied** to the **surroundings** by the lever.

figure A.75 – forces at origin and insertion

Classification of levers

Class 1 lever

This is a see-saw lever with the fulcrum in between the effort and the load. It is found rarely in the body, for example the triceps / elbow / forearm lever (see figure A.76), or the atlas / neck muscles used in the nodding movement.

Class 2 lever

This is a wheelbarrow lever where the load is bigger than the effort, and the fulcrum is at one end of the lever with the load in between the effort and the fulcrum. This is found rarely in the body, the main example being the achilles tendon / calf muscles (gastrocnemeus / soleus) and ankle joint lever (see figure A.78, see page 70). This is used in most running or walking movements with the fulcrum underneath the ball of the foot as it drives the body forward.

Class 3 lever

This class of lever again has the fulcrum at one end of the lever arm, with the effort in between the load and the fulcrum. It has a mechanical disadvantage, the effort is bigger than the load and is the most common system found in body. For example the elbow / biceps / forearm lever (see figure A.77), or the knee / quadriceps / tibia – fibula systems (see figure A.79, see page 70).

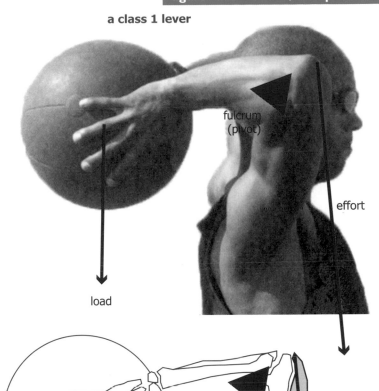

figure A.76 – elbow / triceps lever

a class 1 lever

figure A.77 – the elbow and forearm lever

a class 3 lever

figure A.78 – ankle / calf lever

a class 2 lever

effort

effort

fulcrum (pivot)

fulcrum (pivot)

load

load

figure A.79 – knee / tibia / quadriceps lever

effort

a class 3 lever

effort

fulcrum (pivot)

fulcrum (pivot)

load

load

Effects of the length of lever

The **length of the lever** or **resistance arm** of the lever (**d** in figure A.80) affects the **load** able to be exerted by the lever, and the **speed** at which the hand can move. The longer the lever **d**, the smaller the value of the load for a given biceps strength and value of the **effort arm** (distance between effort and pivot). The longer the lever arm **d**, the faster the load can be applied (as the limb moves through its range - a longer limb - the hand - would move further in the same time).

This means that the hand of a thrower with long arms will be moving faster than the hand of a thrower with short arms if each is turning (rotating) at the same speed.

The **shorter** the **effort arm** the less load can be exerted. The shorter the load (resistance) arm of a person the bigger the load can be. This is why successful weightlifters tend to have short arms.

figure A.80 – the length of a lever arm

effort

fulcrum (pivot)

load

d

Practice questions

1) Sketch the lever system which would represent the action of the biceps muscle in flexing the arm. Show on your diagram the resistance arm of the lever.
   3 marks

2) In figure A.81 of a jumper taking off, name, sketch and label the lever system operating at knee **B** during this action.
   3 marks

figure A.81 – long jumper taking off

3) In softball, what order (class) of lever is shown in the hitting action in figure A.82?
   State **one** disadvantage and **one** advantage of reducing the bat length for a beginner.
   3 marks

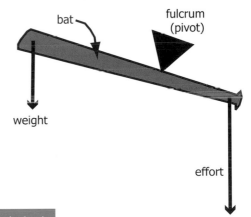
figure A.82 – softball bat

4) Name, sketch and label the lever system which is operating at the ankle of leg **C** when doing the sprint set action illustrated in figure A.83.
   3 marks

figure A.83 – a sprint start

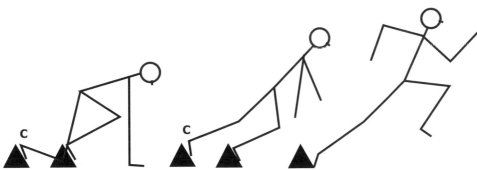

5) a) Figure A.84 shows an elbow joint **A** of a person performing an exercise. Draw a simplified sketch to show the lever system, indicating the various forces operating.
   4 marks
   b) On your diagram draw and label the effort and resistance arm.
   3 marks

figure A.84 – a press-up

6) During physical activity the performer uses a combination of levers to produce movement. Explain why the length of the lever will affect performance.
   3 marks

This content should be delivered in Unit 2, but will be assessed by a question in **Section B of the Unit 1 written paper**.

Principles of training

The aims and objectives of training are to improve performance, skill, game ability and motor and physical fitness. Repeated days of training can be considered as positive stress because training improves one's capacity for energy production, tolerance of physical stress and exercise performance. A well-designed training programme follows a set of guidelines called '**principles of training**' (figure 2A.1).

figure 2A.1 – principles of training

Specificity

Specificity is defined as '**the relevance of the choice of exercise to the activity to be improved**'.

Choices to be made involve energy demands, strength, power, endurance and skill. This notion is thought to be very important for high performance in a chosen sport. For example, the shot putt event requires speed and power developed by stressing the ATP-PC anaerobic energy system. So, in order to putt the shot successfully, the shot putter needs to work on explosive muscular power in training. Hence the training programme must **stress** the **physiological systems** that are critical for optimal performance in the given sport in order to achieve the required specific training adaptations. Similarly, the marathon runner requires endurance which must be obtained by stressing the aerobic energy system. Hence his / her training programme must be largely based on lengthy endurance based runs.

Overload

Overload is defined as '**training activities that are harder, more intense and / or lengthier than the normal physical activity undertaken by an individual**'.

figure 2A.2 – overload

Overload (figure 2A.2) can be achieved by increasing the frequency, intensity or duration of the activity. These terms are also referred to using the acronym '**FITT principles**' described below. Overload places physiological systems under **stress** and the human body responds by becoming more capable of coping with this stress. This training principle applies to muscular endurance as well as to strength and power training.

The major variables used for increasing or decreasing intensity are:

- Sets.
- Repetitions.
- Resistance.
- Rest relief or recovery period.

For example, an athlete performs bench press: 5 sets of 6 repetitions at 85% of 1RM (1 repetition maximum as described below on page 76), and 2 minutes recovery between sets. This exercise would stress the anaerobic fast twitch muscle fibres type IIb of the muscles: anterior deltoid, pectoralis major and triceps brachii.

FITT principles of training

F (frequency) = how often do we train? How often we train will determine the physiologically adaptations achieved. For example, the elite professional sportsperson may be required to train twice a day and thereby achieve optimal physiological adaptations and improvements in performance. On the other hand, a person who just wants to stay fit by attending three aerobic classes a week at their local leisure centre, may notice minor physiological changes such as easier breathing and less tendency to be out of breath when digging the garden.

I (intensity) = how hard do we train? For the elite athlete, training intensity will vary depending on the training emphasis in relation to the periodised year. **Periodisation** is a concept centred around a cyclical load design principle. In this case the training intensity is increased and decreased according to a set pattern, the first two weeks of a cycle may be easy, and the last two weeks very hard. As a general rule, the closer to the competitive phase the harder the workouts. The person who just wants to keep fit for every day living may be content with 3 exercise bouts (walking, swimming or cycling) for about 30 minutes at a level at which he / she can hold a conversation with a training partner.

figure 2A.3 – athlete wins a marathon

Intensity of training can be measured scientifically using lactate testing or calculating the respiratory exchange ratio. Field methods of measurement include Karvonen's training heart rate, weights lifted, heart rate maximum method and a Rating of Perceived Exertion (RPE) using the Borg scale (refer to page 75 onwards).

T (type) = what type of training do we do? Type of training relates to the principle of specificity above. Types of training include:

- Continuous.
- Intermittent.
- Circuit.
- Weights.
- Plyometrics.
- Mobility.

(see page 83 onwards for explanations of these types of training)

figure 2A.4 – recreational cyclist on a 40 min ride

T (time) = how long do we train for or what is the duration of the activity?
The intensity of training and exercise type often determines the duration of the activity. For example an aerobic / weight-reducing training programme should last for a minimum 30 minutes because of the time it takes for fat burning metabolism to commence. A plyometric workout may only last for 10 minutes before fatigue sets in, whereas an ultra distance runner may be unlimited by time during a long-distance run.

Progression

Progression is defined as '**a state of moving onwards, which implies an increase in training load as time goes on**'.

The principle of progression involves the gradual application of the overload principle. You should note that progression could occur without overload, but if overload does not happen, then you cannot obtain the necessary adaptations to body systems such as the muscular system, which would cause improvement in (for example) endurance or strength. The key point about progression is that the sportsperson should be performing at a higher level after the training period than before. In figure 2A.5, progression is steady and over a period of eight months, training intensity increases, and hopefully overload is sufficient to provide long-term adaptations which would lead to improved performance. In figure 2A.6, training intensity progresses

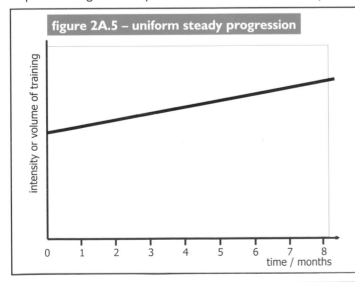

much steeper than in figure 2A.5 for a month before dropping down to a level above the previous starting point. Then training intensity progresses again for another month and so on. The outcome is a cyclic progression with a bigger overload (than steady slow progression) at the end of each cycle.

Over-training

Over-training is explained as '**when the intensity of training and / or volume of training are increased to extreme levels, and there is a lack of recovery within or between training sessions leading to an associated decline in physiological function**'. This situation can lead to extreme **muscle fatigue** and **loss of performance**.

Successful training programmes will include **moderation**, which implies that note is taken of the sportsperson's state of physical health, and when signs of deteriorating performance are detected, training loads will be reduced and recovery times increased until feelings of tiredness are reduced.

Reversibility

Reversibility is also known as **regression** and is defined as '**when training loads are reduced or removed completely, the state of fitness or performance returns to a normal untrained state**'. This is often summed up as '**use it or lose it**'.

This principle explains why performance deteriorates when training stops or intensity of training is reduced. With reversibility, physiological systems revert or **regress** to their normal untrained state eventually. This will not happen immediately, but research has shown that the process begins within 5 days of ceasing training. Interestingly, it is found that adaptations established by longer periods of training remain for longer after training stops, than those produced by a short period of training. In figure 2A.7, training and performance are improving up to the fourth month of the period shown. At this point, a minor injury occurs, and he / she cannot train for the following four months. During this second four month period, performance falls as fitness and strength falls.

figure 2A.7 – regression after training stops

performance standard

point at which trainng stops

0 1 2 3 4 5 6 7 8
time / months

Tedium

Tedium is defined as '**training that lacks variety and causes boredom**'.

Training exercises, drills, or games which are the same (with the same outcomes and feelings) week in and week out, will eventually result in a lowering of motivation as the feelings of mastery of the activity are reduced. In other words, the person becomes used to the outcomes of the activity and his / her drive to continue with the same activity reduces. This can be overcome by setting goals for sessions which vary (even though the activity itself may be the same), or completely change the activity while retaining the same goals (for example goals to improve strength or endurance). Changing activities in training with the specific aim of reducing tedium is called **variance**, and is a crucial feature of a successful training programme.

Warm-up and **Cool-down** are usually considered as essential elements of a training programme, and they are discussed in detail on pages 80 and 81 respectively.

Calculating working intensity

It is possible to calculate working intensities by using a variety of methods. Table 25 compares three methods for rating training intensity.

Table 25 - **classification of exercise intensity based on 20 to 60 min of endurance activity, comparing heart rate maximum, Karvonen's maximum heart rate reserve and Borg's Rating of Perceived Exertion (RPE)**

classification of intensity	relative intensity by HR_{max}	relative intensity by VO_{2max} or HR_{max} reserve - the Karvonen method	rating of perceived exertion Borg Scale RPE
very light	<35%	<30%	<9
light	35 - 59%	30 - 49%	10 - 11
moderate	60 - 79%	50 - 74%	12 - 13
heavy	80 - 89%	75 - 84%	14 - 16
very heavy	>89%	>84%	>16

(From Table 19.3 Wilmore, Costill, Kenney 'Physiology of Exercise 4e', 2008, Human Kinetics)

Heart rate maximum method

To calculate the relative intensity using this method you have to work out the simple percentage of maximum heart rate (HR_{max}). This requires knowledge of the heart rate in near maximal exercise conditions. HR_{max} and percentage of HR_{max} can be estimated as follows:

$$HR = 220 - age \text{ (of the performer)}$$

For a 17 year old this would be:

$$HR = 220 - 17$$
$$HR_{max} = 203 \text{ bpm}$$

Assuming our 17 year old wanted to work at a moderate intensity of between 60% and 79% of HR_{max}, his / her target heart rate zone will be between:

$$60\% \text{ of } 203 = 122 \text{ bpm,}$$
$$\text{and } 79\% \text{ of } 203 = 160 \text{ bpm.}$$

The nearer to 160 bpm the harder the exercise intensity.

This simple method does not take into account differences in fitness levels.

The Karvonen method

This HR method takes into account individual levels of fitness, as resting heart rate is required to work out an individual's training heart rate zone. Note that in table 25 above, the percentage values for HR_{max} reserve are slightly lower than in the HR_{max} column. This is because this method incorporates resting heart rate values and therefore is a more reliable method.

A training heart rate can be established by using the concept of **maximal heart rate reserve** ($HR_{max}R$).
Maximal heart rate (HR_{max}) is calculated by this method (as above) using $HR_{max} = 220 - age$

Our 17 year old would have a maximum heart rate of 203 bpm as in the previous example, and a resting heart rate of 65 bpm.

Maximal heart rate reserve ($HR_{max}R$) is worked out using:

$$HR_{max}R = HR_{max} - HR_{rest}$$

where HR_{rest} is the resting heart rate of the performer, and for our 17 year old:

$$HR_{max}R = 203 - 65 = 138$$

Thus a training heart rate (**THR** – the heart rate at which optimal aerobic training effects can take place during continuous training) can be calculated by taking a percentage of the maximal heart rate reserve and adding it to the resting heart rate:

$$\textbf{THR} = \textbf{HR}_{rest} + \textbf{(required percentage)} \times \textbf{HR}_{max}\textbf{R}$$
$$= \textbf{HR}_{rest} + \textbf{(required percentage)} \times (\textbf{HR}_{max} - \textbf{HR}_{rest})$$

So to work out the target heart rate for **moderate** exercise for the 17 year old of between 50% and 74% of $\textbf{HR}_{max}\textbf{R}$

$$\text{THR}_{50\%} = \text{HR}_{rest} + 0.50(\text{HR}_{max}\text{R})$$
$$= 65 + 0.50 \times 138$$
$$= 138 \text{ bpm.}$$

and

$$\text{THR}_{74\%} = \text{HR}_{rest} + 0.74(\text{HR}_{max}\text{R})$$
$$= 65 + 0.74 \times 138$$
$$= 167 \text{ bpm.}$$

This gives a THR% of between 138 bpm and 167 bpm which is approximately the same as the heart rate corresponding to between 50% and 74% of the $\dot{V}O_{2max}$ as shown in table 25 above.

An aerobic training zone of between 60% and 74% of maximal heart rate reserve (moderate intensity) should be used to ensure a training response when designing aerobic training programmes for most athletes. Progression through the range of training heart rate percentages can be planned as the athlete improves his / her aerobic fitness.

Borg Scale method

The Borg ratings of perceived exertion scale (**RPE**) requires a person to **subjectively** rate the difficulty of the training, using a numerical scale that is related to exercise intensity as illustrated in table 25 above. This means that the person wishing to estimate his / her exertion, would guess at the rating on a scale between zero and 20. The score of zero corresponds to being asleep, and the score of 20 corresponds to absolutely flat out intensity which would bring about complete collapse in under 30 seconds.

Since exercise levels corresponding to higher levels of energy expenditure and physiological strain produce higher RPE ratings, this is an easy and effective method of measuring exercise intensity.

Weights – the one-repetition maximum method

Strength can be defined as '**the maximal force that a muscle or muscle group can generate**', and can be assessed using a 1-repetition maximum test or the **1RM** test.

Weight lifting is a good method to assess 1RM maximal muscular strength.
- Since 1RM represents the highest successful lift
- That can be achieved for one complete repetition of an exercise.
- Having failed at the final lift.

Once the 1RM's values are known, it is then possible to calculate a percentage of the maximum that can be used to establish both anaerobic and aerobic training programmes.

Table 26 sets out the approximate values of loading, sets and repetitions needed to stress the different energy systems available to provide energy to contracting muscle. Values are approximate because different exercises will require slightly different set regimes, and individuals will vary as to how efficient they are at utility of the systems.

Table 26 – **how to use the 1RM method**

	alactic anaerobic energy system	lactic anaerobic energy system	aerobic energy system
when is it used?	flat out exercise up to 8 seconds	flat out exercise between 10-60 seconds	any slow exercise while breathing freely
training load as % of 1RM	80% - 100%	60% - 80%	below 50%
repetitions	less than 3	5 to 12	15 to 30
sets	3 to 5	3 to 5	3
recovery	full recovery	restricted recovery	no recovery

With strength gains achieved as a result of regular systematic training, it is important to retest IRM values at regular intervals (say once a month) so that percentage training values can be adjusted accordingly.

Fitness testing

Fitness testing is a valuable tool that can be used in the planning of a training programme.

 STUDENT NOTE You should refer to your student text book for fuller descriptions of recognised submaximal and maximal fitness tests.

Reasons for testing

Reasons for testing are broad and are summarised in figure 2A.8.
Tests:

- Tend to provide **objective measures** about the individual's current state of fitness / health.
- Attempt to highlight the **strengths** and **weaknesses** of the sportsperson.
- Attempt to evaluate the **effects** of a **training programme**.
- Can be used for **talent** identification.
- Can **motivate** an individual as he / she strives to reach his / her best test scores.
- Add **variety** to training programme.
- Can be **specific** to the individual's sport.

figure 2A.8 – reasons for fitness testing

REASONS FOR FITNESS TESTING: objective, finds strengths, finds weaknesses, evaluates effects of training programme, talent identification, motivator, adds variety, specific

Specific test protocols

Sport specific tests should be appropriate for the subject's age, sex and current fitness. Also, sport specific tests recognise the **specificity** of the test activity, and therefore ensure the variables tested are relevant to the sport. Examples of the specific nature of tests are:

- Use of a flume pool for swimmers.
- Paddle ergometers for swimmers.
- Cycle ergometers for cyclists.
- Treadmill tests for endurance runners.
- Vertical jumps tests for high jumpers.
- Skipping tests for boxers.

Principles of maximal and submaximal tests

Maximal tests

Maximal means that the subject makes an 'all-out' **effort** or undertakes a test to **exhaustion**.

In **anaerobic** work **IRM** represents **one repetition maximum** (see IRM above) which is the maximum possible weight which can be lifted at a certain lift. Performing a IRM represents a maximal test. Other examples of maximal **anaerobic** tests are 30 metre sprint, the Sergeant jump (described in table 27 on page 78) and the Wingate 30 second cycle ergometer test.

A maximal **aerobic** test would be a test to exhaustion, such as the NCF multi-stage shuttle run test, or Cooper's 12 minute run / walk test.

Disadvantages of maximal tests

The main difficulty is in ensuring the subject is **exerting** maximum effort, and the possible dangers of **over-exertion** and **injury**. This issue is dependent on the level of **motivation** (arousal levels) of the performer.

Table 27 - **examples of standardised maximal tests**

test	fitness component	description	advantages	disadvantages
30m sprint	speed	a flat-out timed 30m sprint	easily performed, high correlation with peak anaerobic power	timing errors, differences in footware (trainers / spikes), different surfaces (grass / rubber track)
Sergeant jump	power	two-foot standing take-off, measure between standing two armed reach and highest single hand jumped reach	easy to administer, high correlation with peak anaerobic power	skill factor, height differences between performers
balancing on a beam	static balance	time how long balance can be maintained on the bar on an upturned gym bench	easy to administer	depends on motivation

Submaximal tests

Submaximal means that the subject exercises **below** maximum effort. Data collected from submaximal tests can be extrapolated to **estimate** maximal capacities. Examples of **submaximal aerobic** tests are the PWC-170 test, the Queen's College step test described below, and the Fitech step test.

Submaximal tests are often favoured over maximal tests because there is less stress on the performer and greater reliability of results.

Disadvantages of submaximal tests

Submaximal tests depend on **projection / extrapolation** being made to an unknown maximum, and therefore small inaccuracies / uncontrolled variables can result in large discrepancies in the estimation of the actual maximal values as a result of magnification of results.

Table 28 - **examples of standard submaximal tests**

test	fitness component	description	advantages	disadvantages
PWC-170 test	aerobic fitness	two 6 minute cycle ergometer rides at predicted heart rates, used to extrapolate power output	popular and inexpensive cycle ergometer test	predicted test by extrapolation, fitness levels influence interpretation of results
Queen's College step test	predicted $\dot{V}O_{2max}$	3 minutes of stepping at a set cadence, $\dot{V}O_{2max}$ predicted from HR recovery	easy to administer, cheap equipment	length of leg levers affects results, depends on stepping technique and rhythm, only produces a predicted $\dot{V}O_{2max}$

Your PAR-Q 'Physical Activity Readiness Questionnaire'

You should **administer to yourself** a questionnaire which establishes on **medical** grounds, whether you should undertake demanding fitness tests or not.

Limitations of fitness tests

- Many tests (see figure 2A.9) are not sport **specific** and so do not replicate the specific movement patterns required for the chosen event.
- Many tests are **predictive** because they do not use direct measures and therefore can be inaccurate.
- Many tests do not take into account the sporting **environment**.

figure 2A.9 – limitations of fitness training

specificity of test

predictive tests

personality of tester

not account for sporting environment

time of day

LIMITATIONS OF FITNESS TESTING

validity of test

prior test experience

reliability of test

personal factors

environmental factors

Making a test valid

The concept of **validity** is built around the question '**does each test measure what it aims to measure**?' A test may be valid **for one purpose** but not another. For example the Wingate cycle test may produce a measure of strength endurance but not aerobic capacity.

Making a test reliable

The concept of reliability is built around the **accuracy** of the test results. How **dependable** are the test scores? Will we get **the same result** if the measurement is repeated? This is the **consistency** of test results from one occasion to another.
For example, a measurement of body composition gives a measure of 19% body fat, but the same apparatus gives a measure of 17% the next day. Errors may be induced because of differences in skin moisture and body water content. Therefore the same conditions should be adopted on each occasion if possible.

Factors which could affect test results are:

- Environmental factors (weather, temperature, noise, crowd, test surface).
- Personal factors (health, diet, mood).
- Prior test experience (have you done the test before and will this affect your results?).
- Time of day.
- Personality of the tester.

Standardising test protocols

A test protocol is the way in which a test is conducted. This implies that a test produces **measurable definite results**, and hence **human error and opinion** must not be allowed to influence results. Therefore a test protocol must attempt to **eliminate inaccuracies** using:

- **Efficient** and accurate recording equipment.
- Correct techniques / equipment.
- Use of protocol for **scoring**.
- Elimination of **crowd effects**.
- Controlled warm-up.
- Same conditions for repeated tests.

Physiological and psychological effects of warm-up and cool-down

Warm-up

Figure 2A.10 summarises the issues within warm-up. Warm-up usually consists of a series of low level aerobic exercises which can be sport specific or general in nature (jogging, SAQ, cycle ergometer, stretching). The sport specific element usually includes exercises of increasing intensity up to the moment of game or competition beginning. The aim of this element is to get the sportsperson into the rhythm and flow of their forthcoming activity, practice skills and movements expected later, and to build confidence before event start.

There are two functions of a warm-up, physiological and psychological, both of which prepare the body for the main exercise effort to come.

figure 2A.10 – warm-up

- raises heart rate and cardiac output
- increased oxygen available
- dilates capillaries
- prepare body for exercise
- higher blood pressure
- light aerobic exercise
- **WARM-UP**
- reduced risk of injury
- stretching
- raises body temperature
- enhances rate of ATP conversion
- reduces blood viscosity
- enhances glycolytic enzyme action
- reduces muscle response times

Physiological value of warm-up

- Increase in body **temperature**.
- Which warms muscles and enables better **ATP conversion**.
- Slightly **better blood flow** due to blood viscosity lower at a higher temperature.
- Increases the **speed of nerve** impulse conduction and hence faster reaction time.
- Increase in **heart rate** and **cardiac output**.
- Increase in **volume of air** breathed per minute.
- **Capillaries dilate** with oxygenated blood.
- Increase in **blood pressure** forces blood more quickly through arteries.
- **Stretching** of relevant joints and muscles prepares them for full range action.
- Secretion of **adrenaline** increases the metabolic rate (normal rate at which energy is produced by the whole body).
- **Reduces** risk of musculo-skeletal **injuries**.

Psychological value of warm-up

- Warm-up is a **rehearsal** for skill-related practices (figure 2A.11).
- This improves **co-ordination** of the neuromuscular system.
- Warm-up prepares the body psychologically for training / competition by increasing **arousal**. For example, the New Zealand All Blacks perform the **Haka** as part of match warm-up preparations.
- This arousal will heighten **awareness** of pitch and player positioning and enable focusing on relevant aspects of a game.
- This sort of activity builds **self-confidence** / self-efficacy for the action to begin.

figure 2A.11 – psychological aspects of warm-up

- improves co-ordination
- rehearsal of skills
- increases arousal
- **PSYCHOLOGICAL ASPECTS OF WARM-UP**
- builds self-confidence
- heightens awareness
- enables focusing

Cool-down

The aim of a cool-down (figure 2A.12) is to gradually return the body to its former resting state. This is achieved by performing low intensity exercise such as jogging and stretching. Static stretches during cool-down can increase flexibility of joints.

Physiological value of cool-down

- Keeps muscle active and **capillaries open** for longer to enable **oxygenated blood** flowing to muscles to purge of **oxygen debt**.

- **Flushes** out **lactic acid** and helps oxidise lactic acid thereby **preventing** muscle soreness – **DOMS**.

- Active muscles will activate the skeletal muscle pump for **venous return** of blood to the heart thereby preventing **blood pooling** and dizziness (blood will remain in limbs if muscle action is stopped suddenly).

The outcome of a cool-down should be to allow heart rate to return to its pre-exercise level with reduced injury risk, and to help lower levels of blood adrenaline after a period of high arousal.

figure 2A.12 – cool-down

- continues metabolic processes
- reduces blood pooling
- keeps oxygenated blood flowing
- maintains venous return
- **COOL-DOWN**
- removes CO_2 and lactic acid
- maintains elevated blood pressure
- flushes capillaries with oxygenated blood
- prevents DOMS
- purges oxygen debt

Types of stretching exercises

Types of stretching / flexibility exercises

Flexibility refers to '**the range of motion (ROM) that you can achieve at any joint through any particular movement**' and is joint specific. In simple language this can be expressed as how far you can reach, bend and turn. Joint flexibility depends on the distensibility of the joint capsule, adequate warm-up, muscle viscosity and the compliance of ligaments and tendons. Flexibility is improved by stressing all these components. There are two main types of stretching (figure 2A.13):

- **Static**.
- **Dynamic**.

figure 2A.13 – flexibility / stretching

- active
- passive
- static
- **STATIC STRETCHING**
- PNF
- dynamic
- **DYNAMIC STRETCHING**
- ballistic

Static stretching

Static stretching refers to **stretching exercises that are performed without movement**. In other words, the individual gets into a stretch position and holds the stretch for a specific amount of time.

A static stretch can be performed by placing the body in a position whereby the **muscle to be stretched is under tension. At this point the position is held to allow the muscle to lengthen**. This is a very safe and effective form of stretching with a limited threat of injury. See figure 2A.14 as an example of a static stretch.

figure 2A.14 – hold this static stretch

Active stretching

Active stretching is **slow stretching in which flexibility is achieved without assistance**. This form of stretching involves using only the strength of the opposing muscles (antagonist) to generate a held stretch (held for 10-15 seconds) within the agonist. The contraction of the opposing muscles helps to relax the stretched muscles. See figure 2A.15 as an example of an active stretch. Active stretching is a very effective form of conditioning.

figure 2A.15 – active stretch

Passive stretching

Passive stretching is similar to static stretching, however a **partner or apparatus can be used to help further stretch the muscles / joints**. Figure 2A.16 is an example of a passive stretch in which the floor is assisting the position.

figure 2A.16 – passive stretch

Proprioceptive Neuromuscular Facilitation (PNF)

PNF is a progression on passive stretching, whereby **after stretch is held, the muscle is contracted isometrically for between 6-10 seconds**. It then relaxes and is contracted again, usually going further the second time. Known as the **CRAC** method (Contract-Relax-Antagonist-Contract). The aim of PNF is to toughen up or inhibit proprioceptors (such as muscle spindles and Golgi tendons) in the relaxation of muscle tissue.

Dynamic stretching

This type of stretching refers to **stretching exercises that are performed with movement** and are classified depending on the vigorousness of the bounce. Dynamic stretching uses a controlled, soft bounce or swinging movement, that moves a particular body part to the limit of its range of movement and is a preferred method over ballistic stretching.

Ballistic stretching

figure 2A.17 – ballistic stretch

This type of stretching **involves aggressive, dynamic / rapid / bouncing / swinging movements** during which the contraction of the agonist forces the antagonist to relax. Ballistic stretching fails to allow the stretched muscle time to adapt to the stretched position and instead may cause the muscle to tighten up by repeatedly triggering the stretch reflex. Ballistic stretching should be **used towards the end of a warm-up** because the muscle temperatures are slightly higher than at the start of the warm-up phase. Ballistic stretching is considered to be an outdated form of stretching because of its vigorous nature and risk of muscle tear injury. Activities such as trampolining, rely on ballistic stretching during routine work such as a ten-bounce routine. Figure 2A.17 shows a side-to-side swinging movement aimed at stretching the lower trunk muscles.

Stretching and safe practice principles

This is all about **how** to achieve adequate flexibility that meets the needs of the activity:

*   Stretches should be done when the muscle tissue is warm thereby reducing the risk of injury.
*   Begin stretching slowly at first and hold end points, as in active and passive stretching.
*   Stretching to a painful end point is not recommended.
*   Only use ballistic stretching when the muscle tissue is thoroughly warm since bouncing can cause small muscle tears.
*   Stretch both agonists and antagonists to maintain muscle and joint equilibrium.
*   Good posture before and during the stretch will reduce the risk of injury and ensure that the stretch is correctly directed to the selected joint and muscle(s).
*   Breathe slowly and easily while stretching.
*   Stretching during cool-down can **increase flexibility** of joints because the body is still very warm after full effort exercise.

Training methods

As listed below on page 85 there are several different types of training that can be used to improve fitness levels. Each type is summarised in table 29 on page 85, with examples of sessions and advantages and disadvantages of the different methods.

figure 2A.18 – training methods

Continuous training

Involves continuous activity in which there is **no rest or break** and is normally associated with developing aerobic capacity (VO_{2max}).

The **duration** of the training session should be at least 20 minutes and upwards. Adjusting the pace or effort of the activity can vary the exercise **intensity** (recommended between 60-75% of maximum heart rate) from long, slow distance training to high-intensity endurance training. **Frequency** of sessions at least 3 times per week to benefit from aerobic adaptations.

Fartlek

Fartlek or speed play is a form of continuous training during which the **speed or intensity of the activity is varied** so that both aerobic and anaerobic energy systems and recovery can be stressed.

Intermittent or interval training

This type of training is characterised by periods of **alternating exercise** and **rest**, providing a very versatile training method that enables the individual to perform considerable more work and with greater physiological benefits.
Variables include:

- **Duration** of the exercise period.
- **Intensity** of the exercise period.
- Number of **repetitions** within a set.
- Number of **sets** within a session.
- Duration of the rest intervals (rest relief) or **recovery**.

The exercise **type** and **loading**, number of **repetitions** and **sets**, and length of **rest relief** govern the **adaptive response** produced, thus enabling the individual to select the required intensity of work to stress the relevant energy system:

- **ATP-PC intervals** are characterised by high intensity effort (80-100% of maximum effort) lasting between 3-10 seconds and no more than 2 minutes recovery. Increases ATP-PC stores.
- **Lactic acid intervals** are characterised by medium to high intensity effort (60-80% of maximum effort) lasting between 15-90 seconds with variable recovery depending exercise duration. Increases blood buffering capacity or increased lactate tolerance.
- **Aerobic intervals** are characterised by low intensity effort (below 50% of maximum effort) lasting beyond 20 minutes with short recovery. Increases aerobic capacity or VO_{2max}.

Weight training

Weight training is a form of interval training and can be used to develop / stress several components of fitness such as strength and strength endurance depending on the resistance, number of repetitions, sets and rest relief.

Exercises are normally classed in four groups:

- **Shoulders and arms**: bench press, pull downs, curls.
- **Trunk and back**: back hyperextensions, sit ups.
- **Legs**: squats, leg press, calf raises.
- **All-body exercises**: power clean, snatch, dead lift.

See table 29 on page 85 for details of how to include these exercises in a session.

Circuit training

A type of interval training that provides all-round body fitness, characterised by a number of exercises or stations performed in succession so that different body parts are exercised successively. The training is normally organised to work for a set time period at each station.

Plyometric training

A type of power training **involving eccentric-to-concentric actions at 100% effort** designed to improve elastic strength. Plyometric leg training occurs when, on landing, the muscle performs an eccentric contraction (lengthens under tension) performed quickly so that the loaded agonist muscle stretches slightly prior to concentric action. This stimulates adaptation within the neuromuscular system as muscle spindles cause a **stretch reflex** to produce a more powerful concentric muscle contraction. The throwing and catching of medicine balls is a way of developing elastic shoulder strength.

In figure 2A.19, two athletes are throwing a medicine ball back and forth. The catch phase of this movement is eccentric for the trunk musculature and the shoulders, with the throw movement being concentric in the same muscle groups. Normally this exercise is done too slowly to activate the stretch reflex, but a rapid rebound movement could have the desired effect.

figure 2A.19 – catch and throw as eccentric then concentric exercise – similar to plyometrics

In figure 2A.20, the athlete is performing two-footed jumping (bunny jumps), which would have to be performed quickly to activate the stretch reflex in time with the concentric phase of the jump.

figure 2A.20 – bounding and jumping can be plyometric

Mobility training

Mobility training is discussed above under the heading of stretching and flexibility on pages 81 and 82.

The aim of this type of training is to improve (or maintain) the range of motion over which muscles can act and joints can operate (figure 2A.21). This works on the **stress-overload principle** by forcing the contractile tissues such as muscle tissue to operate at full stretch. Mobility work is best done at the end of an anaerobic training session, during cool-down. This is because the muscular system is usually more relaxed at this time, with muscle temperatures slightly higher than during the warm-up.

figure 2A.21 – mobility training is essential

Practice questions

1) b) Explain why you would use the principles of training when developing a training programme to improve the fitness of 16+ physical education students.

2) b) A group of students wish to create an aerobic weight training programme. Suggest how they could calculate working intensities that would give them optimal strength endurance gains. Illustrate your answer with examples.

3) b) Explain why fitness testing is necessary for both the coach and the athlete?

4) b) The aim of Cooper's 12-minute run / walk test is to run as far as possible in 12 minutes.
What aspect of physical fitness does the 12-minute run / walk measure?
Briefly outline the strengths and limitations of this maximal test as a test for aerobic capacity, and identify some of the external variables that could influence the validity and reliability of this test if it test was performed outdoors on a school field.

5) b) Identify **two** valid and reliable submaximal tests that measure endurance or stamina. Why are submaximal tests often favoured over maximal tests?

6) b) Explain, using examples, why the Illinois agility run test may be of more value to a games player than a 30 metre sprint test.

7) b) From a physiological standpoint, explain why warm-up and cool-down are important within an exercise programme.

8) b) You have been asked to prepare a mobility training session for a group of A-level Physical Education students who wish to improve their flexibility for their chosen individual activity.
Explain, with examples, how you would use static, active, passive and ballistic stretching to create a session in the context of safe practice.

9) b) Your PE group has been asked to devise a running training schedule for an elite 1500m runner. Using your knowledge of both intermittent and continuous training methods show how you could use this information to produce both aerobic and anaerobic adaptations.

10 b) Justify the content of your training programme for an elite 1500m runner, with regard to expected respiratory adaptations.

SKILL ACQUISITION

UNIT 1

SKILLS AND ABILITIES

INFORMATION PROCESSING

LEARNING AND PERFORMANCE

UNIT 2

SKILL ACQUISITION IN
PRACTICAL SITUATIONS

Characteristics and definitions of skill

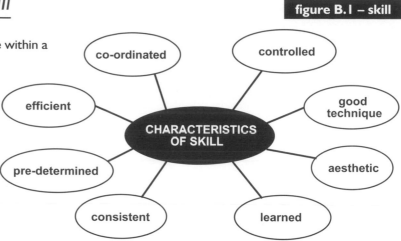

figure B.1 – skill

The term **motor skill** is used to describe a **technique** within a game or sport (for example, passing, hitting, catching, controlling a ball), or in reference to **the sport itself** (diving, tennis, hammer throwing), or a **quality** possessed by a sportsperson. The characteristics of skill (see figure B.1) are that it should be co-ordinated, controlled, with good technique, efficient, or pre-determined by the practice or observation of others performing the skill perfectly. As such the skill will be well-learned, efficient and consistent. The beauty or pleasing nature of a skill is its aesthetic quality (figure B.2).

Difference between motor and perceptual abilities

figure B.2 – squash, a skilful activity?

Characteristics of ability

Ability (see figure B.3) is the foundation for skill learning. A successful sportsperson must be born with a number of relevant abilities. An ability is **genetically determined**, since we are born with our abilities, which means that it is **innate** and **enduring** – it is part of our constitution and will last all our lives. For example, some children can quickly pick up skills (such as catching a ball or riding a bike), whereas other children take much longer and are less successful at any given skill.

Motor (psychomotor) ability

This is about the processing of information about how and when we move. For example, fast reaction time is an ability, a rugby player must react quickly to an oncoming player who changes direction. **Gross motor ability** is an ability in which the performer is able to move using simple muscle movements, for example, being able to run or ride a bike.

Perceptual ability

This is the ability to sense and interpret sensory inputs or information. For example, the awareness of a rugby player of the positions and actions of opponents.

figure B.3 – ability

Ability is an **enduring** trait. We largely hold on to our abilities throughout our lives, for example, riding a bike.

General ability

This does not really exist - we have specific abilities.

Specific abilities

This refers to the fact that skills require different abilities. For example, gymnastics involves balance, strength and flexibility.

Groups of abilities

A good sportsperson may have many different groups of abilities. For example, a good all round sportsman could have different specific abilities such as good hand eye co-ordination and balance which could be transferred to lots of different sports activities.

Difference between skill and ability

Skill is acquired. Skills must be **learned**, which can require an extended process including the copying of expert models. On the other hand, **ability** is an **enduring** trait which can last throughout a person's life, and is genetic in basis. Abilities underpin and contribute to skills. For example, someone with good natural balance, shoulder and hip flexibility, and upper body and wrist strength, has all the abilities necessary to perform a handstand. But practice would be required to actually perform the skill of the handstand.

Types of skill

A **psychomotor skill** is a voluntary body movement with a pre-determined end result, for example, hitting a ball with a bat. **Fundamental psychomotor skills** are basic skills that are learned when young. They form the basis of more complex movements, for example, jumping.
A **perceptual skill** is about being able to interpret information quickly at a given time and to make an appropriate decision. For example, a goalkeeper in football assessing the movement of an opponent approaching.
A cognitive skill is about being able to make sense of a problem and to solve it. These skills affect perception.

Classification of skill

All skills are on a classification continuum. There are several types of continuum:

Environmental influence

The environmental influence continuum deals with a range of skills labelled open to closed. **Open skills** are predominantly perceptual, with no clear beginning / end, are affected by environment, are externally-paced, in response to many actions of others. For example receiving a pass at soccer or hockey. On the other hand, **closed skills** are predominantly habitual, with a clear beginning and end, and are not affected much by environment. For example, an athlete performing a shot-putt. See further examples in figure B.4.

figure B.4 – the environmental influence continuum

OPEN						CLOSED
soccer goal save	soccer pass	tennis stroke		tennis serve	soccer penalty	shot putt

Continuity

The continuity continuum deals with **discrete, serial** and **continuous skills**. Discrete skills are those that have a clear beginning and end, for example taking a penalty kick at soccer. **Serial skills** are those that have a number of discrete elements linked together. For example, the triple jump in which the hop / step / jump are linked into one movement. **Continuous skills** are those that cannot be split up very easily into subroutines, for example, a hockey player dribbling a ball. See further examples in figure B.5.

figure B.5 – continuity continuum

DISCRETE		SERIAL	CONTINUOUS	
weight lifting	javelin throw	high jump	basketball dribble	running

Muscular involvement

The muscular involvement continuum deals with **gross** and **fine skills**. **Gross skills** are those that use large muscle movements, for example, weight lifting. **Fine skills** are those that use small muscle movements, for example, darts. See further examples in figure B.6.

figure B.6 – muscular involvement continuum

GROSS						FINE
weight lifting	javelin throw	netball pass	cricket stroke	golf shot	ten pin bowling	darts / snooker

Pacing

The pacing continuum deals with self-paced and externally-paced skills. **Self-paced skills** are those in which the performer has control over movement, for example, serving in volleyball. **Externally-paced skills** are those in which the environment has more control, for example, blocking in volleyball. See figure B.7 for further examples.

figure B.7 – pacing continuum

EXTERNALLY-PACED				SELF-PACED	
yachting	tennis receiving serve	soccer game	diving	tennis serve	weight lifting

The skill continuum

All skills have elements of **all** the classifications. For example, a golf swing may be predominantly a closed skill but it can be affected by strong weather conditions which would be an open skill characteristic. The swim start in figure B.8 could be said to have gross and closed characteristics, but is it also self-paced and discrete?

Most skills have characteristics which make them near one end of a classification continuum. For example, a batsman in cricket as he plays a shot can be seen to be performing more of an open skill than a closed skill (he has to adapt to the speed and direction of the ball). But the cricket shot does have elements of closed characteristics too. The player has learned particular shots and almost automatically puts them into operation when the ball approaches at different speeds, with different spin, and in different directions.

Practice questions

1) If you were watching a number of performers in sport, what characteristics would you expect the movements of a skilled performer to have?
4 marks

2) By using examples from sport, explain what is meant by fundamental psychomotor skills and why they are so important.
4 marks

3) a) Why is the shot putt often regarded as a closed skill? *2 marks*
b) Using passing skills in a team game, explain what is meant by an open skill. *4 marks*
c) Give one example from sport of each of the following and state why you have chosen your example: continuous skills, serial skills, discrete skills.
3 marks

4) The diagram in figure B.9 shows a profile for the racing start in swimming scaled across four different continua representing the skill characteristics of the movement.

a) Referring to the profile, describe the swim racing start in terms of each of the four characteristics shown.
4 marks

b) Using this same profile chart, sketch a profile which would describe the characteristics of a table tennis serve. *3 marks*

c) Explain why you have chosen your particular characteristic for muscular involvement and environmental conditions.
4 marks

figure B.9 – continuum profile for swimming race start

ENVIRONMENTAL INFLUENCE
closed ←——————————————→ open
CONTINUITY
continuous ←——————————————→ discrete
MUSCULAR INVOLVEMENT
fine ←——————————————→ gross
PACING
self ←——————————————→ external

d) Explain how your profile for the table tennis serve might assist a coach in planning practices for players learning this skill.
5 marks

5) a) You are observing a number of tennis players being coached. There is a mixture of abilities. Explain what is meant by ability, and give examples of motor abilities and perceptual abilities.
4 marks
b) Give **two** types of abilities that are important to play tennis effectively. Why is it wrong to assume that there is such a thing as natural ability?
4 marks

INFORMATION PROCESSING

How is information processed by the brain in such a way as to convert information received from the surroundings into muscular activity? The following model attempts to explain what the brain does during this process.

Whiting's model of information processing

In this model (in figure B.10):

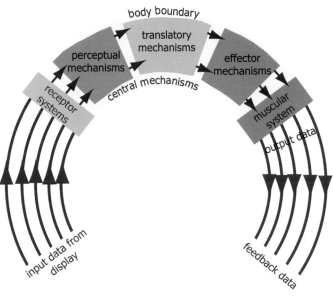

figure B.10 – Whiting's model of information processing

- The **display** refers to the range of actions and things that are happening in the surrounding environment of the performer.

- **Input data from display** involves information from the environment which enters the brain via the **sense organs**. For example, before catching a ball, the catcher sees the ball and is aware of the thrower's movement, or another player shouts to warn of an impending tackle, and the player is then aware of this other player.

- **Receptor systems** refers to the **sense organs** which receive information.

- **Perceptual mechanism** is the part of the brain which perceives the surroundings and gives them meaning.

- The **translatory mechanism** consists of the part of the brain which makes decisions and sorts out and processes the few relevant bits of information from the many inputs from the surroundings.

- The **effector mechanism** is the part of the brain which carries out the decisions and sends messages to the limbs and parts of the body via the nervous system.

- **Output** involves the effector mechanism and muscle movement. The nerves send messages to the muscles which move in order for the ball to be caught.

- **Feedback data** is **information** which is used **during and after** an action or movement which enables a performer to adjust or change performance according to this new information.

Input

Input is directly from the **senses**:

- **Sight / hearing / touch / taste** and **smell** (less useful in the sporting situation), which are linked to the various **receptor** sense organs throughout the body.

- **Proprioception** is a term which describes another form of input via the nervous system (sense organs) which relays information to the brain about the position and angles of joints, and the tension in muscles. This allows the sportsperson to be aware of these factors when deciding to make movements.

Perception and attention

These elements are ideas which should be understood before concepts relating to memory can be explored – see figure B.11.

Perception is **stimulus identification**. As information is received from the environment, the performer needs to **make sense** of it, to **interpret** it and to **identify** the elements which are **relevant** and **important**. Perception consists of three elements:

- **Detection** - the performer needs to be aware that something notable is going on around him / her, where the ball is, where the other players are from both sides in relation to the pitch dimensions, what the goalkeeper is doing - in a field game situation.

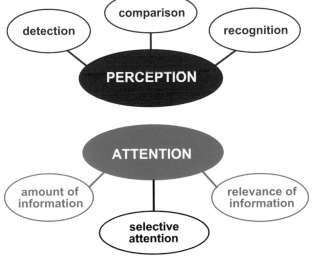

figure B.11 – perception and attention

- **Comparison** - in which the performer will compare what is happening with his / her past experiences of similar situations, where are the players in comparison with set plays rehearsed in a training situation?

- **Recognition** - in which the performer realises that what is happening requires a response or an activity in response, what is the response to the rehearsed set play?

Attention relates to:

- **Amount of information** we can cope with, since the amount of information we can attend to **is limited**, and therefore we have limited **attentional capacity**.

- **Relevance of the information**. The performer must therefore attend to only **relevant information**, and **disregard irrelevant** information. This is called **selective attention**.

Selective attention

This is the process of sorting out **relevant** bits of information from the many which are received. Attention passes the information to the **short-term memory** which gives time for **conscious analysis**. A good performer can **focus totally** on an important aspect of his / her skill which **can exclude other elements** which may also be desirable. Sometimes a performer may desire to concentrate on several different things at once.

When some parts of a performance become **automatic**, the information relevant to those parts does not require attention, and this gives the performer **spare attentional capacity**. This allows the performer to attend to new elements of a skill such as tactics or anticipating the moves of an opponent. The coach will therefore need to help the performer to make best use of spare attentional capacity, and will also need to **direct the attention** of the performer to enable him / her to **concentrate** and reduce the chance of **attentional switching** to irrelevant information or distractions.

Memory

In figure B.12 you can see a model which sets out the various elements of memory and how it works.

figure B.12 – memory

- The **short-term sensory store (STSS)** is the **area of the brain** which receives information and holds it for a **short time** (less than I second) **prior to processing**. Information deemed unimportant is lost and forgotten and replaced by new information.

- **Selective attention** is used to sort out **relevant bits of information** from the many which are received.

- **Short-term memory (STM)** is the **part of the brain** which keeps information for a short period (20-30 seconds) after it has been deemed **worthy of attention**. The STM can carry between 5 and 9 separate items of information which can be improved by chunking (see page 95 opposite for an explanation of chunking). The information can be used for problem solving (**decision making** in which it is decided what to do) or passed on to the long-term memory for permanent storage.

- **Long-term memory** is the **part of the brain** which retains information for **long periods of time** - up to the lifetime of the performer. Very **well-learned information** is stored, and LTM is **limitless** and not forgotten but may require a code for the information to be recalled.

Strategies for improving retention / memory

The following methods of improving retention can be used (see figure B.13):

Knowing how:
- **Educate** the performer about the details of a skill.
- **Explain** what to do and how to do it.

Brevity:
- Be **brief**.
- Do **not overload** the short-term memory which can only hold small amounts of data.

Clarity:
- Keep advice / instruction **simple** and **clear**.
- **KISS** - keep it simple stupid.
- Carefully **separate** similar skills to enable the performer to distinguish between them.

Chunking:
- More information can be held in STM if information is **lumped together** / chunked.

Organisation:
- Organise the process of learning to ensure the information is **meaningful**.

Association or chaining:
- **Link new** information **with old** already learnt information.
- Multiple links can form a chain.

Practice:
- **Practice makes perfect**.
- Perfect practice makes a skill perfect.
- **Repetition** of any information or skill will enable it to be remembered.

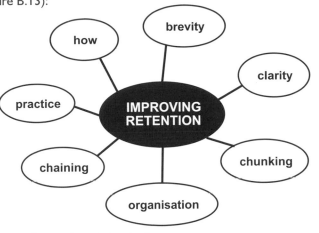

figure B.13 – retention

Mental practice / rehearsal

Mental practice or rehearsal (see figure B.14):

- Creates a **mental picture** of a skill.
- Can be used to **simulate** a whole movement sequence or just part of it.
- Can be used to **imagine** and envisage success and avoid failure in a competitive situation.
- Can provide a mental warm-up in order to promote a state of **readiness** for action.
- And must be as **realistic** as possible to be effective.
- Can be used during **rest / recovery** periods **during** a performance or in between performances.
- Can be used to focus **attention** on important aspects of a skill.
- Build **self-confidence** for an upcoming performance.
- And **control arousal** and induce calmness before a performance.
- Can be used to enable the learner to **memorise** a skill or movement more effectively.

figure B.14 – mental practice

It works by producing **small muscle contractions** in the same sequence as an actual practice, and since the gross movement of the skill does not actually happen, it **prevents** wear and tear.

Decision making

Reaction time, response time and movement time

- **Reaction time (RT)** is the time between the **onset** of a stimulus and the **start** of the response. This is an **inherent ability** or trait. The stimulus could be kinaesthesia, hearing, touch, vision, pain, or smell. From this list, the fastest reaction times occur to stimuli at the front of the list, the slowest to those at the end of the list.

- **Movement time** is the time it takes to **complete the onset** of a movement. **Response time** is the time it takes to **process information** and then to **make a response**.

- **Response time = reaction time + movement time**.

Choice reaction time

Simple reaction time is the time taken to respond to a single stimulus. If **several stimuli** are given but only one must be selected for response, then a choice must be made of which stimulus to respond to. This is the **choice reaction time**. The **more choices** a person has, the **more information** needs processing, and the **longer it takes** to process the information, the **slower** the reaction time. This is **Hick's Law** (see figure B.15, and more explanation below).

Anticipation

This is the ability to **predict** future events **from** early signals or **past events**.

Reaction time can be **speeded up** if the performer learns to anticipate certain actions. Good performers **start** running motor programmes **before the stimulus is fully recognised**. They anticipate the strength, speed and direction of a stimulus, which would enable a performer to partially eliminate the **PRP** (psychological refractory period – see below).

However, **opponents** will also be trying to anticipate the performer's own actions, and a good performer will attempt to **increase** opponents' reaction times by increasing the number of choices of stimulus they have, by, for example, increasing the number of fakes or dummies (Matt Dawson / Jason Robinson in Rugby).

figure B.15 – Hick's Law
showing increase in reaction time as number of stimuli increases

reaction time

number of possible alternative stimuli

Factors affecting reaction time

The following factors affect reaction time, see figure B.16.
- **Age**, the older we get, the slower our reaction times.
- **Gender**, males have quicker reaction times than females, but reaction times reduce less with age for females.
- Increase in **stimulus intensity** will improve reaction time, a louder bang will initiate the go more quickly than a less loud bang.
- **Tall people** will have slower reactions than short people because of the greater distance the information has to travel from the performer's brain to the active muscles. Short sprinters tend to win 60m races.
- **Arousal levels** affect reaction times. Arousal levels are best when the performer is alert but not over aroused.
- The performer must attend to the most **important cues** (which act as a stimulus).
- Factors like body language / position might give a **cue** which enables the performer to **anticipate** a stimulus. For example, identifying favourite strokes or positions, particularly if the play involves an attempted dummy or fake.

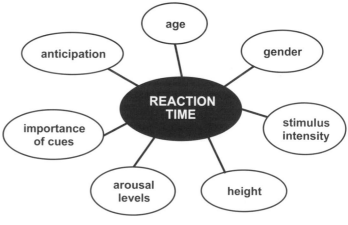

figure B.16 – factors affecting reaction time

age

gender

anticipation

REACTION TIME

stimulus intensity

importance of cues

arousal levels

height

Hick's Law

Hick's law describes the relationship between reaction time and the **number** of stimuli to which a reaction might be expected. This is discussed above in connection with the idea of **choice reaction time**. The point is that the sportsperson has to make a choice between several stimuli – before responding to only one of them. Hick's law (see figure B.15) says that as the number of stimuli increases (and therefore the number of items between which a **choice** must be made increases), then the reaction time increases also. Hence the number of choices is a factor which affects the reaction time.

Psychological refractory period

The psychological refractory period **(PRP)** is about what happens when after an **initial stimulus** (which may cause a reaction), there is a presentation of a **second stimulus**. This has the effect of **slowing down** the processing of information causing a **time lag** (this is the **psychological refractory period**) between the relevant stimulus and an appropriate response. For example, selling a dummy or sidestepping in rugby.

Example

Looking at figure B.18, **S1** (1st stimulus) would be the dummy. **S2** (2nd stimulus) would be the definite move. If the dummy (**S1**) had been the only stimulus then the reaction would have been at time **R1**. In the meantime, **S2** has happened, but the performer cannot begin his / her response to this until the full reaction **R1** has been processed by the brain, so there is therefore a period of time (the **PRP**) after **S2** but before the time break to **R2** can begin. A person who can do a multiple dummy / shimmy (Jason Robinson in figure B.17) can leave opposition with no time to react and hence miss a tackle.

Single channel hypothesis

This hypothesis says that a performer can only attend to **one thing at a time**, so information is processed **sequentially**, that is one after another. Attentional switching would occur by **transferring attention** from one situation to another, so although attention would be **shared** between situations, only one would be attended to at a time (one then two then one then two …). Therefore this can only be done if each situation requires **small** attentional capacity.

Motor programmes and subroutines

Motor programmes

Motor and **executive programmes** are the **general movement patterns** stored in the long-term memory. For example, the general movement pattern associated with kicking a football, striking a forehand at tennis or squash, or performing a pole vault (figure B.19).

A **motor programme** contains **all the information** required to make a movement including which muscles to use, the order in which muscles are used, and the phasing and degree of contraction of muscles. They are formed through repetition of movements. For example, the repetition of a particular swimming dive will eventually cause the swimmer to perform the dive with little conscious effort.

An **executive programme** enables a **skill** to be performed, can be made up of a **large number of subroutines**, and must be **adaptable** so that it can be altered when the environment / surroundings change.

the vaulter has a complex executive programme for this activity

Subroutines

Subroutines are the segments which go toward building a whole movement pattern or programme. They can be structured in **layers** (see figure B.20 as an example for the pole vault) where some subroutines can be in turn broken down into further subroutines which form smaller parts of a skill. Each subroutine is a **short fixed sequence** which, when fully learned, can be performed **automatically without conscious control**. When effectively broken down into subroutines, and learned thoroughly, a skill performed by a sportsperson can therefore contribute to his / her autonomous phase of learning. It is the efficiency of the subroutine process which contributes most to the advancement of the skill into the autonomous phase.

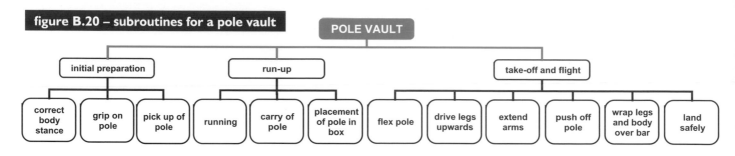

figure B.20 – subroutines for a pole vault

POLE VAULT

- initial preparation
  - correct body stance
  - grip on pole
  - pick up of pole
- run-up
  - running
  - carry of pole
  - placement of pole in box
- take-off and flight
  - flex pole
  - drive legs upwards
  - extend arms
  - push off pole
  - wrap legs and body over bar
  - land safely

figure B.21 – a tennis serve

In the example of a tennis serve (see figure B.21), subroutines would exist for all the components listed in figure B.22, and others not listed!

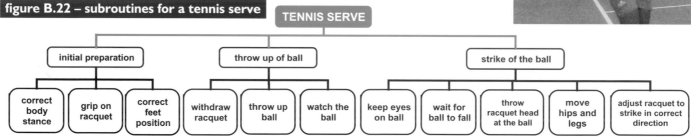

figure B.22 – subroutines for a tennis serve

TENNIS SERVE

- initial preparation
  - correct body stance
  - grip on racquet
  - correct feet position
- throw up of ball
  - withdraw racquet
  - throw up ball
  - watch the ball
- strike of the ball
  - keep eyes on ball
  - wait for ball to fall
  - throw racquet head at the ball
  - move hips and legs
  - adjust racquet to strike in correct direction

Factors affecting the efficiency of the components of the information processing system

Improving response times

Response times (see figure B.23) can be improved using the following tactics.

- **Detecting the cue**, in which the **stimulus** (starter's gun) is sorted out from the **background** (spectator noise).

- **Detecting relevant cues**, in which the relevant stimulus is picked out from other possible ones.

- Choice reaction time is reduced by **eliminating alternative choices**.

figure B.23 – improving response times

IMPROVING RESPONSE TIMES
- decision making
- attentional focus
- concentration
- controlling anxiety
- optimum motivation
- warm-up
- detecting the cue
- detecting relevant cues

- **Decision making**, in which performers work on **set pieces** in open skill situations so that an 'automatic' complex response can be made to a simple open stimulus.
- **Change in attentional focus**, in which the performer practices **switches of concentration** quickly from one situation (for example, opponents in defence) to another (for example, field of play in attack).
- **Controlling anxiety**. Here, we know that anxiety would increase response times, so the performer would reduce anxiety by using **calming** strategies.
- **Creating optimum motivation**, in which the performer / team uses **psyching-up** strategies.
- **Warm-up** ensures that sense organs and the nervous system are in their **optimum state** to transmit information and that the muscles are in an optimum state to act on it.

Practice questions

INFORMATION PROCESSING

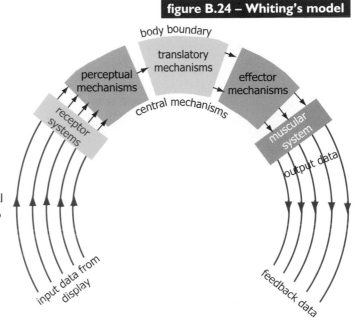

figure B.24 – Whiting's model

1) Improvement in performance of a skill can be better understood by reference to the processes involved. Figure B.24 shows Whiting's information processing model.
   a) Explain the meanings of the terms: **perceptual mechanisms**, **translatory mechanisms**, and **effector mechanisms**, and relate these terms to stages in the Whiting model. *5 marks*
   b) The diagram also shows five arrows entering the perceptual mechanism and only one leaving. What is the name given to this process and why is it necessary? *4 marks*
   c) Identify **three** factors which might help a performer with his / her perceptual mechanisms. *4 marks*

2) Identify the three main receptor systems used by a performer in sport.
   Where is the filtering mechanism found in an information processing model? Explain what happens with information as it passes through this mechanism. *5 marks*

3) Using figure B.25 representing the human motor control mechanism, explain what is meant by short-term memory and long-term memory. *2 marks*
   b) How can information be retained in the long-term memory? *4 marks*

figure B.25 – human motor control mechanism

RECEPTOR SYSTEM → short-term SENSORY STORE → short-term MEMORY ↔ long-term MEMORY / → RESPONSE SYSTEMS

4) a) Using the example of a table tennis player receiving a serve what information would be held in the short-term sensory store, and for how long? *4 marks*
   b) Name and describe the purpose of the process by which information is transferred from the short-term sensory store to the short-term memory. *4 marks*

5) a) Explain the difference between reaction time, movement time and response time? What advice would you give to a sprinter to cut down on reaction time at the start of a race? *4 marks*
   b) Sketch and label a graph to illustrate Hick's Law.
   How does the number of choices available to a performer affect his / her performance? *4 marks*
   c) When taking part in a badminton game, the shuttle occasionally hits the netcord during a rally, and the receiver has to adjust his / her return shot. This causes a delay before the final response can be made. What is this delay called and explain why it occurs? *4 marks*
   d) What factors could affect response time in any game or sport? *4 marks*

6) a) Explain what is meant by a motor programme and give an example.
   How can a programme become a subroutine?   *4 marks*
   b) How is closed loop control used to make a movement more skilful?
   Explain the contribution of the use of subroutines to open loop control and the autonomous phase of learning.   *5 marks*

7) a) Looking at figure B.26, list **six** major subroutines of the executive programme for throwing.   *6 marks*
   b) Briefly explain how the analysis of skills will influence a coach in organising training for javelin throwing as compared with basketball free throw.   *4 marks*

figure B.26 – a javelin thrower

LEARNING AND PERFORMANCE

Learning

The phases / stages of movement skill learning

The **phases of learning** (according to Fitts and Posner see figure B.27) are:

Cognitive

The **cognitive (early)** phase, in which the learner attempts to understand the skill, begins to look at techniques and memorise what is required, begins to practise and repeat the skill according to a simple model, and learns by trial and error. In this phase **guidance** would tend to be predominantly visual, with manual or mechanical guidance also being used, as basic body positions and movements are learnt. Here **feedback** involves reinforcement of success by the coach, with mistakes corrected by reference to the model. This phase applies to the novice player who can require a lot of support in order to achieve success.

Associative

The **associative (intermediate)** phase, in which the learner will understand the skill, and movement patterns will be more fluent and established (can be repeated at a reasonable level without much thought). In this phase **guidance** is more likely to be visual and verbal with some manual guidance to illustrate specific body positions or movements. The coach will give a lot of detail within this guidance. Here **feedback** involves the learner associating the 'feel' of the activity (via kinaesthesis) with the end results. This phase applies to the competent performer who still requires full support from a coach to correct mistakes.

Autonomous

The **autonomous (final)** phase, in which movements are well integrated and automatic, with the learner able to perform without conscious effort. The performer can now give attention to the environment and wider cues about play (such as the position and movements of opponents). **Guidance** would not need to be extensive, but highly specific to situations which the performer would already have realised need attention. Verbal guidance would be the predominant method, with **feedback** being mostly via the learner being able to judge performances and make corrections by him / herself (often with the aid of video

figure B.27 – phases of learning

COGNITIVE PHASE (beginner)
initial learning of basic skill
understanding of the activity
analysis of techniques
use of models

ASSOCIATIVE PHASE
focus on movement
comparison of action with model
error detection and correction
skill still inconsistent

AUTONOMOUS PHASE
(elite sportsman)
action automatic
attention can be given to
environmental aspects of activity
focus on tactics / strategy

analysis of the performance). This phase applies to the player who can perform by him / herself, who can make decisions about tactics without prompting, and whose skill under pressure is stable.

The details of guidance are discussed in section 2 on page 116.

Learning curves

Learning curves are graphs which reflect the relationships which exist between **trials of a skill** and the success or **performance** rate. Learning curves show performances but can also give a good **indication of learning**. They are useful for **goal setting** and recognising the actual ability level of the performer.

figure B.28 – typical learning curve

The **S shaped** curve is a **typical** curve of learning of a gross motor skill (see figure B.28). Learning is **slow** to **start** with as he / she gets to grips with the skill, then the learner begins to be motivated by success and to practise more hence a **rapid** improvement. Finally improvement **slows down** as difficulties are encountered requiring more cognitive effort.

The **positive acceleration** curve shows poor early performances but improves later (figure B.29).

The **linear** curve shows a situation where performance is directly proportional to the number of practice trials (figure B.30).

The **negative** curve shows good early performances but poorer performances in later trials (figure B.31).

figure B.29 – positive / acceleration

figure B.30 – linear learning curve

figure B.31 – negative learning curve

The learning plateau

figure B.32 – the learning plateau

This type of learning curve is one which typically affects most young performers. As learning begins, the learner shows improvement, but as time progresses the curve levels out with not much change if at all in performances over a number of trials (figure B.32). Performance becomes stuck at a certain level – the learning plateau. This happens because:

- The person has **limited ability** and has reached the limits of possible performance, or the training tasks are **too difficult** for the performer.
- The person has reached the **limits** of the **cognitive stage** of learning, and is ready to move to the associative stage – with different ways of learning and guidance.
- There is a **transitional period** before development of a more complex skill.
- The person is **injured** or **overtrained**.
- The person becomes **bored** with the skill learning process.
- The person is **fatigued**.
- **Coaching** has reached the limit of the coach's ability.
- Once a certain level of performance is reached, the person is **less well-motivated** to learn or train.
- Once a certain level has been reached, the skill or power level required to improve further **requires much more time** and intensity of focus.

To avoid a learning plateau

From figure B.33, avoidance of a learning plateau can be achieved by:

- Giving **new goals** that can be reached.
- Giving **praise** that is deserved.
- Giving **new responsibility** (team captain?).
- Ensuring that there are **regular rest** intervals.
- **Maintaining motivation** and employing positive cognitive techniques.
- **Explaining** what the plateau is, and why progress will be made in the future.
- Providing appropriate **feedback**.
- **Varying** types and methods of training.
- Re-establishing **physical fitness**.
- Looking at **technical development** for possible variations or improvements.
- Improving **coaching knowledge**.
- Changing the way in which a **skill is taught**, with whole-part-whole practice.

Motivation

A motive is seen as a cause of behaviour which **energises**, **directs** and **sustains** the behaviour. It can be explained as a **drive** to **strive** to meet the needs of the situation in which a person finds him / herself. The strength of such a drive (or motive) depends on the **person** and the **situation**. Different people will have different types and strengths of motives (drives) to meet the needs of the situation. In a sporting context, the term **motivation** implies the driving and striving to **succeed**, to **win**, to **improve performance**, and to **pursue goals** (having set them in the first place).

Motivation and arousal

Intrinsic motivation

Intrinsic motivation (figure B.34) is the term which describes the **internal** drives or feelings that make us do things.

These feelings come from **within** the performer and involve **enjoyment** of the performance, **satisfaction** of performing, **pride** and the feeling of **well-being** from a job well done.

Extrinsic motivation

Extrinsic motivation describes the feelings coming from rewards **externally** derived (from outside the performer).

These rewards could be **tangible** such as prizes, money, or awards (for example, a gymnastics badge, or wanting to win at basketball because a trophy may be won, or an Olympic medal). Or **intangible** rewards, such as approval, praise or recognition from others, for example, attaining a world record initiates praise by the media, initiates national recognition, and reinforces the glory of the situation. Raising social status is a further intangible reward which would reinforce extrinsic motivation.

figure B.33 – avoiding a learning plateau

figure B.34 – motivation

Arousal

Arousal is a term which describes the level of **inner drives** which forces the sportsperson to **strive to achieve**. It needs to be **under control** and at the **right level** depending on the task. This striving is linked with the concept of motivation.

Drive reduction theory

This theory (see figure B.35) explains why it is sometimes necessary to **vary or renew** the need to learn.

The theory says that the **need to learn** to solve a problem, to learn a skill, or to achieve mastery inspires **motivation**, the **drive** to succeed at the task. This leads to the performer **achieving** the desired outcome (action) which in turn leads to a **reduction in drive** (motivation) to achieve the **same outcome** (since it has already been achieved). This is known as **inhibition**.

The theory explains why people give up sport when it becomes routine, and why changes in for example training venue, training partner, coach or manager, can renew motivation to succeed and continue with a high level of commitment of time and effort.

figure B.35 – drive reduction

need to learn

DRIVE REDUCTION

DRIVE (motive to satisfy need)

action

Motivational strategies

These ideas should aim at avoiding or **reducing drive reduction** (reduce **inhibition** of motivation – see figure B.37) by changing the **importance** of a task (raise its **status**), or **matching** the task to the performer's needs ('you need to do this to be able to progress towards the Olympic Gold').

- A task could be made more **difficult** (and therefore more **challenging** and worthy of motivation).
- A **competitive** situation could be created (in which the task is performed, and the performer might find this more enjoyable and hence motivating).
- **Handicaps** could be introduced into a task to increase the challenge and make the task more competitive.
- A task could be made more **enjoyable** (fun).
- It would be essential to keep the performer **focused** on the task.
- **Change the nature** of a specific learning task to another task with the same aims (vary the task).
- **Models** of a **comparable standard** should be used when demonstrating a task (so that the performer is not overwhelmed by difficulty nor suppressed by the ease of a task).
- A successful coach will have a **large range of learning tasks** which are varied from training session to training session.
- And will use **success** (set achievable goals), **praise**, **encouragement** and **extrinsic rewards** to enhance motivation.

This analysis is also relevant to general lifestyle issues, as well as elite sports performance issues.

figure B.36 – England soccer coaches

frequent change of England coach is intended to improve the performance of the National team by increasing motivation

figure B.37 – motivational strategies

reduce motivational inhibition

change task importance

avoid drive reduction

match task to performer needs

increase task difficulty

MOTIVATIONAL STRATEGIES

use extrinsic rewards

competition situation

diverse learning tasks

handicaps

comparable models

enjoyment

focus performer

vary task

Learning theories

See figure B.38 for a summary of the theories of learning.

Associationalist / connectionist theories

Associationalist theories state that learning occurs as a result of the **association** or connection between a **stimulus** and a **response**. This stimulus-response connection is called the **S-R bond**.

Conditioning

The connection between stimulus and response is due to **conditioning**, which is a form of **training** which makes a certain behaviour into a **habit** (**habitualised** - unvarying). Such a habit is an ingrained and learned behaviour which becomes part of a person's **automatic** response to a stimulus.

figure B.38 – theories of learning

classical conditioning · associationalist · reinforcement · Thorndike · THEORIES OF LEARNING · operant conditioning · insight learning · social learning theory · cognitive theory

A sports example of this would be the instant reaction of a soccer goalkeeper to a penalty taker's strike depending on the penalty taker's stance or body position. Since **learning** involves a **change of behaviour**, learning takes place when a **connection** is made between stimulus and response.

Another example of this could be the baton passing routine during a sprint relay. An incoming runner would shout 'hand', and the outgoing runner would present his / her hand to receive the baton. The shout is the stimulus, the reaching out of the hand the response. Eventually, the response is automatic (and learnt) and the baton will always be passed successfully.

Operant conditioning

Operant conditioning is concerned with **modifying behaviour** and hence **response** to a specific situation. This is the work of **Skinner** who used pigeons to whom he gave food if they pecked at and then hit a table tennis ball with their beaks.

Eventually, by developing the reinforcement (giving of food) when the desired response was achieved, the pigeons were able to knock a ball back and forth between them. This is based on **trial and error**, with the correct response **reinforced**.

This can be used to learn from a **demonstration** that teaches how to perform the skill (shaping), and then **reinforced** after the performer has performed the skill successfully (through knowledge of results). For example, suppose a rugby player kicks when he / she should pass the ball. By rewarding (reinforcing using praise) every time the player passes, gradually the player learns to pass the ball (behaviour has been modified). The learner may not know **why** the response is correct only that it will be **rewarded**. To be effective, a reward will **closely follow** a correct response, and a coach will be concerned **to strengthen a correct S-R bond**, and weaken an incorrect S-R bond.

Reinforcement of learning

Reinforcement (see figure B.39) is concerned with ensuring the correct response is repeated.

Positive reinforcement

Positive reinforcement uses rewards or praise to achieve the desired result. For example, a professional footballer might receive a bonus for scoring a goal, an amateur gymnast might be praised by the coach for a good performance.

Negative reinforcement

This means that rewards are withdrawn if there is a poor performance. For example, the same footballer may not receive a bonus when he fails to score a goal, the gymnast would not be praised if he / she performed inadequately.

figure B.39 – reinforcement

positive reinforcement · negative reinforcement · REINFORCEMENT · punishment

Punishment

This means inflicting retribution on a learner who performs incorrectly. This breaks a bond between the learner's learning process and an incorrect performance. For example, the footballer might be dropped from the team after he fails to score a goal, or a player is sent from the field if he / she fouls an opponent.

Thorndike's laws

Thorndike's laws of exercise (see figure B.40) are concerned with **strengthening the S-R bond**, and hence the concept of reinforcement.

figure B.40 – Thorndike's laws

- **The law of exercise** explains that **repetition** strengthens the S-R bond.

  For example, the more a discus thrower practises throwing the more likely it is that this correct throwing technique will be repeated in the competitive situation. So **practice** is very important.

- **The law of effect** uses **reinforcement** (by praise, reward or observed success) to strengthen the S-R bond. **Satisfying reinforcers** (ones which make the learner feel good) increase the likelihood of a response being repeated.

  For example, if the thrower feels that the movement is correct then he or she is more likely to repeat the movement. A **trial and error** process can produce this effect, since **success** reinforces a response, whereas **failure** forces the performer to try new methods to achieve success.

- **The law of readiness** says that learning can only occur when the **nervous system** (and muscular system) is **sufficiently mature** to allow the appropriate S-R bond to happen.

  For example, the more a thrower is physically and mentally prepared to perform a throw the more likely it is to be performed well. People should learn **simple basic skills** (and become **basically fit**) **before** attempting to learn more complex skills. Also the performer needs to be **psychologically ready**.

figure B.40 – Thorndike's laws

- law of exercise
  repetition
  strengthens S-R
  bond
- law of effect
  reinforcement
  strengthens S-R
  bond
- THORNDIKE
- law of readiness
  nervous system
  is mature

Cognitive / insight theories

Cognitive theories are concerned with **understanding and insight**, and are the work of **Gestaltists** / German scientists who showed the importance of perceiving a problem in its **entirety**. **Intervening variables** are the factors which come between the stimulus occurring and a response being selected.

The learner is involved in the process by absorbing **information** from various sources to understand the '**whole picture**'. He / she needs to know **when, where and why** to use a skill, not just how to perform the skill, and must be able to draw on **previous experiences** and knowledge. He / she must recognise **important cues** (within a game situation) to **understand** the skill learning problem and how it should be tackled. This might be termed **insight learning**.
For example, a tennis serve should be practised as a whole not broken down into parts. Another example, hockey players being encouraged to think about marking strategies against twin centre forwards. This would be a problem to be solved which gives the players more insight and eventual understanding of the problem.

Bandura's observational model of learning

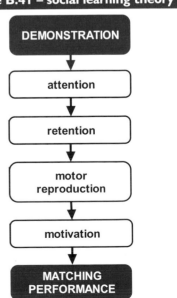

figure B.41 – social learning theory

DEMONSTRATION → attention → retention → motor reproduction → motivation → MATCHING PERFORMANCE

Social learning theory

This theory (see figure B.41) describes learning by **copying** others (**observational learning**).

In this theory, the performer is more likely to copy '**significant others**', those who are seen as **high status role models**.
- **Demonstration** of the skill (by **significant others**), is followed by the learning process which includes **attention** (the learner takes note of the demonstration).
- **Retention** (the learner remembers the demonstration).
- **Motor reproduction** (the learner attempts to copy the movement), and is **motivated** to do so.
- Finally the learner produces a **matching performance** (successful reproduction of the skill).

The learner copies because he / she wishes to be accepted by others or to be held in **high esteem**. Skills are often copied to achieve the **success** that others enjoy and to be **praised**.

Observational learning

Observational learning is at the heart of social learning theory (see figure B.42). Learning takes place via **watching** and then **imitating** what is seen. Imitation is **more likely** if the model is seen as relevant, complies with social norms, and is similar in age or ability. Also, imitation is more likely if the behaviour of the learner has been reinforced, and the performance of the model is seen as successful.

For example, the techniques and tactics of a successful tennis player are most likely to be copied, the behaviour and techniques of a top soccer player are most likely to be imitated.

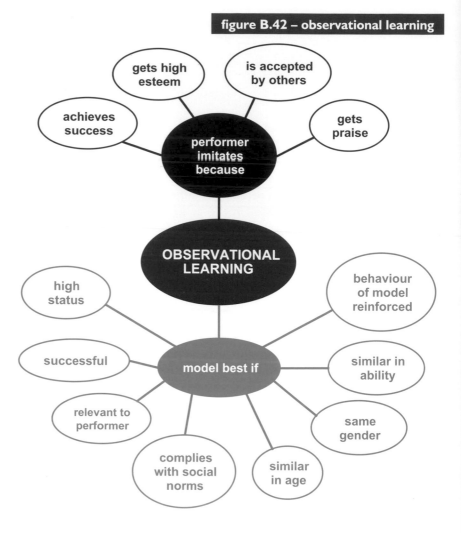

figure B.42 – observational learning

Motor learning, Schmidt's schema theory

Schmidt's schema theory

Schema theory (see figure B.43) explains how sports performers can undertake many actions with very **little conscious control**.

The long-term memory **isn't big enough** to store all the motor programmes required. **Schema** theory says that **generalised motor programmes** exist which can be modified by taking in information while a skill is being performed. Hence the LTM has to store **far fewer** motor programmes, since any **new movement** can be performed by running a schema which **closely matches** the needs of the new movement. The **bigger** the schema the more **efficient** the movement, and large amounts of **varied practice** are needed to improve a schema. **Feedback** is very important to **correct** and **update** a schema.

A **schema** is made up of two elements (see figure B.44).

figure B.43 – schema theory

Recall schema

The first element of a schema is the **recall schema** which consists of all the information needed to **start** a relevant movement. This includes the **knowledge of the environment** (initial conditions):

- Playing conditions (pitch, playing surface, weather).
- Positions of team mates and opposition.
- Condition of equipment (kit, bike, car) and so on.

The recall schema also includes the **response specifications** (the correct technical model):

- Speed and force required.
- Size and shape of movement required.
- Techniques and styles used.

This is used for quick ballistic movements when there **isn't enough time** to process feedback.

Recognition schema

The second schema element is called a **recognition schema** which contains:

- Information needed to **correct errors** and remember **correct performance**.
- **Information** about evaluating the response.
- **Sensory consequences** (knowledge of performance) which would be the feeling and look of the performance.
- **Response outcomes** (movement outcomes) which would be the results of performance and the knowledge of results (how far / fast / many).

This would be important when there is **enough time** to process feedback or for evaluating performance.

figure B.44 – schema

Summary of schema information:

1. **Knowledge of environment (initial conditions)**, for example, a basketballer who is aware of how far he / she is away from the basket.
2. **Response specifications**, for example, the basketballer recognising that he / she must carry out a jump shot because of an opponent.
3. **Sensory consequences**, for example, the basketballer is intrinsically aware of his / her body movements as the jump shot is being performed.
4. **Movement / response outcomes**, for example, the basketballer being aware of whether or not the shot has succeeded.

Transfer of learning

The term **transfer** (figure B.45) describes the influence of one skill on the performance of another.

Positive transfer

This type of transfer occurs when **learning** in one task is enhanced by learning in **another task**. For example, learning a golf stroke may be enhanced by virtue of the fact that the player is a good cricketer.

Zero transfer

This describes the situation where **no transfer at all** may occur even between skills which appear to be similar. For example, learning at squash may have zero transfer from weight training.

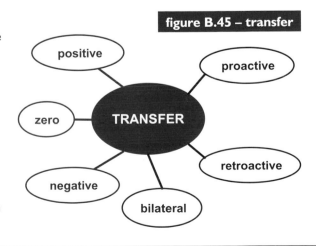

figure B.45 – transfer

Negative transfer

This occurs when the learning of a new task is **interfered** with by the knowledge of a similar activity. For example, the flexible use of the wrist needed for badminton may interfere with the firm wrist needed for tennis.

Bilateral transfer (limb to limb)

This is the transfer which takes place from **one limb to another**, sometimes called **lateralisation**. For example, a soccer player learns to kick a ball with the non-preferred foot, the actions are learnt through reference by the brain to the preferred foot.

Proactive transfer

This type of transfer refers to the influence of one skill on a skill **yet to be learned**. For example, having learned the forehand drive in tennis, the action is then modified to the forehand drive with top spin.

Retroactive transfer

This type of transfer is where there is a negative influence of one skill on a skill that has **previously been learned**. For example, a hockey player learns the flicking skill which may have a negative effect on the previously learned push (the push pass may be lifted unnecessarily).

The impact of practice on improving learning

figure B.46 – transfer

Variable practice

Variable practice (see figure B.46) is a method in which practice **conditions are varied** to encourage the formation of **schema**. Schema are: '**the patterns in the brain which enable a sportsperson to perform skills with fluency and competence**', and are discussed above. Practice activities would include a number of different activities which could be performed in different ways. Conditions should be as **realistic** as possible in **as many situations** as possible, as near to the **competitive** / match situation as possible. The method is relevant to **open skills**.

Distributed practice

Distributed practice is a method in which training sessions include **rest intervals** which could involve mental practice. Sessions would be short and spread over time with recovery periods between. This is good for the **beginner** and most **skill learning**, gives **time to recover** physically and mentally and is good for potentially **dangerous** situations.

Massed practice

Massed practice is a method in which practice is done with **no rest intervals** with sessions **long in duration**. A single training session lasting a relatively long time, in which all the activities are performed one after the other. This method is good for '**grooving**' of skills and to encourage an **habitual** response, is good for **discrete skills** of short duration, but can lead to **fatigue** and boredom and there may be elements of **negative transfer**.

Overlearning

Overlearning involves a learned skill that is **habitual** because of many **repetitions**. **Motor programmes** / schema are formed and performed '**automatically**' in response to a game / sporting situation (stimulus). This means that **attention** can be directed **peripherally** to **other elements** of a game (for example, tactics or strategy).

Mental practice

Mental practice is discussed in detail above on page 95, and again in the unit 2 section on page 115.

Goal setting

The main function of goal setting (figure B.47) is to increase **motivation**. The feeling of satisfaction gained from achieving a goal brings about this motivation. Goal setting can also be used as a means of **managing anxiety** or stress.

figure B.47 – goal setting

Goals can be **short**-term, **medium**-term or **long**-term. Short-term goals can be used as targets for single training sessions, or what can be expected after a period of training. Long-term goals may or may not be achieved, but are placed in the background of a performer's mind and can underpin everything he or she does. Kelly Holmes had the ambition (goal) of getting an Olympic gold, and she **eventually** did this – twice! This goal motivated Kelly to keep going through injury and disappointment, to keep her training through bad weather and good times.

Goals (figure B.48) should be:
- **Easily** attained initially and therefore **realistic**.
- **Incremental**, a little bit at a time.
- **Challenging** but **achievable**.
- **Progressively** more difficult.
- **Training goals** should be planned around **overall goals**.

Goals are either:
- **Outcome oriented**:
  - Towards the end result of the sporting activity.
    For example to win a race.
- **Performance oriented**:
  - Judged against other performances.
    For example to beat his or her best time.
- **Process oriented**:
  - Obtain an improvement in techniques.

figure B.48 – goals should be?

Effective goal setting

Goals (figure B.49) should be:
- Stated **positively**.
- **Specific** to the situation and the performer.
- **Time phased**, to be achieved in 1 week or 2 months for example.
- **Challenging**.
- **Achievable**.
- **Measurable**, so that you can actually say exactly whether or not a goal has been achieved.
- **Negotiated** between sportsperson and coach.
- **Progressive**, from short-term to long-term.
- **Performance oriented** rather than outcome oriented.
- **Written** down.
- **Reviewed** regularly (with downward adjustment if necessary - in the case of injury).
- **Achievement oriented** rather than failure oriented.

figure B.49 – effective goals

Failure to achieve goals should be followed by resetting of goals to maintain the performer's **self-esteem**.

S.M.A.R.T.E.R. goals

SPECIFIC
   directly related a sporting situation.
MEASURABLE
   progress can be assessed.
ACCEPTED
   by both performer and coach.
REALISTIC
   challenging but within the capability of performer.
TIME PHASED
   a date is set for completion.
EXCITING
   inspiring and rewarding to the performer.
RECORDED
   written down.

Practice questions

LEARNING AND PERFORMANCE

figure B.50 – performance of a gymnast

1) Figure B.50 shows the improvement in performance of a gymnast over a period of time.
a) Name the stages **A**, **B** and **C** shown on this chart and explain their significance to the gymnast.
   6 marks
b) Identify the characteristics of a performer in phase **C**.
   4 marks
c) How might the type of mental practice change in the last phase of learning?   *4 marks*

2) According to Fitts and Posner, learning passes through three stages. Use an example from one of your practical activities to describe the key characteristics of each of these stages.
   5 marks

3) a) Describe what is meant by the term feedback, and briefly describe **three** functions of feedback.   *5 marks*
b) Where possible explain the kinds of feedback available to a performer which would be classified as:
   i) Intrinsic and internal.
   ii) Extrinsic and internal.   *4 marks*

4) Explain how feedback differs through the associative and autonomous stages of learning as a performer makes progress.
   4 marks

5) A pole vaulter makes rapid progress when first learning the event, but then reaches a plateau of performance.
a) Explain what the plateau is and why it might occur.   *4 marks*
b) What strategies could be used to improve from the plateau level?   *4 marks*

6) a) What sort of motivation methods would you use to motivate a beginner in gymnastics?   *4 marks*
b) How would the motivation methods used for a skilled performer differ from those used by the beginner?   *3 marks*

7) a) Explain how you would use operant conditioning to teach a sports skill of your choice.   *5 marks*
b) Describe what is meant by reinforcement and give examples of different types.   *4 marks*

8) a) Using examples from sport explain what is meant by the S-R bond. *4 marks*
   b) Explain how a coach in a sport could ensure that a correct response follows a particular stimulus. *5 marks*

9) a) In racquet sports, coaches give demonstrations to aid skill development. Identify the stages of Bandura's model of observational learning, giving an appropriate example of each stage to illustrate your understanding. *4 marks*
   b) Explain the cognitive theory of learning as proposed by Gestaltists and apply this to a practical situation. *4 marks*

10) Stimulus-response bonding has been used to explain how a physical skill can be learned. What is a stimulus-response bond and how can a Physical Education teacher ensure that it is strengthened when teaching swimming or athletics? *6 marks*

11) a) Using examples from sport, identify **four** items of information stored as schema. *4 marks*
   b) Comparing the skills of throwing the javelin and taking a free throw at basketball, explain how the skills are related using schema theory. *4 marks*

12) How could a teacher of Physical Education use his / her knowledge of schema theory when planning a practice session for a named activity? *5 marks*

13) Explain **four** different types of transfer of learning. *4 marks*

14) a) Using a practical example, explain what is meant by the term transfer in skill learning. How can transfer be detrimental to performance? Give a practical example. *5 marks*
   b) How can a teacher or a coach ensure that as much positive transfer takes place as possible in a training session? *5 marks*

15) A coach reinforces good performances in training with praise. Why does this reinforcement work rather than punishing poor performance? Explain what is meant by reinforcement and punishment in this case. *5 marks*

16) a) Explain the difference between massed and distributed practice. *2 marks*
   b) Justify the choice of practice conditions for a training session of a sport of your choice. *6 marks*
   c) Name **two** characteristics of the task, and **two** attributes of the learner which might lead you to decide which method (massed or distributed) of practice to use. *4 marks*

17) a) What are the **main** positive effects of setting goals in sport? *2 marks*
   b) Show what is meant by short-term goals and long-term goals by using examples from sport. *4 marks*
   c) As a coach how would you ensure that your goal setting was as effective as possible? *6 marks*

This content should be delivered in unit 2, but will be assessed by a question in **Section B of the Unit 1 written paper**.

Factors to consider when developing skill and planning training / coaching sessions

Students should note that many factors under this heading have already been discussed during the work on Unit 1. The following list is a summary of issues which you may require to note when planning your training.

What is the nature of the skill to be learned?

Is it open or closed, discrete or continuous, gross or fine, or self paced or externally paced?

Where a skill fits onto the skill continuums will determine how you set up its practice.

For example, a **closed** skill such as putting the shot or a tennis serve will require a lot of basic repetition of the **same** movement during practice, whereas an **open** skill such as passing a soccer or hockey ball will need repetition of movements which **vary** according to the receiver's position and distance from the passer.

Where do you rate the ability of a performer?

If he / she has weak motor ability, then it will be unlikely that such a person could learn complex skills requiring a large degree of hand eye co-ordination such as badminton or tennis. But such a person may be able to run or swim effectively.

Where is the performer in relation to his / her stage or phase of learning?

Is he / she in the cognitive, associative or autonomous phase of learning?

If you are lucky enough to be in the autonomous phase, then your skill will be well-learnt and stable under stress. You will be able to make your own adjustments without guidance to most of the movements you make, but may occasionally need the advice or help of a coach during the performance situation. On the other hand, if you are in the cognitive phase, you will need extensive help from a coach or teacher, and will need plenty of practice of basic skill movements with extensive feedback from a coach about the success of the practice in order to avoid a learning plateau.

How well motivated is the performer?

If your motivation is intrinsic, then you will not need reminding to turn up to training or practice. On the other hand, if your motivation is extrinsic, you will need an incentive to complete a training regime, although success in this exam should be sufficient!

Teaching styles

Teaching style determines the way in which information is transmitted to the learner.

Mosston's spectrum of teaching styles

In this method (see figure 2B.1), the style is determined by the proportion of decisions the teacher or the learner makes. From figure 2B.1, style A has all the decisions made by the teacher, and style M has all the decisions made by the learner. Style G has roughly half made by both teacher and learner. The more decisions made by the teacher, the more authoritarian the style (this means that the teacher tells the learner what to do – and the learner obeys this and follows exactly what the teacher says). The more decisions made by the learner, the more free-form the style and what is done is decided by the learner, and the teacher goes along with this completely. There are four main styles (figure 2B.2):

- **Command**.
- **Reciprocal**.
- **Discovery**.
- **Problem solving**.

figure 2B.1 – spectrum of teaching styles

A B C D E F G H I J K L M

teachers' decisions

learners' decisions

A B C D E F G H I J K L M

figure 2B.2 – teaching styles

command   reciprocal

TEACHING STYLES

problem solving   discovery

Command style of teaching

This style involves mostly the teacher making the decisions. It is authoritarian with the teacher / coach telling the learner what to do (place A or B in Mosston's spectrum). For example, in a hockey small game situation, the coach calls 'freeze' to preserve pitch position. The coach decides on all the drills and activities to be done in a training session.

This is **good** for:

- **Novices** (who need to be told what to do).
- **Quick responses** (discipline would be expected, and immediate action to the coach's commands expected).
- **Dangerous situations** (like rock climbing or canoeing).
- **Hostile groups** (a coach would expect attention to his / her instructions, without group members being involved with their own antagonisms).
- **Large groups** (where if too many different things were happening at once, there would be chaos).

The command style is **not good** for:

- **High level performers** (where it would be expected that the performer would know what to do, and make all adjustments to performance during the occasion by himself / herself).
- **Social interaction** (where the coach would expect members of a group to chat and get to know one another – this could not happen if the performers would have to listen to the coach and concentrate on obeying his / her instructions).
- **Creativity** (where the performer would be expected to initiate his / her own ideas about what to do).

Reciprocal style of teaching

This style involves learners becoming teachers of others for part of the teaching process (between D and J on the Mosston spectrum). The teacher / coach would set the task and monitor its progress, but the learners would for example work in pairs and teach one another. Or, in swimming, the coach teaches the skill of a tumble turn to some of the swimmers, who in turn then teach others.

This is **good** for:

- **Social interaction** (it would be important for the learner groups to communicate and interact with one another to complete the tasks).
- **Giving responsibility** (group members would need to take it upon themselves to complete the tasks).
- **Personal development** (the process would rely on group members to initiate the organisation of the tasks).
- **Feedback** (self-realisation of how good a performance is – or peer group information as to the quality of performance may have more impact).

The reciprocal style is **not good** for:

- **Discipline** (the style allows some freedom of movement and action within the learner group).
- **Correct information delivered** (the method allows for learners to interpret information as they feel is best, and sometimes inaccuracies in what is to be done can happen).
- **Beginners** (beginners need to be told what to do).
- Those who have poor communication skills.

Discovery style of teaching

This style involving decision making by the performer / learner. The teacher / coach would guide the learner to find the correct movement by giving clues or asking questions of the learner (between H and K on the Mosston spectrum). For example, the coach tells players in a hockey team to work out for themselves the strategies for a penalty corner. The players already know the rules for penalty corners, they just have to decide on the positions and movement of the players and who strikes the ball and so on.

This style is **good** for:

- **Creativity** (the learner can decode from his / her own feelings about a situation to perform certain tasks).
- **Motivation** (people who perform their own tasks are often highly motivated by their 'ownership' of the activity).
- **High level performer** (who knows what to do after many years of practice, and who can make complex decisions based on experience).

The discovery style is **not good** for:

- **Efficiency** (the way in which a learner decides to perform a task may not always be the best / most efficient way).
- **Learning correct habits** (sometimes people may need to be told what is the correct way to do things).
- **Motivation** if things go wrong (sometimes people will get disheartened if their choice of activity proves to be incorrect).

Problem solving style of teaching

In this style, the teacher / coach would set a problem and the learner would decide (without prompting or help) how to solve the problem or perform the tasks (between L and M on the Mosston scale). There would be no limits set by the coach, and the aim would be to develop the cognitive abilities of the learner. There would be no correct solutions, only those decided by the learners.

The advantages and disadvantages of this style are similar to the discovery style, but should perhaps only be used when there are no correct outcomes to a task, where performers are experienced / expert, and there are no time limits to the process.

In a true teaching / coaching situation, a mixture of styles would be used according to the situation, the task, and the stage of learning of the performer.

Methods of presenting practice

This reflects the ways in which a skill can be taught to facilitate learning and maximise performance.

Factors affecting choice of method are:

- **Type** of skills to be taught.
- **Complexity** of the skill.
- **Classification** of the skill.
- **Environment**.
- **Ability** level of the **performer**.
- **Motivational** level of the performer.

See figure 2B.3 for the different methods of organisation of skill practice, and figure 2B.4 for the details of how the different methods are organised.

figure 2B.3 – organisation of practice

The whole method

In this method, the skill is **practised in total** should be preferred **where the skill / task**:

- Is of low complexity or is a simple task.
- Has high organisation.
- Consists of interrelated subroutines.
- Has discrete skills of short duration (the movement is rapid / ballistic).
- Cannot be broken down into parts.
- Or requires temporal / spatial co-ordination.

figure 2B.4 – practice methods

WHOLE METHOD
whole practice only

PROGRESSIVE PART METHOD
part A - B - parts AB - part A - B - C - parts ABC - part A - B - C - D - whole ABCD

WHOLE - PART - WHOLE METHOD
whole (ABCD) practiced - then parts A - B - C - D practiced separately - then whole (ABCD)

Examples of skills / activities where the whole method would be appropriate are:

- Somersault or tumble in gymnastics.
- Dart throw.
- Snooker or pool shot.
- Tennis serve.
- Soccer penalty kick.

The **performer**:

- Would be experienced.
- Has high levels of attention.
- Is in the later stages of learning.
- Is older and highly motivated.
- And uses distributed practice.

The progressive part method

In this method, parts are practised separately, then combined into slightly bigger elements for practice, which in turn can be combined into the whole movement or bigger parts for further practice and so on. This method is suitable for:

- Complex tasks / skills.
- Helps chaining of complex skills learned independently.
- Skills which have limited attentional demands.
- Skills which require co-ordination of spatial / temporal components.
- Skills which have a good **transfer** to the whole movement.

The whole-part-whole method

This method is a **combination** of whole and part methods which has the advantage of flexible application to almost any task and any situation depending on the stage of learning of the performer and the task difficulty. A learner would first practise the whole movement and identify difficult components, which would then be practised separately. These difficult components might be different for different people. When sufficiently fluent, the parts can then be re-combined into the whole movement for further practice.

Types of practice

STUDENT NOTE

For types of practice refer to page 108 for notes under heading 'The impact of practice on improving performance'. See figure 2B.5 for a summary of types of practice.

Mental practice or rehearsal

The functions of mental practice are summarised in figure 2B.6. Mental practice:

- Creates a mental picture of a skill.
- Can be used to **simulate** a whole movement sequence or just part of it.
- Can be used to imagine and envisage success and avoid failure in a competitive situation.
- Can provide a mental warm-up in order to promote a state of **readiness** for action.
- Must be as **realistic** as possible to be effective.
- Can be used during **rest / recovery** periods **during** a performance or in between performances.
- Can be used to focus **attention** on important aspects of a skill.
- Can build **self-confidence** for an upcoming performance.
- Can control **arousal** and induce calmness before a performance.

figure 2B.5 – practice conditions

figure 2B.6 – mental practice

Mental rehearsal works by producing small muscle contractions in the same sequence as an actual practice, and since the gross movement of the skill does not actually happen, it **prevents** wear and tear. Top performers in sport use this technique to iron out difficulties when not actually engaged in physical activity. They can focus on what their situation requires and use mental practice even when walking down the street or in domestic circumstances.

Methods of guidance

See figure 2B.7 for a summary of methods of guidance.

figure 2B.7 – types of guidance

VERBAL
it is explained to the learner what to do

VISUAL
the learner watches a model

GUIDANCE

MECHANICAL
using a mechanical aid to fix the learner's body positions

MANUAL
supporting or physically moving a learner's body

Visual guidance

This method works mainly through **demonstration** (by **video** / poster, by human **live** model, or by demonstration of techniques by a **coach** or teacher).
This demonstration should:

- **Be realistic / appropriate / not too complex.**
- Emphasise **relevant** aspects of a skill.
- Be **repeated**.

Visual guidance is very important in the **cognitive** early stage of learning:
- The **learner** should be **attentive / retentive**, and should be **capable of matching** the demonstration (performer at the appropriate level of learning).
- The performer would learn by **watching** and **imitating** a **model** who should be of **high status** and technically **competent / correct**.
- **The coach** should **reinforce** correct copying of skills.

Verbal guidance

This method is used often to **accompany visual** guidance and is used more with **competent** performers at a later stage of learning. The amount of verbal guidance must be **controlled** and the **quality** of this guidance is important for effective coaching / teaching. Verbal guidance can be used for **conditioning** a response (giving reinforcement).

Manual guidance

This method (figure 2B.8) uses **physical support** (as in a coach supporting a gymnast during an asymmetric bar movement or performing somersaults), or **placing** limbs in correct positions (as for a novice thrower). This helps with **kinaesthetic** awareness, is useful for giving **confidence**, particularly for **beginners**, and is useful for **safety** reasons.

Mechanical guidance

This method uses a mechanical **aid**, for example:
- Stabilisers on a bike (see figure 2B.9).
- Flotation devices for swimming.
- Belay ropes for climbers.
- Somersault rig for trampolinists.

figure 2B.8 – manual guidance

figure 2B.9 – mechanical

This type of guidance gives **confidence** and ensures **safety**, gives some idea of **kinaesthetic** sense of movement, but must **not to be overdone** because this form of kinaesthesis is not the same as the real thing. The performer can become **over-reliant** on the mechanical device used.

Feedback

Feedback is a term which describes the way in which information is received by a performer about a performance either just completed, or sometimes during the performance itself.

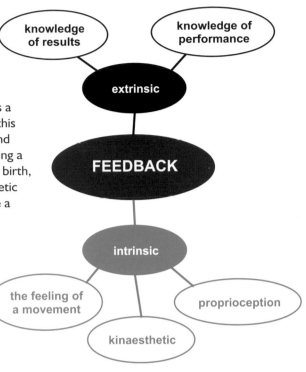

Intrinsic feedback

This form of feedback takes place when the feeling of a movement tells a performer whether it was successful or not (see figure 2B.10). Part of this is **kinaesthetic** and is provided by the **proprioception** within joints and muscles which tells a person of the muscle tension and joint angles during a movement. This is an **ability** which is usually a part of the person from birth, and is genetic and enduring. A person who has more effective kinaesthetic feedback about movements made by his / her body is more likely to be a successful sports performer.

Extrinsic feedback

This can have two forms:
The first is **knowledge of performance**:
- Where information is obtained about a performance. For example, its **quality / rhythm / aesthetics** from a coach, video, or from the press / TV.

The second is **knowledge of results** in which a performer has:
- Information about the **outcome** of a performance.
- Success or failure, or the distance / height / time performed.
- Information can be from a number of sources, the coach, video, or press / TV.

Feedback dependency

Feedback dependency occurs when some performers can become **dependent** on feedback:
- For example, from a coach or significant other about the quality of performance or technical competence.
- If this feedback is withdrawn or cannot be given then performance **can deteriorate**.
- This might occur in a field event athlete in a major games who cannot function without feedback from a coach about his / her technique, and who therefore will fail.

Terminal feedback

This occurs **after** a performance has finished which is important because it **strengthens the schema** in learning.

Concurrent feedback

Concurrent feedback occurs **during** a performance and has the aim of improving skills or techniques **while a performer is in action**.

Positive feedback

Positive feedback is feedback which gives information aimed at a **constructive** development of performance. It uses positive reinforcement, **praise** and **encouragement** about good performances, and the knowledge from poor performances which gives insight about **errors and their possible correction**. For example, a coach who praises a performer and encourages him / her to repeat the skills being praised will be giving positive feedback.

Negative feedback

This type of feedback is information which could **depress performance** and would consist of negative reinforcement or negative criticism about **poor** performances. For example, in this case, a coach who repeatedly feeds back information about faults, and gives little help about how to correct them would be giving negative feedback.

Figure 2B.11 summarises the types of feedback used in sport.

In the case of a squash player (figure 2B.12), in open play the skill is an **open** one (movements are altered according to the position and direction and action of the other player, the stroke played, and the subsequent direction and speed of the ball). Feedback to the player occurs during the movement, and he alters his position, stance, movement pattern and stroke outcome in response. Part of this feedback is **kinaesthetic**, in that his position, speed and posture are sensed by the orientation of his limbs and tension in his musculature, and changes are then made according to the sensations and feelings from this – in response to the game situation. His perception of the game situation (knowledge of the environment) and interpretation of what to do next (response specifications) can be thought of as an element of a **recall schema**.

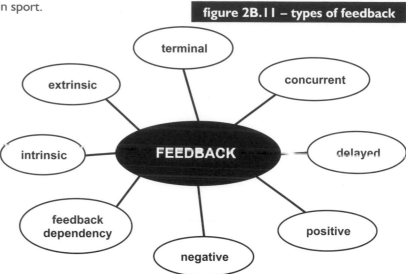

figure 2B.11 – types of feedback

terminal

extrinsic

concurrent

intrinsic

FEEDBACK

delayed

feedback dependency

positive

negative

figure 2B.12 – squash requires feedback

Question layout

This section is examined as question 7 of the Unit 1 question paper. This question will have two parts a) and b), one part each based on the physiology and skill acquisition content listed for Section B of Unit 2. Answers will be expected to be in essay format (not bullet points or single word answers). The bulk of the marks will be awarded for the style and presentation of an answer which includes enough factual content as outlined below. Up to 8 marks will be given for each part of the answer, to a maximum of 12 marks for both parts. Marks for each part will be given according to the following band range descriptors as described in table 31.

Candidates are expected to put their answers in the context of a practical scenario, adopting the point of view of one of the roles:
- **Practical performer**.
- **Official / referee / umpire / judge**.
- **Leader / coach**.

Table 31 - **band range descriptors for questions 7.**

band range	band descriptors
7 - 8	addresses all areas of the question. has accessed at least seven points from the marks scheme. few errors in the spelling, punctuation and grammar, and correct use of technical language.
5 - 6	addresses most of the question. has accessed at least five points from the mark scheme. few errors in the spelling, punctuation and grammar, demonstrates use of technical language although sometimes inaccurately.
3 - 4	addresses one area of the question. has accessed at least three points from the mark scheme. errors in spelling, punctuation and grammar and little use of technical language.
1 - 2	attempted to address one area of the question. has accessed at least one point from the mark scheme. major errors in spelling, punctuation and grammar, with no use of technical language.

Each question would follow one or other of the following formats

1) You have been asked to develop the skills and fitness of a group of 17 year old sportspeople who wish to improve performance in a team game.

2) You have been asked to develop the skills and fitness of a group of 17 year old sportspeople who wish to improve performance in an individual sport.

3) You have been asked to develop the skills and fitness of a group of 17 year old sportspeople who wish to improve performance in a racquet game.

4) You have been asked to develop the skills and fitness of a group of 17 year old sportspeople who wish to improve performance in an outdoor pursuits activity.

Practice questions

figure 2B.13 – spectrum of teaching styles

1) a) Figure 2B.13 shows Mosston's spectrum of teaching styles in terms of decision making in the learning process.
   Identify the teaching style at A, and explain its consequences for teaching method.
   What are the advantages and disadvantages of this teaching style in teaching a sport or sport skill?

2) a) What is meant by the reciprocal teaching style and what are its drawbacks?
   What are the **main** advantages of the discovery method of teaching?

3) a) Generally a skill should be taught as a whole as far as possible. Give reasons for this.
   Some skills need to be split up into parts to be taught effectively. What are the advantages and disadvantages of this type of skill presentation?

4) a) Explain the difference between massed and distributed practice.
   Justify the choice of practice conditions for a training session of a sport / game of your choice.
   Name **two** characteristics of the task, and **two** attributes of the learner which might lead you to decide which method (massed or distributed) of practice to use.

5) a) Other than visual guidance, what other **main** methods of guidance are there? Give a practical example for each.
   How would you optimise the use of visual guidance in teaching motor skills? What are the drawbacks of this method?

6) a) Identify **two** different mechanical items which might assist movement skill learning.
   Give reasons for the use of these mechanical items to help a learner come to grips with a motor skill.

7) a) Explain how feedback in a sports skill learning situation helps the sportsperson improve performance.

8) a) Define the term feedback, and briefly describe **three** functions of feedback.
   How would you make feedback effective when teaching a motor skill?

SECTION C

OPPORTUNITIES FOR PARTICIPATION

UNIT 1:1
INTRODUCTION TO CONCEPTS

UNIT 1:2
CURRENT PROVISION
FOR ACTIVE LEISURE

UNIT 1:3
ROLE OF SCHOOLS AND
NATIONAL GOVERNING BODIES

UNIT 1:4
POTENTIAL BARRIERS
TO PARTICIPATION

AN INTRODUCTION TO THE CONCEPTS, CATEGORISATIONS AND BENEFITS OF PHYSICAL ACTIVITY TO BOTH THE INDIVIDUAL AND SOCIETY

Introduction

The intention of this section is to clarify what we mean by studying a series of related **concepts**, **categories** and **benefits**. However, it is also necessary to look at the **cause** of problems and so, while focus is on **activity**, we also need to be aware of the effects of **inactivity**.

figure C.1 – children's activities as play

Physical activity and healthy lifestyles

The focus is on **physical activity** as a necessary experience for the development of a balanced, active and **healthy lifestyle** (see the model in figure C.2). This is a wider concept than physical activity as a recreational and sporting experience. It is a **lifetime commitment**, which involves **healthy attitudes** in all walks of life, both work and leisure.

Physical activity

Physical activity is taken to be gross motor movement, where major parts of the body are highly active. It is a necessary feature of modern society, valuable in itself, but important as part of the broader concept of having a **healthy lifestyle**. We therefore need to link a **healthy lifestyle** with **physical exercise** as it should exist in physical and outdoor recreation, physical and outdoor education, and various levels of sport.

Physical exercise

Physical exercise describes human activity in which the body, or parts of the body, are moved **vigorously**. The **sedentary** nature of modern life fails to give us the physical activity our bodies need for a long and active life. The **causes** are:

- The increased availability of **transport**, as opposed to the need to walk or run.

- The widening availability of **non-exercise based** recreational activities, such as computer games.

- The actual increase in **leisure time**, which can mean less time spent being physically active at work or in physical recreations.

How to achieve the benefits of physical exercise

To achieve the **benefits** of physical exercise, recommendations by leading authorities emphasise the value of:

- **Regularity**, with a degree of **intensity** sufficient to increase the heart rate over a period.

- The intention of **sustaining** this improved condition, thus promoting **long-term health**.

- Giving the individual a more **balanced attitude** towards personal fitness.

- For example, a minimum of exercise three times per week of 20 minutes duration and raising the pulse and breathing rates to 70% of maximum.

figure C.2 – healthy lifestyle

For these reasons, **lifetime sport** or **life-long physical activity** are valuable goals in life. They would enable people to live longer with fewer health complications and with a greater enjoyment of a full and active life.

Inactivity

Inactivity and bad eating habits have led to the problem of **obesity** in our society, particularly as it affects young people. Individuals, parents, schools and the media must take their share of the blame.

In the case of **children**, physical inactivity is the result of:

- Constant **car use**.
- **Limited physical education** on the curriculum or extra-curriculum.
- The **discouragement of vigorous play** activities in the playground.
- Many cases of **school fields being sold off** or not being fully utilised.

Obesity has also led children to avoid physical activity, because of its competitive nature and their discomfort in physical education kit. However, programmes are being designed to encourage obese children to join exercise and sports groups. Future policies must promote programmes for child obesity, ensuring **opportunity**, **provision** and **self-esteem** for this group. Certainly, **play** and safe **play areas** should be important family, school and community objectives.

THE CHARACTERISTICS AND OBJECTIVES OF A VARIETY OF PHYSICAL ACTIVITIES

The use of terms like characteristics and concepts are interchangeable, whereas objectives are what you hope to get out of the experience.

Play

Here we consider play as **a child's activity**-experience, with definitions, characteristics and objectives (figure C.3).

A definition of play is that '**it consists of activities from which you get immediate pleasure without ulterior motive**'.

The **characteristics** of play lie within this principle of **immediate pleasure**, even though play does not always have a happy ending! In the first instance there are the elements of free choice of **time** and **space**. There would be no direct concern with how long children play or where they play.

The **spontaneous** nature of play is fundamental and this is normally linked with its **intrinsic value**. They are hoping to have **fun** for its own sake.

figure C.3 – play

CHILD'S PLAY — immediate pleasure — no ulterior motive — activities — have fun for its own sake — exists in its own time and space — spontaneous — preparation for life — non-serious

Child's play

Play at the child level is supposedly **non-serious** and presumed to be of little value other than for **enjoyment**. But many educationists would now recognise that play not only motivates children, but improves skills and social awareness.

For a child it can be argued that play is a chance to **master reality**. Make-believe allows children to solve problems in a world of their own making as a preparation for life.

Children's play does not always involve physical activity or encourage physical exercise. Significantly, one of the major issues linked with child obesity is the popularity of video-games at the expense of the physical street play so common a century ago (figure C.4). We need to look at the expansion of sedentary activities by children in their free time. The expansion of play areas with exciting equipment now requires the interest (supervision) of a parent to ensure safety. Hence many playground games are no longer allowed at school.

figure C.4 – street games in early 20th century

A more refined definition of play

A more **academic** approach to play has been made by a number of psychologists, particularly by Huizinga, who recognised that play existed in its own time and space, and that rules were freely accepted just to make the activity work. However, he also considered that moods found in play could change from interest to rapture very quickly. This would mean that festive feelings could reach extremes of exultation and tension, with mirth or tears arising from intense experiences. When you take some of these comments into account, sport and play seem to have a lot in common!

So, if we go to a skateboard park and watch young people or look at children making a chain (figure C.5) you can ask the following questions

- Is it a **voluntary** experience?
- Are they **free**?
- Might this be a **special experience** for them?
- Can it create **order**, can it lead to harmony?
- Are they sharing a **common social experience**?

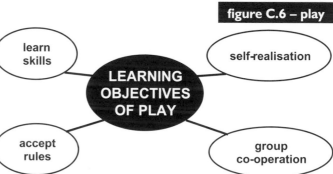
figure C.5 – children playing trains

Objective of play

The **objectives** of play are more difficult to explain as, in the simplest terms, there is only one objective and that is **to have fun**.

However, adults may encourage play as an **activity**, because it occupies children and perhaps keeps them out of trouble. But also, if they see play as a **learning experience** there are other objectives (figure C.6). These learning objectives might include helping children to:

- Learn simple skills.
- Improve self-realisation.
- Learn to play in a group.
- Learn to accept the rules identified by the play group.

That is, they can learn how to **master reality** through the **medium of play**.

figure C.6 – play

learn skills · self-realisation · **LEARNING OBJECTIVES OF PLAY** · accept rules · group co-operation

Adults at play

In respect of **adults** or young adults at play, activity, fun, non-serious, pleasure, and spontaneity are valid.

- Adults do tend to want to organise their play more than children.
- Adults put play in a context in which rules and structure are more important.
- Adults view the outcome with a little more seriousness than would children.

For example, the annual **Gloucestershire Cheese Rolling event** is held as an activity for adults. It has no serious context other than that of winning, is regarded as fun by most taking part, and is an excuse for robust physical acts. The festival context builds the event to an intense experience, which in 2008 led to several broken limbs, and the sense of achievement of arriving at the bottom of the hill in one piece!

Examples of adult play are street or beach games of soccer (figure C.7), basketball, street hockey and so-on. Kick-abouts without formal kit or pitches fall into this category.

figure C.7 – adults at play – beach games

Benefits of play

Immediate benefits derived from the activity itself:
- **Freedom to engage** in their chosen activity.
- **Enjoy the immediate pleasure** of playing, particularly when it is a group activity.
- If play is of a physical nature, then there are the **benefits of exercise and the performance of physical skills**.
- If the activity has a structure, then repetition and simple **rule agreements** take place.

- Play can therefore lead to **simple team and friendship building**.
- And increased levels of **individual and group confidence**.

Developmental or **educational benefits** of play:
- Play becomes the driving force for **educational objectives** in physical education and more general life skills.
- Benefits of **lasting value** hinge on the assumption that **play is an experience** as well as an activity.

Ultimately, childhood and society are enriched by the play motive. It gives each individual the chance to be active, to make friends, and to take a place in a child's community.

Physical education

A definition of physical education is 'the **formal educational process of acquiring knowledge and values through physical activity experiences**'. Therefore physical education is an area of educational activity in which the main concern is with **vigorous bodily movement**.

figure C.8 – overlapping physical issues

Our initial notions about what happens within physical activities in a school lies in the overlapping boundaries between **curriculum** physical education and **extra-curriculum** sport and physical recreation during the school day (figure C.8). Both curricular and extra-curricular activity should imply desirable knowledge and values as part of the **formal curriculum** of any school or college. There is also **playtime activity**, which can add recreational opportunities in a play environment, and should therefore be taken into account as part of the school experience.

To move on to more detail, a **National Physical Education Curriculum Document** identifies certain activities which should be taught in all schools. Athletics, gymnastics and dance, games and contests, outdoor activities and swimming are important areas of study, where **opportunity** and **provision** allows. The document also recognises that the health, fitness, and safety awareness of individuals are essential elements within this experience. This hopefully leads to a **healthy lifestyle** being established among **young people**, with a view to the retention of lasting **interests and values**.

Characteristics of physical education

The **characteristics** of **physical education** are that it represents physically challenging experiences within an educational institution. There are **physical** and **educational** values from such a curriculum programme. Extra-curriculum **sport** allows an emphasis on competitive experiences, and **physical recreation** should represent a broad band of physical activity outside the curriculum (see figure C.8) as well as at playtime. Most of the physical activities on the curriculum are compulsory, but extra-curricular activities are optional. Such optional activities normally involve free time and the opportunity for children to participate in personal choices. Extra-curricular activities should still be seen to be part of the ethos of the school.

The general aims of this subject area are to enthuse young people into the value of these physical experiences at both curriculum and extra-curriculum level and thus encourage a healthy lifestyle. Values are summarised as long-term objectives in figure C.9.

figure C.9 – physical education

Objectives and benefits of physical education

The benefits of physical education (figure C.10) are:

- All children have regular, compulsory physical activity which ensures a level of vigorous health related exercises.

- The activity includes strengthening, mobilising and co-ordinating activities designed to establish sound levels of **health and fitness**.

- **Skills and techniques** are taught in all the required physical activities.

- Children are coached at their optimum level.

- Children are also given opportunity for **competitive experiences** in individual activities and games.

- Best achieved in an **enjoyable** atmosphere with the objectives of promoting **health**, **effort** and **prowess**.

figure C.10 – benefits of physical education

- **Social** skills can be developed through the experience of performing in groups and teams.

- Qualities of **leadership and response to leadership** are combined to develop a respect for others.

- This involves the development of sound **competitive** and **co-operative** attitudes.

- **Cognitive** benefits arise from the considerable mental involvement in **understanding** skills and tactics and **decision-making**, when performing them in physical activities as part of a process of **problem solving** and **strategy building**.

- Acceptable values can be learnt through the acceptance of rules and regulations as part of a **moral code**.

- Involvement in physical activities present opportunities for **ethical judgements**, reflected in a willingness to resist the **temptation** to break rules and practise gamesmanship.

- The opportunity is given to learn about **oneself** in critical situations and develop an awareness of others, potentially stimulating the development of **self-realisation** and **socialisation**.

- **Emotional** benefits can occur, where **personal control** is necessary in excitable competitive situations.

- The opportunity for **self-expression** is given in many creative situations.

- Physical education can be a **medium** where there is an opportunity for **creativity** and an **appreciation** of successful performance by others and as such a **taste of excellence**.

- There is an alternative test of self, where an individual or team **experiences success** as a result of a high level of **commitment** and a strong element of **vitality**.

We are a sporting nation, but one with a tendency to watch rather than play. The primary role of **physical education** is to inculcate physical activity values in a way which encourages a life-long commitment to healthy physical exercise in society. However, what is started in the school must continue to be promoted in an adult society which values a healthy lifestyle.

Leisure and recreation

Definitions

There are a number of definitions of leisure:

'**It is an activity, apart from the obligations of work, family and society, to which the individual turns of their own free will**'.

'**It helps people to learn how to play their part in society, it helps them to achieve societal or collective aims, and it helps the society to keep together**'.

This second definition suggests that leisure has a social function, not just free time. This makes it more than an **activity**, but also an **experience**.

A third definition could be, '**leisure consists of relatively self-determining activity experiences that fall into one's economically free-time roles**'.

Characteristics of leisure

A useful step is to check out the types of activities which might fit into what you understand as leisure.

Figure C.11 gives you a number of activities to pick from. Thinking about these activities, you need to decide which activities you think are leisure and which are not leisure. This will help you decide on the **meaning** of the word **leisure** better than any definition.

In order to qualify as leisure (figure C.12):

- An **activity** has to be in your **free time**, but you may want to do nothing, to **relax**, to **recuperate**.
- This might not be physical, however, as it might be a case of **mental rekindling**!
- You **choose** to do it.
- It has **social** values.
- It helps to know yourself better (**self-realising**).
- To get on with others better (**socialising**).
- To better understand the society you live in (**culturally civilising**).
- It could be **recreating**, since recreation, physical recreation and even sport can be forms of leisure activity! That is as long as they are your choice! See figure C.13.
- You must like and **enjoy** the activity.

figure C.11 – leisure

examples of **LEISURE ACTIVITIES**

- watching and listening
- playing games and competing
- visiting and communicating
- dancing and romancing
- playing instruments and painting
- inventing and discovering
- walking and jogging
- reading and writing
- gardening and constructing
- daydreaming and relaxing

figure C.12 – characteristics of leisure

LEISURE

- activity
- free choice
- relax and recuperate
- mental rekindling
- self-realising
- socialising
- civilising
- experience

figure C.13 – rock climbing as outdoor recreation

Recreation

By definition, recreation is a **positive aspect of leisure** and is widely described as **active leisure**. Its **characteristics** (figure C.14) are similar to leisure in that it carries the individual and group away from the usual serious concerns of life. The attitudes derived from recreation involve relaxation (from mental anxiety). **Contentment** should be a product of the recreational process.

The objectives are similar to leisure, but with a narrower, positive expectation of outcomes:

- Improved **mental well-being**.
- Improved **physical well-being**.
- **Creative** opportunity.
- Ongoing **commitment**.

Add to this the social and cultural factors identified with leisure and you have positive values at a family, community and national level.

figure C.14 – recreation

Active leisure as physical recreation

The term **active leisure** normally identifies with **committed** forms of recreation, which often fit into identifiable groups. This may include art classes, music and poetry groups or historical society membership, as well as physical recreation and outdoor recreation.

Definitions

A definition of active leisure is '**recreational commitment in a specific form of active leisure**'.

A definition of physical recreation is '**the recreational pursuit of a range of physical activities, where the level of challenge is well within the capacity of all those participating. This is physical exercise in a recreational environment, which has a positive effect on maintaining a healthy lifestyle**'.

This definition can also include **outdoor recreation**. Outdoor recreation has a number of unique features as **recreational physical exercise in a natural environment**.

Characteristics of physical recreation

The sorts of activities included under the labels of physical and outdoor recreation include all physical activities which involve recreational rather than sporting values. Those listed in the diagram (figure C.14) are examples only, but the recreational dimension is often identified in the title chosen for the activity. For example, bathing rather than swimming, jogging or riding rather than racing.

Physical activity at a recreational level may not be competitive. Examples would include hitting a ball over a net, a kick-about, or a low-level match in which friendly participation is the whole point of the activity.

STUDENT NOTE

Note that **effort** and **prowess** would be among the main characteristics of a competitive **sporting** game or activity. Friendly participation would be firmly left to the non-serious recreational performer.
It is important to note that the recreational approach could be more pleasant and long-lasting than the intensity of sporting activities.

The recreational dominance means that the concept is similar to **play**. It means that:

- Those involved tend to **co-operate** rather than compete.
- Those involved tend to re-create **pleasant** experiences and refresh body and mind through **companionship** (figure C.15).
- There are elements of **physical vigour** and commitment.
- It depends on the individual and is moderated by **long-term participation** objectives and to meet the capacity of the whole group.
- It is in a sense **non-utilitarian**, in that the gain lies more in **intrinsic** involvement rather than extrinsic rewards.

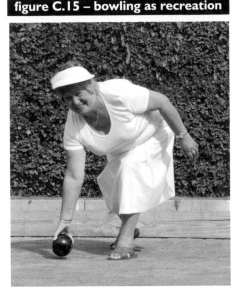

figure C.15 – bowling as recreation

Objectives of physical recreation

The objectives of physical recreation and outdoor recreation are:

- To engage in a **physical challenge**, which is pleasurable and has lasting health value.
- To involve the use of activities and skills, which maintain our general fitness.
- To give us **experiences**, which give us pleasure and satisfaction.
- They should be **self-realising** in a lifetime context.
- To endorse long-term friendships.
- To be culturally rewarding.

These objectives mean that physical recreation is more than an activity. It is an experience which can be life enhancing and last a lifetime.

figure C.16 – active leisure

Benefits of physical recreation

The benefits are that **physical recreation**, as with other forms of **active leisure** (figure C16):

- Allows individuals to have time to **relax** and **recover** from work and areas of responsibility.
- It is normally **enjoyable**, where a person would be pursuing healthy physical activities.
- A person would be happy to undertake these activites in a non-serious atmosphere.
- There can be considerable **health values** arising from this active physical experience.
- There is **skill learning** and the **social contact** of friendship groups.
- The freedom associated with these activities can help the development of **self-esteem** and give **creative opportunities** to individuals as well as groups and clubs.

While we are producing sporting prowess, we are increasingly a nation of spectators, glued to television and the terraces. We have a problem of obesity in our society and the only hope for us is to become more physically active. Whether this is through a better controlled diet, regular visits to fitness clubs, the continuation of the physical skills we learn at school, or joining sport or rambling clubs, the focus of our society must change. The rewards are of feeling better, making new friends and probably living longer.

Outdoor education

It is important to establish what outdoor education has in common with the other physical education activities and then why it should be looked upon as a different and valuable experience.

As part of physical education, a definition of outdoor education is '**the formal educational process of acquiring knowledge and values through outdoor activity experiences**'. This is an area of educational activity in which the main concern is with vigorous bodily movement.

The difference is its location in the **natural environment** of water and mountain and the **challenging nature** of this experience.

It is normally convenient to focus on four types of activity (figure C.17):

- The two **water activities** of canoeing and sailing.
- The two **mountain activities** of endurance hill walking and rock climbing. All these should include the notion of camping in the natural outdoors.

Canoes are used in swimming baths and climbing walls are found in sports halls, but these are nothing more than convenient opportunities to practise outdoor activity skills in a safe environment.

Characteristics of outdoor education

As with physical education, there are **overlapping** boundaries between:

- **Curriculum**, which may be compulsory lessons or extended field weeks.
- **Extra-curriculum**, where club groups may operate.
- **Playtime activity**, where this is safe to do so.

The **national physical education curriculum** recognises that outdoor activities are valuable physical and educational activities. All children should experience these activities where opportunity and provision allows. This type of activity can lead to a **healthy lifestyle** being established among **young people.**

In addition to the **characteristics** of physical education, with its unique combination of the **physical**, **educational** and **recreational** values, outdoor education offers **adventure in a challenging natural environment**. Figure C.17 should give you the key words associated with this form of education, with particular focus on the relevance of **discovery**, **challenge**, **excitement** and **risk**.

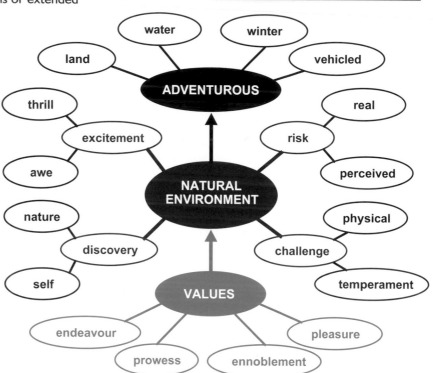

figure C.17 – outdoor education

The **objectives** of this educational area build on these characteristics, but also more general objectives already outlined for physical education.

Benefits of outdoor education

In **physical terms**, it is suggested that the outdoor education experience:

- Expands the **boundaries of health** as a result of spending time in the fresh air.
- Presents situations requiring **unexpected physical challenges** and a different kind of **physical prowess**.
- Involves an additional dimension by taking children out of the school and urban existence into the less predictable natural environment.
- Set at a challenging level, **risk** has to be estimated and reduced to what is perceived risk rather than real, by qualified staff.

figure C.18 – outdoor education

It is argued that many of the **educational benefits** (figure C.18 on facing page) are enhanced in this challenging and often beautiful environment. Particularly:

- **Leadership** skills.
- **Problem solving**.
- **Strategy building**.
- The opportunity to learn about **oneself** in critical situations.
- An awareness of others.
- The emotional experience of the **thrilling**, but also **awesome** moments.
- The additional quality of experiencing and learning to appreciate the **natural world** and its beauty.
- Through individual and **group experiences**.
- Which require a high level of **commitment**.

Outdoor and adventurous activities

This area of experience should be seen to start as part of **outdoor education**. It can develop into **outdoor recreation** and a commitment which carries them into **adventurous outdoor activities**.

If the definition of outdoor education is '**the formal educational process of acquiring knowledge and values through outdoor activity experiences**'. The term **outdoor recreation** (figure C.19) defines the less controlled experience of **recreational physical activity in a natural environment**, which defines the **characteristics** of the activity.

figure C.19 – outdoor recreational activities

OUTDOOR RECREATION — healthy lifestyle, natural environment, co-operative, physical challenge, risk awareness, sense of achievement, adventure, frontier experience

These activities can also have a positive effect on maintaining a **healthy lifestyle**, because of the likelihood that these activities can be experienced for many years. Outdoor recreation takes the experience learnt in **outdoor education** and encourages individuals to continue appreciating and visiting the countryside.

Hazards

There are potential hazards from outdoor activities, when walking, climbing, sailing and canoeing, and winter sports. The principles of avoidance of unnecessary risk are:

- Not to go out into open country on your own.
- Of knowing your own and the group's limitations.
- Being prepared for all climatic and accident eventualities.

This means that recreational characteristics apply such as co-operative rather than competitive engagement. The hope is to have pleasant experiences and to refresh body and mind through experiencing fresh air and exercise with friends.

Objectives of outdoor and adventurous activities

The **objectives** are recreational, but with risk awareness:

- To experience a rewarding escape into the natural environment.
- To face the pleasure of the unpredictable alongside the adventure associated with the unexpected.
- To be aware of individual and group experience and limitations.
- To prepare accordingly.
- To see this as a chance to be physically active and yet be able to appreciate the beauty of the countryside, our coastline and rivers.

Risk and adventure

It is important to be aware of the levels at which **adventure** should exist (figure C.20). The principle is that in outdoor education, risk must only be perceived and not real.

- The **first level** is a basic, safe **experience**, perhaps paddling a canoe in a swimming bath, canal or still water. Alternatively it might be rock climbing on slabs or easy climbs. This in itself will present anxieties, but must become a successful, safe experience.

- The **second level** should be a **challenge,** but not dangerous, for example, paddling should be in safe, white water or surf, or taking on carefully guided recognised climbs, again with successful, safe outcomes (figure C.21).

- The **third level** is a test of self and others in a '**frontier experience**', taking the canoeist into graded rapids or distance sea paddling and high surf.

- The **fourth level** is **misadventure**. It is a point where misjudgement occurs and with it real risk. This is an unacceptable experience in outdoor education which, regrettably, can happen through negligence or as an unpredictable development.

The third and fourth levels would not normally be part of the outdoor adventure curriculum in schools without specialist leadership.

figure C.20 – adventure

risk - fourth level	→	misadventure - real risk
risk - third level		frontier experience
risk - second level		challenge - not dangerous
risk - first level		safe experience

ADVENTURE

High level performance at outdoor pursuits

This area of **adventurous outdoor activity** takes us into the sporting dimension of high level performance and commitment to outdoor pursuits. The significant difference here from outdoor education is that the responsibility is taken away from the educational establishment and is held by the individual or the associated administration which is responsible for that individual's safety.

This takes performers into and beyond the third level of adventure, where the aim is to test oneself and others in a **frontier experience**. Sadly, there are occasions when there are instances of **misadventure** in this dangerous environment. This is because of the unpredictability of the natural environment and the irresponsibility of some adventurers.

The **characteristics** of this high level performance activity differ from outdoor recreation. The same activities are simply taken to the upper limit of an individual's capability. We are now talking about the high levels of fitness and advanced skills required by canoeing in extreme or competitive conditions, by long distance or competitive sailing, and by altitude or severely testing rock. These activities are, by choice, extreme challenges at the upper level of an individual or group's capability.

figure C.21 – outdoor adventure

Objectives of high level adventurous outdoor activity

The **objectives** are now personally directed towards achieving excellence:

- To **test** the effort and the prowess potential of an experienced performer.
- To **engage** in a challenge or competition with total commitment.
- To be aware that co-operation and comradeship could win the day.
- To **succeed** through the use of sound strategies, awareness of problem solving needs and good judgement under stress.

Ultimately the thrill of each success becomes a **taste of excellence** and a **sense of achievement**, until the next challenge.

Benefits of outdoor recreation

- To have time to **relax and recover** from work and areas of responsibility, but in this case at **a pleasurable level in the natural environment**.
- To enjoy outdoor recreation, but with an **exhilaration** arising from the **perceived risk in challenging situations**.
- To be non-serious, but in an atmosphere of caution followed by a strong feeling of **achievement with success**.
- To take advantage of considerable **health values** arising from these active outdoor experiences including the **fresh air**.
- To learn new techniques and share the experience with others.
- To use the **freedom** associated with these activities to help the development of **self-esteem.**
- To give **creative opportunities** in the natural environment, enhanced by an **awareness and appreciation** of areas of natural beauty.

STUDENT NOTE

Note that these recreational freedoms are dependent on equality of **opportunity**, **provision** and **esteem**, ideals not necessarily achieved by everyone today in our affluent society. However, just as we should fight for equality, so we need to make a greater use of the advantages we already have to live a healthy lifestyle. Occasionally, we must get out of that car and walk or jog or ride a bike.

Benefits of adventurous activities

The **physical benefits** lie in:

- The successful **testing of elite skills**.
- The proving of individual prowess.
- The capacity for that individual to make **other performers** part of that progression.
- The **avoidance of misadventure** In the future.

The **personal** benefits enable the adventurous individual to:

- **Test commitment** and **experience**.
- Learn from this in an atmosphere of **co-operation** and **comradeship**.
- Succeed in these challenges as a result of talent and resolve.
- Advance **self-development**.
- Experience problem solving strategies, sound judgement, and the maintenance of personal control under stress.
- Pass on to others the wisdom gained from the experience.

Hopefully, the exhilaration of each success is a reward in itself, a **taste of excellence**.

Maybe our society has gone soft, that we are prepared to allow a few enthusiasts to compete and take our money. If each and every one of us took that one step towards excellence, just one rung up the ladder, then our society would be that much more vital and **participating** instead of **complaining**. If only we all tried to go that extra mile!

Sport

Sports and pastimes are commonly used terms which describe a variety of sporting activities. Modern sport has many of the features and values which have evolved from the traditions built many centuries ago. Regular **institutionalised sport** was a 19th century European development of **athleticism** and **Modern Olympism**. In both cases, **sport** reflects the **culture** to which it belongs, and therefore **cultural variables** play a large part in its development.

Definition

A definition of sport is '**an institutionalised competitive activity that involves vigorous physical exertion and the use of relatively complex physical skills, where participation is motivated by a combination of intrinsic satisfaction associated through the activity itself, and external rewards earned by high level performance**'.

The advantage of this rather complex definition is that it identifies the physical exercise and physical skills criteria in physical recreation and physical education. This is within the two levels at which sport can operate, as a recreational activity and as an experience involving excellence.

Characteristics of sport

The characteristics of sport (figure C.22) include:

- Individual physical activities and games.
- Have the character of **play**.
- Take the form of a **struggle** with oneself.
- Involve **competition** with others.
- Are **institutionalised**.
- **Regular** and organised.
- Regulated by a code of **behaviour**.

figure C.23 – sport at university – the Loughborough HIPAC

figure C.22 – sport

The characteristics and benefits of **physical recreation** are carried into **sport** and adjusted to meet the stringent requirements of **sporting excellence**.

It is important to make the point that to achieve sporting excellence there must be:

- The **organisational** support including a professional administration.
- An efficient **selection** process.
- Top **facilities** and centres of excellence (see figure C.23).
- An elite system of **coaching** and **funding**.

Sportsmanship, gamesmanship and fair play

figure C.24 – sportsmanship reigns

However, it is not just what you play, but how you play in a sport that is important. If the sporting activity involves competition, then it should always be performed with a **spirit of sportsmanship** (figure C.24). The ideal view is that there can be no true sport without the idea of **fair play**.

In sport, we have problems of violence on the field and the use of performance enhancing drugs. This tells us that the ethic of fair play is under attack. Without fair play, sport as an educational vehicle and as a noble pastime is doomed. It is possible to look at games on the television or during school sport and test the behaviour of performers. The behaviour will vary from the high point of players making moral decisions to the other extreme of deliberate violence against others. Fair play will exist as long as you at least accept the referee's decisions, but it's better if you accept the rules of play.

- In an ideal world, the notion of **fair play** is paramount, where the spirit in which the activity is played is more important than a win-at-all costs attitude.
- Sportsmanship is **functional** if the rules of a game or sport are accepted, or the decisions of a referee or umpire are accepted.
- Sportsmanship is **dysfunctional** if a performer has no regard for others, or deliberately subverts the rules of a game in order to gain advantage.
- The term **deviance** describes behaviour in which people find a way around the rules, however they are framed.

Deviant behaviour can be institutional, group specific, or individual, and is either:

- **Voluntary** - the performer decides to take drugs.
- **Co-operative** - the performer decides to take drugs, because all his friends are doing so.
- **Enforced** - a former East German swimmer took drugs because her coach gave them to her.

Alternatively, **gamesmanship** is defined as '**the intention to compete to the limit of the rules and beyond if you can get away with it**'.

Some professional performers and coaches maintain that, '**you get away with what you can**', an admission that potential rewards, millions in sponsorship and wages, can outweigh moral considerations.

Categories within sport

Numerous attempts have been made to **categorise** sports, none of them perfect, but the one in the supporting chart (figure C.25) is reasonably sound.

A primary division into **individual activities** and **games** shows seven groups of individual activities, most of which have variations within each group.

Similarly, in games, given the structural difference of team and partner games, there are four groups, each representing a difference in their basic structure.

The theory is that all the major activities and games will fit into one of these groups, but it is relatively easy to show that there are exceptions. Archery has certainly changed over the centuries and basketball is a tricky one to put in place on the chart. Nevertheless figure C.25 helps because it can be established that each group has activities with a common structure and emphasis on certain objectives.

figure C.25 – sport activities

Objectives of sport

The objectives of sport vary according to the performer's place on the continuum from recreational sport to sporting excellence. But if you assess these at a personal level, then each performer should set out to do his or her best (this is the meaning of **prowess** and **effort**, key features of how a performer should approach **sport** as opposed to **recreation**).

In **physical terms**, the objectives of sports are:

- To give the maximum **effort**.
- To make the most of your skills and tactical knowledge.

In **behavioural terms**, the objectives are:

- To encourage co-operation as a team and yet **compete** as hard as you can.
- To work on **strategies** and problems arising from competitive challenges.
- To learn to **play fair** in competitions and games as part of your personal development.

- To help others, particularly if you have a **leadership** role.
- To **control your emotions** under pressure.
- To help you to **express** yourself.
- To recognise that sport is about **commitment**.
- To feel good, to be **creative**, to value the activity.
- To **appreciate** the performance of others.

These are the **noble objectives of sport**. Sadly, there is also the negative side of the coin, where the code of '**win-at-all-costs**' is dominant, and abuse and cheating become the dysfunctional behaviour alternative. Despite greed and the excessive ambition of individuals and nations, the **Olympic Code** is worth saving.

Benefits of sport

The **physical benefits** of sport are summarised in figure C.26. These benefits allow individuals to recover from the stress of work by pursuing **healthy** sports in a happy atmosphere, as well as learning physical **skills** through friendly **competition**.

However, as the intensity of the sporting experience increases (towards **excellence**), so does the importance of **physical endeavour** and the need for **physical prowess**.

The **personal benefits** of intrinsic sport also involve:

- Elements of **recreational** opportunity, where the **freedom** to choose what sporting activity to do is a rewarding experience.
- Participation, in itself, can be fulfilling in the **enjoyment** sense, but also in terms of **personal achievement**.
- An experience of partner and team sport is likely to increase **social skills** in pressure situations.
- In the more formal coaching environment, **personal benefits** of sport, and particularly high level sport, include qualities of **leadership**, and sound competitive and **co-operative** attitudes.
- **Decision-making**, opportunities to learn about oneself and others in competitive situations.
- Benefiting from at least an occasional taste of excellence.

The potential **moral benefits** of **sport** arise from competition, and so it should always be performed with a spirit of **sportsmanship** and **fair play**.

figure C.26 – benefits of sport

RELATIONSHIP BETWEEN PLAY, PHYSICAL EDUCATION, LEISURE, RECREATION AND SPORT

There is a firm **relationship** between **play** and all the other named activity-experiences, because the basic concepts of play are common to them all. They are all determined by:

- **Time**, how long?
- **Space**, where?
- Elements of **spontaneity**.
- Retain a varying degree of **intrinsic** value.
- There is a strong **enjoyment** factor.
- With immediate **pleasure** in anticipation and preparation.
- And where psychologists suggest that play helps children to **master reality**.
- Give the participant levels of **confidence** and **experience**.
- Which helps them to **cope with reality**.

A common **relationship** between **physical education** and the other activity-experiences is its physical commitment for vigorous exercise. It is true that this physical element does not always exist in play or leisure, but it often does. The additional key point is that physical activity triggers the emotional, social and cultural development as a result of this engagement.

figure C.27 – sea canoeing adventure

A common **relationship** between **leisure, recreation, active leisure** and **play** is the association with free time and choice, together with the emotional rewards of enjoyment and appreciation. Sport in school and society, particularly at a lower level, has this element of choice, freedom and fun.

The firm **relationship** between **elite sport, physical education** and **outdoor and adventurous outdoor activities** is the commitment in terms of organisation and rigour. In this case teaching, coaching and adventure expectations are high (figure C.27), developed as part of a progressive programme, aiming for optimal understanding and performance.

Comparing and contrasting

To compare one concept with another seems an excellent way of testing your understanding. It means putting any two types of activity alongside each other and identifying similarities and differences.

Comparing play with physical education

All young children play and the play-way is seen as an important teaching style with children at nursery and primary schools. The motive of play in terms of **enjoying** physical activity should permeate the whole physical education programme. They differ insofar that physical education is an important educational subject area and so is a structured programme. The principle of child-centred work exists in dance and gymnastics encouraging degrees of spontaneity and mastering skills and techniques. These techniques might be played out in extra-curricular clubs, and can be seen to be a mastery of life and sports skills.

Comparing play with leisure, recreation and active leisure

There is very little difference conceptually between these types of activity. They all match the play motives of free time and space, spontaneity, and intrinsic immediately pleasurable activity. They also enable the mastering of life experiences in a person's free time. Differences lie in the age group involved and the interpretation of what it means to the group. Children's play is so immediate and intrinsic that there seems little possibility of instilling lasting values. Adult awareness as a result of active leisure is such that skills are more obviously developed, with possible increased self-realisation, socialisation and cultural awareness. These may be transferred into life skills.

Comparing play with outdoor and adventurous activities and sport

The play concepts are squeezed out of the other activities as expectations are increased. The notion of play (the concept of playing games) is closely linked with a desire to retain the fun element in sport. This is at the same time as keeping a belief in the honour of **playing** the activity rather than an extreme commitment to the win-ethic. It is the reduction of intrinsic values in favour of extrinsic ones which is the dominating contrast, together with a need to succeed in sport. This **need to succeed** is even more dominant in the hostile and dangerous adventurous environment.

Comparing physical education with leisure, recreation and active leisure

Curriculum physical education is compulsory and so in opposition to the free time basis of leisure and recreation. Nevertheless, an objective of physical education is to introduce children to a series of recreational activities, particularly physical recreations, as a part of active leisure and a healthy lifestyle. Extra-curricular sport and recreations in the school are normally on an optional basis, even if attendance at team practises is expected.

Comparing physical education with sport and outdoor adventurous activities

The common ground is the **serious** intentions of these three groups of activities. Sport and outdoor adventurous activities are optional but hold a committed path towards **professionalism** which binds performers to clubs and sponsors. One of the primary objectives of physical education is to prepare young people for an active lifestyle. Those children who are talented and committed may go on to achieve excellence in sport or outdoor adventurous challenges.

figure C.28 – marathon start

For outdoor adventurous activities, children are in the care of qualified teachers responsible for the children's well-being. Similarly, coaches, instructors and leaders are responsible for their charges, particularly important where risk, injury and recovery are concerned.

Comparing leisure, recreation and active leisure with sport

Some regard these as opposites because leisure and recreation are seen to be free relaxing activities, while sport is very much dynamic, obsessive and pressurised. It is far wiser to see this as a continuum.

At the extreme leisure end of the continuum we can relax and rest. As we move along the continuum, we would become more active and take part in some form of physical recreation. At the other end of the continuum, we may undertake intense exercise options.

At the active end of this continuum, the person may select one or two recreative activities to play more regularly and take more seriously (and even become a professional). Although the two ends of the continuum have totally different characteristics and objectives, they are still the same activities. Any one person can and should continue to experience the pleasurable moments of watching a marathon, enjoying a fun-run, or testing him or herself in the London Marathon (see figure C.28).

Comparing leisure, recreation and active leisure with outdoor and adventurous activities

It is easy to see that there is nothing relaxing and enjoyable in the middle of an extreme outdoor adventurous situation. People would be striving, determined and focused, and would find the exercise exhilarating, thrilling and exhausting. These feelings are more likely during and after a supreme test of self and others.

As mentioned in the previous section, this is a journey from leisurely to extremely adventurous situations. It is to taste freedom on the one hand and excellence on the other, but also to feel able to engage in both worlds. Young people, introduced to outdoor activities at school, might well select one outdoor activity and take it to an advanced level.

So, perhaps a person should seek to encompass the whole field of activity-experiences, so that all individuals have the opportunity to taste freedom. This would enable such a person to experience the immediate pleasure of active leisure. This person would be able to select activities which would allow him / her to use his / her talents and taste excellence, but most important of all, to retain a love of healthy lifetime physical activity.

Practice questions

1) Identify possible physical objectives of a major game, swimming or athletics as part of your Physical Education programme.

3 marks

2) What are the **main** educational qualities of outdoor education? Illustrate your answer using a specific outdoor activity.

3 marks

3) Identify **four** characteristics of sport using a game to illustrate each of them.   *4 marks*

4) Discuss the **main** similarities and differences between physical recreation and sport.   *4 marks*

5) a) In the UK and Europe people participate in sport, leisure and recreation. Define and outline the differences between these three forms of activity.   *3 marks*
   b) How can a school provide opportunities to participate in both sport and recreation?   *3 marks*
   c) Outline the basic requirements needed to undertake sport or recreation.   *3 marks*

6) a) Leisure is time in which there is the opportunity for choice. Use an example of a leisure activity to explain this statement.

4 marks

   b) Explain the changes which occur as the concept of leisure is narrowed to reflect a 'Sport for All' campaign.   *4 marks*

7) a) Select a children's play activity and use figure C.29 to explain the characteristics of play which should be evident while they participate in this activity.

4 marks

   b) Explain why it is thought that when children play they increase mastery over reality whereas adults at play tend to be escaping from reality.

4 marks

figure C.29 – play

8) Briefly discuss the view that play is more than an activity, but also a valuable experience.   *5 marks*

9) Outdoor education is a means of approaching educational objectives through adventurous activities in the natural environment.
   a) Select an outdoor adventurous activity and explain it in terms of four levels of adventure.   *5 marks*
   b) Use Figure C.30 to explain values associated with an outdoor adventurous activity of your choice.   *5 marks*

figure C.30 – an outdoor activity

The public, private and voluntary sectors

The main **function** of the public, private and voluntary sectors of sport lies in the area of **funding**.
With this mixed arrangement it is important to explain the characteristics of each, but also to recognise their strengths and weaknesses.

The public sector

The primary **goal** of the **public sector** is to act as the central source of funding for sport in the United Kingdom. There are two main strands to this sector and an explanation of these is in effect an identification of the main **characteristics**.

The first strand is the funding through the **normal taxation** process. At a **national level** this is allocated as part of the budget and normally involves Government contributions to major projects, like the 2012 London Olympics. Also, **local authorities** contribute to their own projects, such as local sport and leisure centres and school facilities, which would be financed directly through the Council Tax, and through indirect sources such as the **PFI** (Private Finance Initiative).

The second is the funding through the **National Lottery** (see figure C.31) which has five strands:

- Health, Education and the Environment (33.33%).
- **Sports (16.67%)**.
- Arts (16.67%).
- Heritage (16.67%).
- Charities (16.67%).

The **Sports** element encompasses the Sports Councils, Governing Bodies, sports coach UK, and the Youth Sports Trust. The total for the **2005 / 2006** year was **£3.3 billion**.

There is some overlap between the two areas, for example, the **National Lottery**, through the **Youth Sports Trust**, funds activities in schools, which are mainly run and funded by **Local Authorities**.

figure C.31 – lottery funding in the UK

good: additional money available for sport, support for professional sports and excellence, also grassroots projects
bad: still not sufficient for needs, a better balance between public and private funding required

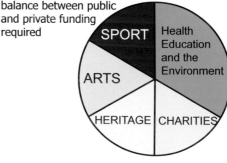

The private sector

The primary **goal** of the **private sector** reflects our mixed economy, insofar that traditionally the private sector of sport has always tended to fund itself. Consequently, this funding is largely directed towards the private provision of sports facilities. These include those available on a pay as you use basis, such as a few golf clubs, but many are by subscription and some are privately funded country clubs, requiring substantial incomes to join.

There are multi-sports clubs based in most towns and cities, which often cater for conditioning, squash, rugby, hockey, and cricket. For example, David Lloyd centres, which include tennis as a special facility, and specific conditioning centres like Total Fitness and LA Fitness. The large Soccer and Rugby Clubs employ a substantial team of organisers, coaches and medical support staff, as well as the players, and this to a large extent is dependent on private funding by spectators who watch games.

figure C.32 – volunteer funding

unpaid organisers

unpaid coaches

club member's subscriptions

poor areas do badly

match fees

VOLUNTEER FUNDING

potential talent lost

local authority facilities

coach expenses paid sometimes

small grants from lottery

The voluntary sector

The primary **goal** of the **voluntary sector** reflects another traditional feature of sport in the United Kingdom, which is the willingness of sport enthusiasts to give their time unpaid (see figure C.32). The characteristics of this sector, therefore, are of coaches and organisers making unpaid contributions most evenings in private or self-funding clubs.

Self-funding normally comes from members' subscriptions in a club, or fees taken from players for playing a game. Local authorities in the form of sports centres, athletics tracks, swimming pools, school gyms and sports halls, and playing fields often provide the facilities. In addition, facilities used in this way can be small scale privately owned pitches or games clubs, who rent out the use of their grounds or buildings.

The voluntary sector often operates through the **Governing Bodies** of individual sports, which also receive funds from the public sector often via the **National Lottery**. Additionally, this voluntary sector has an opportunity to apply for **grants** from the lottery system to improve their facilities, such as a new clubhouse, set of kit or a minibus, but not usually to pay administrators or coaches. Evidence suggests that some 90% of our administrators and coaches are volunteers who are sometimes paid expenses by local clubs.

The advantages and disadvantages of the public, private and voluntary sector provision

Public funding

The **advantages** of the **public** funding programme (see figures C.33) are that money is available from national and local taxes, and the amount available has been increased over the years. In figure C.34 we outline the factors which affect public provision. This includes initiatives which are part of the political and local government activity which is aimed at providing sport to the Nation. The details of this provision are discussed below on page 142. The main **disadvantage** is that public money is required for other commitments and often these take precedence over sporting needs.

As a result the amount is always limited and so sport has to turn to other sources for funding, such as commercial money, which is not as evenly distributed. Commercial money invariably looks for a visible return for its money and so is often attracted towards successful sports, rather than those in need who can offer little publicity.

Private funding

The **advantage** of **private** funding is that it reduces the use of public money where clubs have independent means. This reflects our free enterprise traditions, but the **disadvantage** is that this money is to some extent only available to those with money, when the need is to support those without sufficient funds. British sport has always been led by private clubs and in some sports the most successful ones have become professionalised. However, they have to maintain solvency by balancing income with expenditure. Certainly, with some association football clubs, this has become an uncontrollable downward spiral towards bankruptcy.

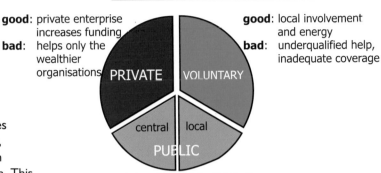

figure C.33 – sports funding in the UK

good: private enterprise increases funding
bad: helps only the wealthier organisations

PRIVATE

good: local involvement and energy
bad: underqualified help, inadequate coverage

VOLUNTARY

central | local
PUBLIC

good: taxation is fair, distribution by consensus
bad: shared by all charities, inadequate amount for sport

figure C.34 – efficiency of provision

FUNDING — ORGANISATION — GOVERNING BODIES
sport for all — INITIATIVES — Sports Mark Active Mark
TOP Sport — TOP Play
nine priority sports

Voluntary funding

The **voluntary sector** approach is at the heart of British sport and its main **advantage** is that it encourages enthusiasts to help, particularly in the local community. It represents the lowest tier of activity, reduces the need for public and private funding and, without doubt, grass-roots sport as we know it would founder if it were not for these committed individuals.

The **disadvantage** is that volunteers are increasingly hard to come by. This reflects a fundamental change in attitude by many retired performers, parents and public figures. It is also partly because parents increasingly expect specialist support from coaches. There is little doubt that anxiety is also felt by volunteers in the face of increased safety regulations. Unfortunately, despite more paid coaches being available, potential talent is being lost and deprived areas often miss-out.

The concept of 'best value' in relation to the public sector provision

'**Best Value**' is a key government policy set out in the **Local Government Act 1999**. The act requires all providers of public services to consider the best value for money of what is planned, as well as the value of the experiences offered. This must be placed in the context of our mixed system of provision for sport as a result of our sporting tradition. This tradition is a product of our **culture** and our particular brand of **democratic society**, which is a reflection of our current economic and political system.

The factors relevant to the notion of efficiency of provision for sport in the UK are outlined in figure C.35, with a discussion below on pages 154-158 concerning the details of the bodies mentioned.

It is not a perfect arrangement, but we do not have the commitment of a **socialist society**, like **China**, where the Government has taken control of funding sport, nor do we have the **capitalist wealth** to allow commercial interests to supply the bulk of funding as in the **USA**. We also lack the drive of **Australia**, where the energy comes from a young **athletic culture**, compared with the relative apathy of our ageing society. However, there is no justification for falling behind other West European countries.

figure C.35 – efficiency of provision

- DCMS
- UKsport
- UK sports institutes
- Private Finance Initiative (PFI)
- Sport England
- sports coach UK
- **SPORT PROVISION**
- Celtic Sports Councils
- Youth Sports Trust (YST)
- National Governing Bodies (NGBs)
- English Institute of Sport (EIS)

The post-war political trend for Western Europe has been to make the State increasingly responsible for national standards in sport. This is undoubtedly the result of the globalisation of sport, where the massive increase in opportunity and provision has led to increased funding, competition and ever increasing standards of performance. This follows from sport moving from private, largely amateur objectives to professionalisation.

We are increasingly dependent on the **public sector**. If, with the problem of accountability, we want to remain a leading sporting nation, we must use the funding from the public sector wisely. We are increasingly dependent on it and there is a limited amount the Government is prepared to allow. As a result, unlike China, the U.S.A. and Australia, we are forced to establish '**best value**' and unfortunately, this also means a selection process of 'most worthy'.

However, in terms of the Government Policy Document '**The Value of Sport**', the following outcomes are expected from provision of sport **as well as the use of the facilities for sport**:
- Improved health.
- Reduced crime.
- Economic regeneration.
- Improved employment opportunities.

PFI and its implications for the future

The **Private Finance Initiative** (**PFI**) is the government's method of bringing facilities up to the 21st century without incurring a large capital expenditure. The PFI is being applied to schools in general (not just the sports facilities) and public sector facilities like hospitals, and civil service and council buildings. Also included are almost all other public service buildings and projects.

The way this works is that the land is sold to the private sector buildings firms, who build the buildings at their own expense, and then lease back the facilities to the local authorities. The advantage of this process is that the government does not have to find the money from our taxes to pay for the buildings and facilities, and that these facilities are being provided **now** rather than spread out over the next 20 to 30 years. The main disadvantage is that the **revenue** expenditure is larger than it would have been when using the old method of government only expenditure – but of course we now have wonderful new facilities to use. Another disadvantage is that facilities are not **owned** by the school (or hospital) and use of facilities out of main hours have to be negotiated and paid for.

Hence, dual use by both schools (daytime), and community (evenings and weekends) of sports facilities is seen to be a major contributor to the 'Best Value' criteria, with the PFI companies as the commercial drivers of the process.

Olympic Games funding

London 2012 is now a major focus for sport spending up to 2012. There is a new National Lottery game to specifically fund the 2012 project, which hopefully will have a large legacy of fantastic sports facilities for the use of the population of the Greater London area. It is expected that funding will also be available for other projects on a National scale linked to the games. This includes training facilities for the teams attending the games – who will be billeted across the country prior to the games. Additionally, there are major plans to improve the infrastructure (roads, transport systems, housing) to support the locality of the games itself. In this context, the '**Best Value**' concept is most likely to be seen to be working to the advantage of the Nation.

Historical, social and cultural factors

The development of **physical education** and **sport** reflected changes in British society and, therefore, it is important to place **social and cultural** changes in the context of elitist **institutions** like the **English public schools**.

The English Public Schools between 1800 and the present

The context is the time span from the early 19th century up to the present day. We will now look at the major changes which occurred in society and these institutions and the possible influence on increased participation today. It is essential that you have a basic understanding of how society changed during this period as it influenced **development and change** in the institutions.

The early 19th century marked the beginnings of **three social revolutions** in England.

The **agrarian revolution** (figure C.36) involved the gradual movement of workers from the countryside to the larger towns.

This agrarian revolution was caused by:

- The emergence of a **gentry** class.
- The **enclosure** of much of the countryside.
- The growth of the **Methodist** Movement.
- The gradual increased significance of **respectability** in early Victorian society.
- The **poor wages** of the rural working class.
- The gradual **mechanisation** of tenant farms.

figure C.36 – agrarian revolution

- enclosure
- emergence of gentry
- growth of Methodists
- **AGRARIAN REVOLUTION**
- respectability
- mechanisation of farms
- low wages of rural workers

This latter point was also a reflection of the **industrial revolution**, which had begun in the mid-18th century, but mushroomed over the next century to give increased power to the middle classes and better wages for the industrial working class and greater prosperity for the country at large.

This gave rise to the **urban revolution**, which marked a massive rise in the population, as industrial and commercially well placed towns grew in size and national significance. This was alongside a new **Muscular Christian Movement**, supporting rational recreation and with it the concept of **amateurism** in sporting activities.

The English Public Schools

The so-called major **public schools** originated many centuries earlier, but were gradually adopted by the upper class as a necessary educational experience for their **boys**.

Nine of these schools increased in size and were identified in the **Clarendon Report** (1864) and later called the **Barbarian Schools** by Matthew Arnold. These **Clarendon Schools** are Eton, Harrow, Rugby, Shrewsbury, Charterhouse, Westminster, Winchester, St. Paul's and Merchant Taylors. The first **seven** of these were boarding schools and were at the centre of a later expansion of boarding schools as middle class copies throughout the country.

figure C.37 – public schools

- gentry
- boys
- fee-paying
- **PUBLIC SCHOOLS**
- endowed
- boarding
- non-local
- spartan
- trustees

Over the rest of the century both groups were responsible for the development of public school athleticism, which in turn had a major influence on sport and sportsmanship in the United Kingdom and the World.

Figure C.37 outlines the determining features of the public schools of that time.

Public school definition

A definition of such a school is 'an endowed place of old standing to which the sons of gentlemen resort in considerable numbers and where they reside for eight or nine years to eighteen years of age'.

The characteristics of these schools are identified in the model (in figure C.37), where each component had a positive effect on the growth of athleticism.

Athleticism

Athleticism was originally defined as 'a muscular Christian view of manliness reflecting physical endeavour and moral integrity'. By the end of the 19th century, athleticism had become so popular that some authorities felt that it was undermining other educational values. Hence a second critical definition was given as 'the exultation and disproportionate regard for games, which often resulted in the denigration of academic work and in anti-intellectualism'.

The growth of this movement is best broken up into three stages:
- **Schoolboys recreations**.
- **Arnold and Christian gentlemen**.
- **Corinthian Athleticism**.

Schoolboys recreations

It is a case of linking developments in the schools with changes in society. At the beginning of the 19th century, communications were limited to carts, stage coaches and wagons. Only the **very wealthy** had the **time, money** and **transport** to travel any distance. As a result they were the only people with the tradition of their sons attending boarding schools away from home. It is important to mention that at this time the daughters of the very wealthy either had governesses or went to **academies** near to home (figure C.39).

Recreations within the first stage followed local folk customs and practices. With game laws in place, hunting and shooting were controlled by the upper classes, and traditional festivals were held in the towns and villages on occasional holy days and chartered fair days. The upper class played a courtly role and the lower classes made the most of a festival day, which of course was a day off from the grind of work.

The **boys** therefore took local **folk activities to school**, so that there were regular fights, mob games (figure C.38), cricket (of course), swimming in the river or open pools, and boating. Very few schools had hounds, so the young boys became the hares and the seniors chased them labelled as hounds.

Arnold and Christian gentlemen

By the third decade of the century, a **new breed of headmasters** were **reforming** their schools and starting to link Christianity with the Ancient Greek model of Mind, Body and Spirit. They chose to link the energy identifiable in the games and sports with education. The Headmaster would have led

figure C.38 – mob games

figure C.39 – cricket in an early girls academy

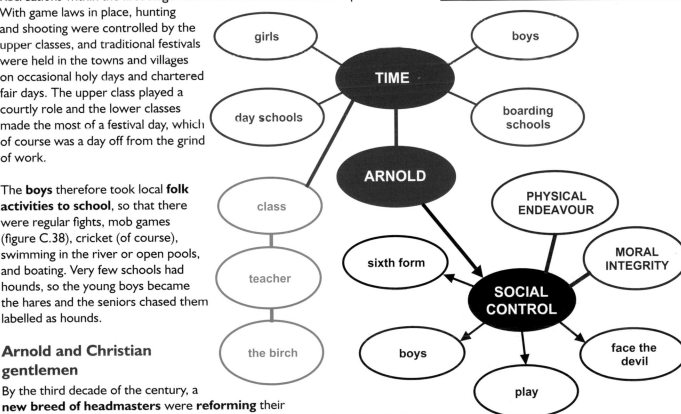
figure C.40 – Arnold and social control

the revised programmes, with prefects and junior members of staff establishing basic rules. House matches allowed healthy, social competition.

Social control (figure C.40, page 145) was an important objective of this process, in an attempt to reduce the bullying and lawlessness in the schools. Thomas Arnold is known to have led this reform, but much of his reputation comes from the book Tom Brown's Schooldays, rather than research evidence. In the eyes of Arnold and others, the **desire to produce Christian gentlemen** was central and the moral code of **fair play** was introduced at this level.

Corinthian athleticism and the emergence of rational recreation

With more regular play of games and sports, written rules were established. But because this was an internal programme, each school devised its own version of rules depending on the facilities available. Only the game of cricket had a set of universal rules across several different schools throughout the country at this time. Football and fives rules were different in each school. Swimming was popular wherever there were lakes, ponds or rivers available, as in the Duck Puddle bathing pool at Harrow (figure C.41).

At Eton boating was encouraged instead of swimming in the Thames, but Shrewsbury and Eton established safety rules that only those boys who could swim, could row.

As the schools and society changed to meet the energy and reforming zeal of Victorian England, so the lesser gentry and **industrial middle class** presumed the right to public boarding school education. They were not allowed into the Clarendon Schools and so they built new ones. These new schools had extensive sports facilities, were built in attractive spa towns and other wealthy areas, and were linked by the new **railway** system.

figure C.41 – the Harrow School Duck Puddle

figure C.42 – lacrosse as a girls' game

Middle class developments

The middle classes were not only wealthy and industrious, they wanted the status previously reserved for the gentry and they felt that the **public schools** would at least give that to their sons. Meanwhile, with some upper class women gaining access to Oxbridge, these women opened boarding schools for their daughters. This was eventually taken up by the middle class with a **girls' high school** opening in every major town.

Sport in public schools was now **widespread**, as teachers moved schools to obtain headships and took the notion of sport as part of a school with them. But certain idiosyncrasies remained, such as soccer and rugby having separate codes and fives having several versions. **Regular play** and **written codes** evolved as senior boys continued with sport at the **universities** and, as **old boys**, they continued to encourage athleticism in their old school and in amateur sport.

Girls' schools started with callisthenics and girls also played organised games based on similar principles to the boys. Established men's games were generally avoided. The girls played **hockey** and **lacrosse** (figure C.42) in the winter and **lawn tennis** in the summer, but cricket was often limited to junior girls.

Spreading the message

With the lead coming from university graduates, there was a focus on the things men had learnt at school and university. These men were experienced **all-round** sportsmen, often getting 'blues' in several sports at university. They formed **elite clubs** (for example, Leander for rowing and the Corinthians for cricket and soccer), setting a high standard of sportsmanship. This process was the basis of early **amateur governing bodies** and the birth of **rational recreation**.

See figure C.43 for an outline of the factors affecting the birth of rational recreation via the public schools.

The next step

In turn, young men drawn from the middle classes went back to their factories, commercial businesses and schools. There, they set up clubs for children, friends and salaried workers. This expansion led to benevolent businessmen forming **social and sports clubs** for their **workforce**. With this impact **physical education** was carried into grammar schools and later into primary and secondary comprehensive schools.

All this development reflected the improved wage structure for working men and the provision of town sports facilities. Specialist teacher training colleges were set up where physical educationists were trained.

The code set by the Governing Bodies held true to the amateur ethic until the last 30 years, when they reluctantly allowed amateur rules on financial aid to be revoked. Today, **professionalism** has taken over the status of most sports, but Governing Bodies continue to also represent grass roots development which has remained amateur. However, with media coverage showing regular examples of **gamesmanship and cheating**, it is increasingly difficult to maintain the importance of sportsmanship in sport. In spite of this trend in society, the teaching of **fair play** is still a basic principle underlying the role of physical education as an educational vehicle.

figure C.43 – the influence of non-local elements of 19th century public schools

Diagram nodes: NON-LOCAL — activities, popular recreation, regions, schools, EHCWWRS. MELTING POTS — universities oxford cambridge, teachers, clergy, industrialists, estates, army, career, rational recreation, colonial.

The development of physical activities within state elementary schools

The 20th century opened with the **Boer War** in South Africa and the extremely bad publicity which was given to Swedish drill in elementary schools, where blame was placed on the poor standard of physical fitness of young soldiers.

The Model Course

The result was an imposition of **military drill** by the War Office called the **Model Course** in 1902 (figure C.44). Regular soldiers went into the elementary schools (our present primary schools), and instructed boys and girls in a set of fixed exercises, originally designed for army recruits.

The aims were explicitly:

- To increase **fitness to fight**.
- To improve **discipline** at work and war.
- To help children to **understand hardship**.
- To teach them to be familiar with military **weapons**.

figure C.44 – exercises from the 1902 course

The content consisted of a series of set exercises by numbers and included marching and drill with staves, which took the place of rifles. The teaching method was direct **instruction**, with the whole class doing the same thing at the same time to numbers, as in the army itself.

It is difficult to understand what life was like, particularly in the larger towns at this time. Working class children were really poor, many suffering from malnutrition often without warm clothing and receiving harsh treatment at home. To read or see some of the Charles Dickens' stories will help you to understand that these children needed individual treatment and kindness, rather than oppressive instruction. Even girls were taught these drills even though there was no prospect of them joining the army.

The 1904 syllabus

Teachers and school authorities eventually rebelled against this oppressive system. Within two years the Model Course was thrown out and replaced by a Ministry of Education syllabus (the 1904 syllabus, see figure C.45) which reverted to the **Swedish** style of **Physical Training**, and was taught by **teachers**.

The objectives now hinged on:

- Sound **educational** principles.
- Some military exercises continued.
- All the exercises were based on **scientific principles**.
- Exercises were linked with health and **physical fitness**.
- A strong **disciplinary** approach, in the belief that this was necessary for working class children.
- The use of simple apparatus depending on its availability.

figure C.45 – exercises on the yard 1904

The content of each lesson was controlled by a carefully devised syllabus of **fixed exercises**, with some development as children progressed. These exercises systematically worked through different parts of the body in the belief that this would improve physique, fitness and general health. Some old style military elements, like marching, were still practised, partly because many schools did not have teachers with any training in the Swedish approach.

The teaching method remained direct with the whole class working **in unison**. To some extent this was necessary because of the **large groups**, the small playground space, and little or no apparatus available. Children were trained in lines with boys and girls doing the same exercises by numbers.

1909 and afterwards

The 1904 syllabus was followed by one in 1909, where the latter reflected the increased number of exercises envisaged, and an awareness that an increasing number of teachers were now trained to do this work.

figure C.46 – 1912 games in elementary schools

This Edwardian period reflected the affluent lifestyle of the upper classes. But the middle class gained confidence and status influenced by the dynamic energy of the great 1907 Liberal Government. The middle class sons and daughters were grounded in public school athleticism and this contributed to the volume of sport increasing in the Nation.

It was a time of improved wages and working class trade unionism. There was an acceptance that the tradesmen and skilled workers not only deserved a status in society, but that the working class in general should have increased work and leisure opportunities. Probably the most significant factor in the context of physical training, however, was the awareness that a healthy workforce was essential in an industrial nation. In 1912 attempts were made to include playground games for older children (figure C.46).

The 1919 syllabus

The First World War brought a halt to progress and delayed the next syllabus until 1919. This disastrous war not only led to a massive loss of life, but was followed by a 'flu' epidemic which almost killed as many survivors of that war as were actually killed in the war itself.

However, when a war ends, the winning side often has a spirit of idealism. This was reflected in the 1919 syllabus in that for the first time a separate programme was identified for children under seven years old. The main new element was the introduction of **play activities**, and with it the first signs of a 'free' approach and the recognition that children could learn through play. This resulted in guided teaching as well as direct instruction. Unfortunately, the rest of the syllabus remained formal with standard exercises done in unison.

At a conceptual level, therefore, the objective of learning through play was identified. But the major intention remained to improve the health and fitness of children, with some recognition of skills being learnt. This was happening in largely middle class grammar schools and middle class society, with the development of organised sport and games even in the smallest communities.

With the exception of play activities for the under sevens, the sophisticated structure of fixed Swedish exercises were continued, but with more alternatives and progressions.

This teaching style was certainly affected by play activities, largely because many schools had been run by women during and after the Great War, and pressure to return to a military policy was resisted. However, the formal exercise framework set limits on improvisation. Class teaching in lines continued, largely because classes were very large and facilities very limited.

The 1933 syllabus

figure C.47 – 1933 syllabus included gymnastics

The recovery of living standards in the UK continued into the 1930's and sport became popular among all classes. Also, between 1920 and 1930, secondary schools were being built in all towns to support those who did not go to grammar or private schools. These were built with good physical education facilities and so it was no surprise when the **1933 syllabus** was published that it contained games (figure C.47). This was the last syllabus, but certainly the most detailed and progressive. It took the **Swedish scientific principles** and presented them in a 20th century social setting. This reflected the emergence of a literate working class and an easier progression into skilled labour and trades.

The concepts still included the notion of health and fitness, but increased the significance of skills. Classes were decentralised into group work at the end of each lesson. This was the first step in recognising the importance of the individual child, and encouraged the extension of play activities for older children. This was now possible because there was normally a playground and at least the use of small equipment. These advances meant that physical training was changing into physical education.

figure C.48 – movement on frame apparatus

The influence on activities was considerable. Although systematic exercises were continued, there was a section in the syllabus which involved individual activities like cartwheels together with gymnastic skill which depended on the apparatus available. Minor games and relays became commonplace, and rotating group activities allowed small numbers to work in a rotating series of gymnastic skills. The teaching method in general was direct training, but during the introduction and group work, there was teaching at an individual level. In addition, for the first time there was also a competitive fun element in parts of the average lesson (see figure C.48).

Figure C.49 summarises the factors which outline the social setting in which physical education was able to grow between 1900 and 1950.

Post 1945

The Second World War not only meant that women teachers had to take the place of men (who were in the Forces), but there was considerable bombing which destroyed many of the schools. After the war, a major building programme resulted in a large number of new junior and secondary schools being built with indoor and outdoor sports facilities. Additionally, this war had been fought in a different way and so commando techniques using assault courses gave educational advisers the idea of adventurous apparatus. Also there was a double revolution involving idealistic aims of freedom of the individual and gender equality.

figure C.49 – social setting 1900-1950

- commercialised and spectatorism
- increasing diversity
- decentralised
- increased free time
- increased sporting standards
- **SOCIAL SETTING 1900-1950**
- respectable working classes
- financial crises
- industrial slumps
- universal education

The outcome was a Ministry book called '**Moving and Growing**' (see figure C.50 for an example of the type of activity) and a support text of activities called '**Planning the Programme**'. These changed the face of physical education, by putting the well-being of the individual child first. This meant that the children had a chance to select the activities they practised and were able to experience two new approaches called **Educational Gymnastics** and **Modern Dance**. These programmes were designed to engage children's interest and imagination, with skill sequences produced through guided rather than direct teaching.

figure C.50 – modern dance theme in action

In this way activity and skill learning were seen as an alternative way of achieving health and fitness in a post-war world, during which our Welfare State was established and child poverty was markedly diminished.

Over the last twenty years, some of this free expression has been reduced, given the pressure presented by rising standards and competitions in sport. The focus has to some extent changed from guided theme work to specific skills, with particular emphasis on games skills and tactics. Certainly the quality of specialist teacher training has helped this diversity of knowledge and the 'A' Level in PE gives teachers a sound theoretical background in their subject.

Characteristics of the key stages of the national curriculum for physical education

The belief that education in schools was best left to an advisory inspectorate, professional bodies and school staff, was shaken in the 1980's by a drop in standards. The result was the issue of a **National Curriculum** identifying four key stages in the Education Act of 1996. These key stages are coded as **Key Stage 1** (**KS1** – years 1-2, ages 5-7), **Key Stage 2** (**KS2** – years 3-6, ages 7-11), **Key Stage 3** (**KS3** – years 7-9, ages 11-14), and **Key Stage 4** (**KS4** – years 10-11, ages 14-16).

In this Education Act, physical education was recognised as a non-core **foundation subject** which made it compulsory, with a note that **two hours a week** of physical activity, including the National Curriculum for Physical Education and extra-curriculum activities, should exist in all schools. This applied throughout all key stages. The reaction by school staff was that this was less than the best primary schools were already doing, but subsequent trends have been to increase primary PE time to approaching an hour a day.

Today's curriculum offers children of different ages a variety of activities (table 32). It is a compulsory part of education and is becoming increasingly important as the health of the nation is decreasing due to increases in obesity and heart disease. The government currently aims to increase the exposure of physical activity among school age young people to 5 hours per week (called the **5-hour offer**).

National Curriculum for Physical Education 'PE makes your heart beat faster'.

Summaries of the activities (table 32), concepts (table 33) and principles (table 34) are to be found in the following three tables.

Table 32 - **National Curriculum for Physical Education – activity list**

KS1 (5-7yrs)	KS2 (7-11yrs)	KS3 (11-14yrs)	KS4 (14-16yrs)
games	games	games	games
gym	gym	gym	
dance	dance	dance	
	swimming	athletics	
	and a choice between athletics & OAA	and a choice between swimming & OAA	and one other area of activity from KS 2 & 3

Figures C.51, C.52, C.53 show examples of types of activity at KS2 or KS3.

figure C.51 – KS2 sports day

figure C.52 – KS2 outdoor activities

figure C.53 – KS2 swimming

Table 33 - **National Curriculum for Physical Education – basic concepts**

KS1 (5-7yrs)	KS2 (7-11yrs)	KS3 (11-14yrs)	KS4 (14-16yrs)
natural enthusiasm for movement	play, skill experiences and enjoyment	become more expert in skills and techniques	achieve physical competence and confidence in a range of activities
explore and learn about their world	development of imagination and creativity	understand what makes a performance effective / begin to apply this to own and others' activity	achieve physical skilfulness and discover abilities / aptitudes / enable the confidence to get involved in exercise and activity out of school and later
watching, listening and experimenting	co-operation and competition	begin to take initiative and make decisions for self and others	gain knowledge of the body in action, promoting health and well-being / personal fitness
individually, in pairs and small groups	rigour of athletic experiences	identify types of activity preferred	decide on roles in terms of performer / coach / leader / official / choreographer
skills in movement and co-ordination	challenge of the natural outdoors	take a variety of roles including leader / official	learn competitiveness / creativity / face up to challenge
enjoy expressing and testing themselves	.	.	learn how to plan / perform / evaluate

Table 34 - **principles of the National Curriculum**

KS1 (5-7yrs)	KS2 (7-11yrs)	KS3 (11-14yrs)	KS4 (14-16yrs)
fundamental motor skills	furthering of motor skills	refine motor skills	undertaking different roles – official / player / coach
sequences of movement	co-ordination developed	learn rules / tactics of games	preparing training programmes for specific sports
individual and pair work	more complex movement patterns	learn more complex movements	refining skills and tactical knowledge
understand and recognise effect of exercise the body	experience, understand and maintain sustained period of exercise	learn how to prepare for and recover from activities	understand theoretical principles on which exercise programmes are based

These were the far-reaching aims, which teachers were obliged to make a basis of their programme, with the expectation that an inspectorate would assess the level achieved through **OFSTED**.

STUDENT NOTE

The National Curriculum booklet for Key Stages 3 and 4 will be available in your school or college and you will be able to identify the aims of each of these.

Key Stage 3 for 11-14 year olds is at present under review, but is part of an on-going progression from primary to secondary education. Sadly, in the past, many secondary school departments knew nothing about the programmes going on in the primary school and, anyway, a mixed school intake meant the non-existence of an overall pattern. This handbook has been a useful source of information as to the stage of accomplishment of this age group. This is particularly while part of the country is still operating a middle school system, while others have returned to the secondary intake at 11+. An excellent development in specialist secondary schools is that of appointing staff with special responsibility to liaise with their intake primary schools.

Key Stage 4 is terminated by the **National GCSE Examination** and this is offered by several Boards, with minor variations but the same general characteristics.

The factors influencing the provision in schools

Three terms are normally used to encompass the factors influencing physical education provision in schools. These are **opportunity**, **provision** and **esteem** (figure C.54).

figure C.54 – the provision axis

Opportunity

Opportunity means that you look at:

- The **time** you have in school or college for physical education and sport.
- Also **time** spent in physical activity outside school.
- You need to explain the **level** at which these initiatives are available to you.
- The **degree** to which staff are able or willing to meet the initiative objectives.

Provision

Provision takes you into limits imposed by the **availability** and **affordability** of facilities, their quality, quantity and convenience, and the existence of adequate **equipment** and its affordability.

Esteem

Finally, the impact of these initiatives depends on:

- The **esteem** you and your friends have in relation to them.
- The **attitudes** of the teachers and head teachers.
- The **attitudes** of significant others, such as family, friends and those involved in promoting these initiatives in the community.

Efficiency of provision

To **evaluate** this area, you need to include influences (see figure C.55 on page 153) outside the school such as funding, organisation and the impact of governing bodies. It is then possible to discuss the **impact** of these **initiatives** on young people, and this requires a balanced analysis of significant **agencies** and administrative **factors** and the degree to which these are **efficient** or **deficient**. The easiest way is to see this is in a number of linked tiers as in figure C.55.

To **evaluate** the impact of sports' performance initiatives on young people and school club links, you need to make a case using **your** knowledge and experience **in** and **out** of school. The **initiatives** are easily identified from those already described. These initiatives can be looked at in terms of their influence on the **school curriculum** and **extra-curriculum** in your school, and also for yourselves and other young people in your **community**. Probably the best way is to retain a **focus** throughout on how **efficient** or **deficient** these initiatives are and use a framework known to you, such as looking at them in terms of **opportunity**, **provision** and **esteem**.

The effects of developing school-club links

In 2000, Sport England produced the document 'A Sporting Future for All', which led to an action plan 'The Government's Plan for Sport'. This document set out the government's plans for modernisation of organisations involved in sport, and produced '**Game Plan**' (2002), which sets out a strategy (figure C.56) for delivering the nation's physical activity objectives.

Game Plan

This acknowledged the fact that a large number of British people take part in sport or physical activity without Government involvement, but states that Government has a role in widening opportunities to participate in order to:

- **Reduce the growing costs** of inactivity in terms of the health of the population.
- **Improve success** in international competition.

Four recommendations were made:

- **Grass roots participation** - the focus would be on disadvantaged groups, particularly women, young people, and older people. Barriers to participation and failures in provision of coaching and facilities are identified as worthy of development.

- **High performance sport** - the priority for funding of sport at the top level would be made. This includes the identification and development of talent which could aspire to top level performance.

- **Mega sporting events** - the assessment of the balance of benefits and costs should be taken by Government before agreeing to hosting top events.

- **Delivery** - National investment in sport has to be justified in terms of whether or not organisational reform would work, and how the voluntary, public and private sectors can co-operate towards common goals.

figure C.55 – efficiency of provision

figure C.56 – Game Plan

In terms of school sport, official policy asserts that education has a pivotal function in improving participation in sport (it is also acknowledged that sport can have an equal effect on education).

Facilities available in schools are often not used except during school hours, and voluntary sector facilities are often used only at the weekends or evenings. One of the main aims of policy is to link together both education and voluntary sectors so that facilities are used more efficiently.

Initiatives

Physical Education and School Sport Club Links

The Physical Education and School Sport Club Links (**PESSCL**) strategy (figure C.57) is a policy jointly delivered by the **DfES** (Department for Education and Schools) and **DCMS** (Department for Culture, Media and Sport). This strategy has eight components:

- **Sports Colleges**.
- **School Sports Partnerships**.
- **Gifted and Talented**.
- **Swimming**.
- **Step into Sport**.
- **School / Club links** (see page 153).
- **QCA PE and School Sport Investigation**.
- **Professional Development**.

The main aim of this strategy is to improve the participation of 5 to 16 year olds in physical activity. It will be expected that all children will spend at least two hours per week on high quality physical education or sport. A recent survey has found that in 2007 86% of children between KS1 and KS4 achieved the '2 hour offer'. The government is putting into place plans for five hours of quality PE / sport per week for this age group, known as the '5 hour offer'. This will include extra-curricular sports / activities.

figure C.57 – PESSCL strategy

Sports Colleges · School Sports Partnerships · professional development · PESSCL · Gifted and Talented · swimming · QCA PE and School Sport · School / Club links · Step into Sport

Sports Colleges

Sports Colleges were established by the **Youth Sports Trust** to bring into action the government policy on school academies for sport in the age group 11 to 16. There are approximately 475 Sports Colleges in England and Wales (in November 2008), each with extra funding for facilities and staff to improve participation and develop excellence in sport among their pupils. Such facilities and expertise should also be available to feeder junior schools.

These schools are particularly targeted for the 2 hours per week of PE or sport for every child. They aim to improve the expertise of their staff (in terms of coaching and knowledge of sports), and make all possible use of new technologies when encouraging and developing participation in physical activity.

School Sport Partnerships (SSPs)

Sports colleges are at the centre of the SSP infrastructure (see figure C.58). School Sports Partnerships (SSPs) are groups of schools working together to develop PE and sport opportunities for all young people.

A typical partnership consists of:

- A partnership development manager (PDM).
- Up to eight school sport co-ordinators (SSCos).
- Between 30-45 primary and special school link teachers (PLTs).

A **PDM** is a full-time role usually based within a Sports College. They manage the SSP and develop strategic links with key partners in sport and the wider community. For example, part

figure C.58 – a typical SSP model

PDM in a Sports College · SSCo · PLT

of their role is to link school and local facilities (that tend to operate separately from the schools sector) to large numbers of school pupils who participate in and enjoy physical activity in school, but find it difficult to continue once school finishes. This applies to weekends and school holidays for younger school pupils, as well as what happens when students leave school or college at 16 or 18.

An **SSCo** is a member of the PDM's team based in a secondary school and who concentrates on the day-to day task of improving school sport opportunities, including out of hours school learning, intra and inter-school competition and club links, across the local family of schools within the SSP.

PLTs are part of the PDM team, based in primary and special schools. Their role is to improve the quantity and quality of PE and sport in their own schools.

Those going to Higher Education have their university facilities available (but not necessarily used to the full), and such students have postponed the break from a relatively organised and well-structured sporting existence. When people leave full-time education, many of them do not know how or where to join a club. Since most people in this category have to work for a living, these clubs or opportunities must offer 'out of working hours' sporting arrangements.

Hence the function of the SSP is to provide links from schools to clubs and co-ordinate use of facilities. In addition **Sports Competition Managers** assist in the provision school-based competition. A highly successful example is the growth of the **Sports Hall Athletics** annual competition, which starts at a local school level and proceeds to the National finals.

Started in September 2009, Further Education Colleges have designated a specialist physical education manager to stimulate or encourage increased participation in physical activities.

Gifted and Talented

The Youth Sport Trust manages the Gifted and Talented strand of the government's Physical Education, School Sport and Club Links (PESSCL) strategy.

The YST supports schools in identifying and supporting talented pupils in PE and sport, by helping them realise their full potential - both in sport and education - through a co-ordinated support programme. Gifted and Talented programmes focus not only on high achievers but also on those who show sporting potential, including pupils at risk of underachieving and those from disadvantaged areas.

Swimming

Currently, the Government is encouraging (with grant aid) free swimming for school children and pensioners. This scheme will operate up until the 2012 London Olympics.

Step into Sport – Sportsleaders UK

Sport relies on 1.5 million volunteer officials, coaches, administrators and managers. The government has identified a gap in the plans for expansion of participation of people in sport at all levels. This is the need for more instructors / coaches / leaders in sport. The purpose of the **Step in Sport** programme is the increase the quality, quantity and diversity of young people engaged in volunteering and leadership.

- **Sportsleaders UK** is a trust (formerly The British Sports Trust) which provides opportunities for young people aged 14–19 particularly to obtain a qualification which can be recognised by those organising sports events at local or national levels.
- **Sportsleaders UK** can give experience in how to organise activities and how to motivate and communicate with people.
- **Sportsleader courses** encourage volunteering in community activities and aim to reduce youth crime by including vulnerable young people in positive activities.

There are **four** levels of awards (promoted by Sportsleaders UK / YST):

- The Junior Sports Leader Award (**JSLA**) for 14-16 year olds, graduated into **3 STEPS**:
  1. **STEP ON:** Students learn to plan, manage and run their own sports season as part of their PE programme.
  2. **STEP IN: TOP Link** focuses on how schools can utilise KS4 (14-16 year olds). Students become active volunteers. For example, supporting inter-school competition. Volunteers are awarded the NGB Introductory Leadership Award.
  TOP Activity extends into how to plan, manage and deliver festival of sport and dance.
  Both TOP Link and TOP Activity form part of the TOP programme (see figure C.60 on page 156).

3. STEP OUT: This aspect of Step into Sport is on the movement of young people from school-based volunteering to community-based volunteering through the provision of placements in high quality community clubs. Young people are supported by their school mentor and county sport partnership (CSP) to source a volunteer placement. The final stage of the STEP OUT programme is the **Step into Sport On-line Volunteer Passport** and it allows every young volunteer to log and manage their volunteering online and supports volunteers to qualify in NGB specific coaching awards.

- The Community Sports Leader Award (**CSLA**) for the 16+ age group.
- The High Sports Leader Award (**HSLA**) develops CLSA award holders to be able to lead specific groups such as the disabled or junior children, includes first-aid and event management, and can lead to sports coaching awards.
- The Basic Expedition Leader Award (**BELA**) is aimed at people who would like to safely lead outdoor activities and organise overnight camps.

Active Sports

The **Active Sports programme** (figure C.59) is a Sport England initiative aimed at encouraging an increase in participation through liaison between local providers such as schools, clubs, local authorities and community groups.

A young person wanting to continue with sport (after leaving school) will eventually be involved in:

- Continuing involvement in club sport.
- Continuing involvement in a sport's governing body performance programme.
- Fast-tracking into the world class programme.

figure C.59 – Active Sports

- governing body
- club sport
- world class programme
- **ACTIVE SPORTS**
- World Class Programme
- Active Schools
- Active Community

Hence this is the **sport** view of the school – sport partnership (via the DCMS). The participation targets are looked at from the point of view of individual sports and in terms of the adult / community population.

There are **three** strands to Active Sports:

- **Active Schools** - looks at opportunities for children to participate at foundation level.
- **Active Communities** - looks at reducing the post-student gap.
- **World Class Programme** - looks at talent identification, linking the most talented potential performers with the Governing Bodies' structure for development into National Team membership.

TOP programme

- Two elements of the TOP programme have already been mentioned above – TOP Link and TOP Activity in relation to the Step into Sport initiative.
- This is another Youth Sports Trust organised programme for children to experience sporting activities, which they would not normally encounter. This includes equipment for each targeted age group, and the training and provision of teachers to deliver the activities.
- For example, **TOP Tots** caters for children 18 months to 3 years to learn and understand about simple games and activities. **TOP Start** is for children aged 3 to 5 years to have a go at a broad range of activities, and so on (see figure C.60).

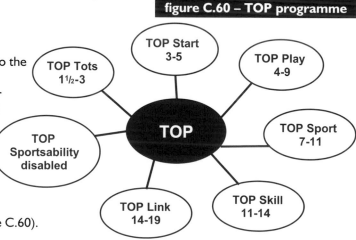

figure C.60 – TOP programme

- TOP Tots 1½-3
- TOP Start 3-5
- TOP Play 4-9
- **TOP**
- TOP Sport 7-11
- TOP Sportsability disabled
- TOP Skill 11-14
- TOP Link 14-19

Young Ambassador's Programme

Each year until 2012, school sport partnerships across England will recruit two young people each year, selected by the PDM, to take on the role of **Young Ambassador** for two years.

In their first year, they work in their local communities championing sport and the ethos and values of the Olympic and Paralympic movement. In their second year, they take on a mentoring role with the new Young Ambassador intake. By 2012, there will be 5,000 young people that will have been trained through this programme.

For further information about all these initiatives visit: www.youthsportstrust.org

The role of national governing bodies

The ultimate opportunity for the British Government lies in the success of the **2012 Olympic Games** in London. People from virtually every nation will be there or observing by television.

If this has **political** and **publicity** value, then **financially** the Games are a huge outlay and gamble, not only in their commercial success, but the long-term value of holding them.

The advantages to **British sports men and women** are available if we can take them. The effort made to get performers up to standard will be unequalled over the next few years and will be reflected in funding and positive attitudes to physical education and sport after that.

figure C.61 – London 2012 logo

Take note of the London 2012 logo (figure C.61) and the slogans:

- 'Winning just got easier'.
- 'We are LondONErs'.

UK Sport

UK Sport is responsible for managing and distributing public investment and is a statutory distributor of funds raised by the **National Lottery**. This body is accountable to Parliament through the Department for Culture, Media and Sport (http://www.culture.gov.uk), and UK Sport's aim is to work in partnership to lead sport in the UK to world-class success. Its goals are given the title '**World Class Performance**' which is aimed to meet the challenge of the 2012 London Olympic Games.

The home countries of the United Kingdom are served by subdivisions of **UK Sport**, in effect the Home Country Sports Councils: **Sport England, Cyngor Chwaraeon Cymru, Sport Northern Ireland**, and **Sport Scotland** and they distribute lottery funding to the grassroots of sport.

See figure C.62 below for a diagram of the bodies involved in UK sport which promote participation.

figure C.62 – bodies promoting participation

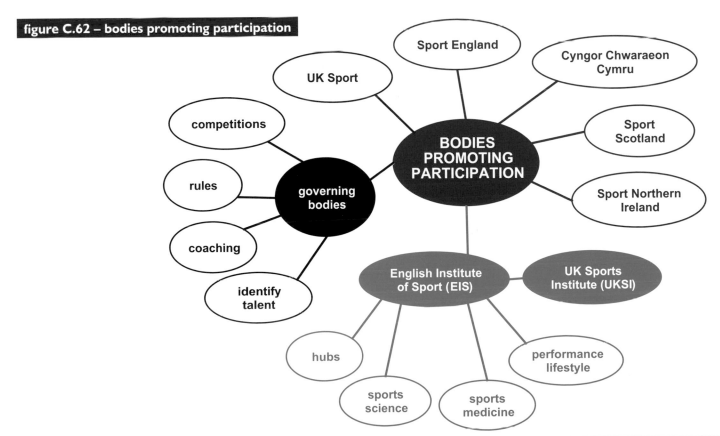

The UK Sports Institute

The **UKSI** is a body, funded by UK Sport and the Lottery, which co-ordinates elite sport development in the UK. Its **Athlete Medical Scheme** has replaced the **British Olympic Association's Olympicare** to provide the UK's top Olympic and Paralympic athletes with free injury treatment. It also organises and sponsors world class **Coaching Conferences,** which presents the UK's top coaches with opportunities to gain new insights and skills to develop future World, Olympic and Paralympic Champions.

The **UKSI** devolves its regional responsibilities into the **Home Country Institutes**, for example, the **English Institute of Sport** (EIS).

The EIS is a network of world class support services:
* Nine regional **multi-sport hub sites**.
* An evolving network of **satellite** centres.
* The **Performance Lifestyle Programme** which provides supplementary career and education advice.
* Sports science and sports medicine:
    * Applied physiology.
    * Biomechanics.
    * Psychology.
    * Medical consultation and screening.
    * Nutritional advice.
    * Conditioning and performance analysis.
    * Sports vision.

UK governing bodies

These bodies are responsible for:
* Establishing the rules.
* Organising national competitions.
* Coaching within each individual sport.
* Picking teams for international competition.

NGBs operate within the **international governing body** umbrella, for example, the IAAF for athletics, and FIFA for soccer. Those with **Olympic** participation will select teams for the Olympic Games and will abide by the Olympic rules for eligibility in respect of residence and drug status, and hence are obliged to implement a stringent anti-drug enforcement policy. **Governing body** and **government policy on participation** revolves around identifying talent and giving as many young people as possible the opportunity to learn and develop their sport.

Government and governing body initiatives

These initiatives are discussed in figures C.55 and C.60 on pages 153 and 156 respectively.

* **Sport for All Active Programme**:
    * The **Coaching for Teachers Programme** through sports coach UK.
    * **Sports Mark** for secondary children.
    * **Active Mark** for primary and middle schools.
* The **Youth Sports Trust**:
    * **TOP Sport**.
    * **TOP Play**.
    * **Sports Development Officers**, whose salaries are funded jointly by the YST and local authorities.
* Community focus on **target groups** and **disadvantaged areas**, with awards and competitions in the community for young people. Sports administration is jointly held by schools, governing bodies, clubs and local authorities.

A **five year development programme** produced by Sport England includes **nine priority sports** for development:

* Athletics.
* Basketball.
* Cricket.
* Women's football.
* Netball.
* Hockey.
* Rugby union.
* Swimming.
* Tennis.

Excellence and participation in sport in the United Kingdom

The sports development pyramid

This is a participation pyramid (figure C.63) which demonstrates how from a broad base or **foundation** activity, where many people try things out and play many different activities, a proportion of these people would progress to **participation**, where particular sports become important at the basic competitive level.

A smaller number become involved at a higher level, which involves training and directed activity where **performance** is improving, and from this group would emerge a much smaller group who would have the talent and ability to reach a stage of excellence which could be described as **elite performance**.

figure C.63 – sports development pyramid

excellence — National standard. public recognition.

performance — coaching & development. done at club & regional levels.

participation — increasing leisure options & HRF awareness. promoted via extra-curricular sport.

foundation — learning basic skills, knowledge & understanding, often delivered in PE programmes in schools.

Sporting excellence

The notion of sporting excellence presumes that individuals have the potential talent, ability and enthusiasm, have the coaching **opportunities** to continue to improve, and the **provision** of facilities near enough to be feasible for regular travel. The **multi-sports High Performance Centres, 'hubs'** provided by the **Sports Councils** and the **Institutes of Sport** for elite sportspeople, are intended to be located within 1 hours travel time of a million people, and 30 minutes travel time of 250,000. What is happening is that **Governing Bodies** are insisting that members of the **World Class Performance (WCP)** groups locate themselves near to a hub, so that coaching and medical support can also be provided simply and at less cost. Membership of a **WCP** group or **National Squad** carries great intrinsic and extrinsic **esteem** in terms of adulation from the press and people who follow the sport. This stimulates high motivation to succeed.

Practice questions

1) What were the **main** components of the 1902 Model Course? — *3 marks*

2) What were the **major** changes which reflected post-Second World War attitudes to movement in physical education lessons in schools? — *5 marks*

3) Describe the basic organisational framework of Sport in the UK. — *4 marks*

4) Young people often fail to continue with sport once they have left full-time education. Explain the reasons why this might happen. — *3 marks*

5) Explain the advantages of offering activities such as tennis and basketball as part of a physical education programme in year 11 in school. — *4 marks*

6) Identify the theory behind the sports development pyramid and explain the intentions behind each section. — *6 marks*

7) Discuss the changing attitude to sport in the elite 19th century Public Schools and its affect on the emergence of amateur sport in the UK. — *5 marks*

8) Discuss the role of Sports Colleges in the development of School Sport Partnerships (SSPs). — *4 marks*

9) UK Sport is responsible for managing and distributing a sporting programme. How do the UK Sports Institutes co-ordinate elite sport development within the UK? — *4 marks*

The terms which reflect equal opportunity in British sport

Participation in physical activity and the achievement of **sporting excellence** by young people are affected by social status, personal financial circumstances, ability to travel and having the time to participate.

Additionally there are the specific areas of **discrimination**. These are gender, disability, status, ethnicity and age. Once again it is possible to examine these areas of discrimination using the dimensions of **opportunity**, **provision** and **esteem**.

See figure C.64 for a summary of terms.

Opportunity

In terms of **mass participation** in physical activity, the **opportunity** lies within the facilities available (privately or publicly funded), or the willingness of the sportsperson to pay for them.

figure C.64 – equal opportunity

opportunity

discrimination

EQUAL OPPORTUNITY

prejudice

stereotyping

inclusiveness

In order to **participate**, people must have the **time** and **money**, and be able to **travel** on a regular basis to a facility. Some sports centres give **special rates** to unemployed or elderly people, specifically to improve participation in these groups. Choice of sport may be restricted, depending on where a person lives, and this influences the **provision** for sport.

For example, if he or she lives in a rural situation, it may be impossible to travel to a distant town to take advantage of the provision of rowing, tennis or athletics facilities. However, these people may be able to afford weight training equipment in the home, or go road running around the local lanes. To enable more people to participate within a local facility, it will be important for a centre to be included on public transport routes, and to be well-equipped and clean. It is important that people have the desire to participate and that is where **self-esteem** needs to be boosted. This idea is linked to how people view their place in sport and in society, where social status and **peer group participation** may be a major influence. Having friends who take part in sport is a powerful incentive to join in.

Discrimination

Deliberate **social discrimination** is largely a thing of the past in that, legally and by general public consent, discrimination should not exist in our **democratic society**.

In the past, there have been groups of **advantaged** people, primarily reflecting **social class** differences. Also the traditional place of **women** in society, and attitudes to **disabled** people have produced discrimination. In addition, newly arriving **ethnic** groups, particularly those from the old colonies, have been discriminated against on their arrival. There is little doubt that vestiges of this discrimination still exist among groups of people, but this is being fought against at individual, group and government level, especially in sport. The best example of this is probably the association football slogan '**Let's Kick Racism out of Football**'.

Stereotyping

In most cases of discrimination against groups of people in our society, **stereotypes** have been formed (figure C.65), largely justifying the **presumed inferiority** of these groups. Basically, stereotyping concerns the attitudes of parts of the population about the place and capability of other parts of the population. Usually, this takes the form of assumed inferiority, which may be based on **tradition, gender, genetics / ethnicity, wealth, age** or even a resistance to change.

figure C.65 – stereotyping in sport?

An example of stereotyping which presumes **superiority** in certain activities is that of the attitude of some of the white population to participation of black people in sport. The stereotype is that black people are more likely to be good at sport, but less likely to be good at academic studies. Here the stereotype has a plus and a minus **assumed** capability. Another example is that of **women** in strength, endurance and contact sports. The stereotype assumes that female sportspeople are less capable at these activities.

Inclusiveness

It has been a fundamental feature of Government policy in recent years to **include all members** of society in whatever activities are available to the majority.

figure C.66 – disabled athletics are included?

This contrasts in the past to the effective **exclusion** of certain parts of the population from some activities which most people would normally expect to do. On a very basic level, the attitude of the majority of the population to the disabled 100 years ago was to separate certain disabled people into inferior education facilities. The most disabled were locked up in asylums (mental hospitals). Such people were looked after, but not allowed participation in main-stream society.

Today there is a very strong move to engage disabled people in all aspects of society including sport (participation in the Paralympics is an example of this, see figure C.66), and this is an example of **inclusiveness**.

The same thing used to happen to some extent for the elderly. Stereotypes of the elderly used to be that people over 60 were past it, and not capable of enjoying sporting activity. Nowadays, older people are **included** in all plans for sports facilities – and this can be productive for health as well as **self-esteem** and confidence of the people involved.

Government policy on inclusion encompasses a much wider brief than sport. Unemployment, poor skills, low incomes, poor housing, high crime, bad health and family breakdown are the very broad reasons for this policy. Sport as a vehicle for improving health and reducing crime is therefore an important element of official inclusion policy.

Prejudice

Prejudice can be defined as '**a prejudgement of a person, group, or situation usually based on inadequate information or inaccurate or biased information which reinforces stereotypes**'.

Prejudice is the outcome of negative attitudes and stereotyping by one part of the population towards another part of the population. An example of this is that women are often excluded from male dominated sports clubs or events. It is expected that females will not be interested or want to participate in the sport in question (golf, rugby, boxing). A further element of prejudice is that the minority feelings or opinions about the situation are ignored. People prejudiced against female participation usually do not listen to or believe arguments that women should be allowed to participate.

For these reasons, **target groups** have been identified in sport so that all participants can have equal opportunity to participate. This is an on-going campaign in this country where the slogan of '**Sport for All**' is not yet achievable because of continued discrimination. This is also because of inadequate funding and lack of available facilities for the under privileged.

Barriers and solutions regarding certain target groups

Disability

The term **disability** implies loss of ability in certain activities due to **impairment**. Impairment covers various categories including:

- Mental, visual, and hearing impairments.
- Cerebral Palsy.
- Les autres.
- Quadriplegic and paraplegic conditions.
- Amputees.

There has always been a conflict of attitude between ability and disability in the context of sport, since most conditions have little or no effect on the capability of a person to **participate** in and enjoy sporting activities. **Opportunity** is often limited by the **attitudes** of the able-bodied (figure C.68), and also by the low **self-esteem** by some who suffer from impairments. The main issue being tackled is **access**, where public sport facilities are now required to have ramps and wide doorways to allow wheelchair access. The **Paralympic Games** and numerous marathons have highlighted disabled people's potential success at world level.

Social class

The underlying exclusiveness of certain activities lies in the traditional division of British society into **social classes**. Historically this has been based on power, where the strong dominated the weak in terms of the wealthy controlling the poor. For example, the serfs used to till the land belonging to the landed rich. This was due in the first instance to the ownership of land, and later due to the control of the workplace in industrialised Britain. Additionally, women, the disabled, the aged and immigrants have been discriminated against as part of these social constraints.

Because sport was part of these **exclusive** phases in the growth of our society, discrimination can be identified in sport as it reflected **power and influence**. For example, only the upper class was allowed to hunt in the 18th century, only the gentry

figure C.67 – mob football, a social class thing?

went to the public schools in the early years of 19th century athleticism. Only the middle class and above could afford bicycles until the end of the 19th century and so on.

Today, there are traditions where certain groups try to maintain their class identity through sport. For example, sports involving horses still have an upper class association, while certain games are popular among working class groups. In the case of football, this is probably the result of historic links with traditional mob football (figure C.67). None of these activities are exclusive, but represent vestiges of a past in which there was resistance to change because of tradition, cost and fashion. There has been no direct attempt to target the more exclusive upper class sports other than the recent ban on hunting, which was based more on its presumed cruelty than its exclusiveness.

Ethnicity

Race and **ethnic** difference issues include the view that **Asian** communities who have emigrated from Kenya and Uganda into Britain have not regarded sport as a career route. Others from the Indian sub-continent have been too busy surviving and coping with the English language to participate widely in sport. In some areas, Asian soccer and cricket leagues are producing good teams with outstanding players. Many female Asian Moslems have tended to have had limited opportunities in sport.

figure C.68 – Vonette Flowers

The first black woman to win a medal at the winter Olympics

The **Afro-Carribean** ethnic community brought cricket with them and love their cricket and have shown outstanding ability in boxing, soccer and athletics.

Some of this may be a reflection of American cultural attitudes, with its high profile and role models in boxing, American football and basketball. Nowadays, black British sportspeople, male and female, have a substantial place in all our sporting activities and demonstrate a natural ability and enthusiasm. There are relatively few soccer spectators with an ethnic background, probably due to resistance from existing fans. Racism on the ground has been largely stopped as a result of the policy of '**Let's Kick Racism out of Football**'.

Gender

Traditionally, **women** have participated less in sport than men. This was because **Victorian attitudes** to women led to females being excluded from rational sport on the grounds that it was too manly and could endanger childbirth. **Fashions** among the upper and middle classes in terms of restrictive clothing prevented freedom of movement and also discouraged women from vigorous activity. This was extended to include any activity which brought women's femininity into question, such as competition, sweating and display of bodies.

Upper class women, with abundant **free time and status**, excluded themselves from this **stereotype** and developed selective sports on their own private land and in private schools. On the other hand, lower class women were obliged to work to supplement their husband's wages, as well as bring up their families. This meant that lower class women had very **limited free time** and no place in working men's sports. Modern feminist movements have advanced the rights of women in sport, but this trend is still resisted by some men and women. Only a minority of games involve women on equal terms (for example equestrianism).

Combat sports such as boxing and wrestling are generally deemed undesirable for women. Ladies' rugby is becoming increasingly popular, even though in many cases women have only associate membership in male clubs.

Figure C.69 outlines the factors which limit modern female participation in sport via the elements of opportunity, provision and esteem. That an outstanding athlete like Paula Radcliffe (figure C.70) should succeed in having her profile enhanced, and that anything to do with her health and well-being should be of interest to the UK's media, is a comment on how far gender equality has moved in this country. There is still a long way to go.

figure C.69 – the gender axis

figure C.70 – Paula Radcliffe superstar

Age

There is little doubt that our education system is trying to give physical education the status it should have and the opportunity to give children every opportunity to participate in sport, and for the talented to be recognised through the introduction of specialist schools and colleges for sport. However, in the private sector there is still a resistance to **junior** membership in clubs.

Restriction on **elderly** participation in physical recreation and sport is due to the **outmoded stereotypical views** that exercise by the old can be fatal, that to be elderly is to be inactive, and that ageing makes one incapable of enjoying competitive physical activity.

In reality, regular physical activity and sport for the elderly is most **valuable** in terms of physical health (figure C.71), morale and self-esteem. **Opportunities** have increased in which many sports governing bodies have their veteran / masters policy which has resulted in a huge uptake for each veteran age group. **Access** to centres offering exercise and recreational facilities has been a major problem, but non-peak periods during the day are now offered free or at low cost to the elderly in many sports centres. The main problem is the lack of **esteem** of elderly females brought up as non-participants in sport, but aerobics has grown in popularity with this group of women.

figure C.71 – exercise while ageing

This identification of **age** with **disability**, represents a minority group within each of the three main discriminated groups and is easily overlooked, but should be an additional area to recognise as a focus for **inclusiveness** in sport.

Practice questions

1) Opportunities available to people in society determine participation in sporting activities.
   a) Explain the term 'inclusiveness'. — 2 marks
   b) Explain the term 'stereotyping'. — 2 marks
   c) Explain the term 'prejudice'. — 2 marks

2) Identify the problems faced by the disabled in the sporting context and outline ways in which some of these problems have been addressed. — 5 marks

3) Mass participation in sport includes a policy of 'Sport for All'.
   Why is the chance to participate desirable, but the policy of 'Sport for All' difficult to implement? — 6 marks

4) Discuss the terms opportunity, provision and esteem in the context of female discrimination in sport. — 5 marks

5) The National Sports Councils have a role to play of identifying and targeting minority sub-cultures who for various reasons do not fully participate in Active Sport.
   a) What are the **main** reasons why young women do not have as high a profile as their male counterparts in sport in the UK? — 4 marks
   b) Suggest **four** reasons why young children should be discouraged from specialising in a particular sport too early. — 4 marks
   c) Suggest reasons why women over 47 years of age participate in sport less than any other minority sub-group. — 4 marks
   d) Explain the contradiction that there are many black professional soccer players, but very few black soccer spectators. — 4 marks

6) Suggest reasons why rugby football is still only played by a small proportion of women. — 4 marks

7) Explain the popularity of track and field athletics to Afro-Caribbean (A-C) performers. — 4 marks

ANSWERS TO QUESTIONS

SECTION A – UNITS 1 & 2
ANATOMY & PHYSIOLOGY

SECTION B – UNITS 1 & 2
SKILL ACQUISITION

SECTION C – 1, 3 & 4
OPPORTUNITIES FOR PARTICIPATION

UNIT 1 – HEALTH, EXERCISE, FITNESS & NUTRITION

1) Name and define **two** main components of health-related fitness required by an elite swimmer. Explain how these components are used in this sport.

4 marks

Answer

- *Muscular endurance.*
- *Flexibility.*

Explanation:

- *Muscular endurance is needed to maintain repeated contractions of working muscles in training and racing situations without undue fatigue.*
- *Flexibility is needed to produce an efficient and effective stroke, for example the butterfly stroke requires great flexibility.*

2) a) What is meant by the term specific fitness?

2 marks

Answer

- *Specific fitness is a task-oriented definition.*
- *Based on the ability to perform specific aspects of sports or occupations.*

b) Compare the fitness components essential for an elite sprinter with those required by an elite marathon runner.

4 marks

Answer

- *Sprinters and marathon runners need completely different components of health-related and skill-related fitness.*
- *Sprinters need strength, flexibility, power, speed,*
- *Reaction time, good balance and co-ordination from starting blocks into full speed running.*
- *Compared with an elite marathon runner who relies on stamina.*
- *And muscular endurance.*

3) a) Using a sport of your choice, identify **two** main components of health-related fitness required and explain their importance.

4 marks

Answer

- *Example, sprinting.*

Components of physical fitness relevant to sprinting:

- *Dynamic strength needed as muscle groups exert maximal force.*
- *Speed needed because in sprinting person needs to move limbs at maximum rate.*
- *Flexibility required because range of movement at joint site, such as the hip joint which needs to be at full extended during the rear leg driving phase.*

b) Power is a major fitness component required by high jumpers. Define what is meant by power.

2 marks

Answer

- *The rate at which mechanical work can be done which tests bodily strength.*
- *Measured in joules per second or watts.*

c) Describe a recognised specific test for measuring the power output of a high jumper.

3 marks

Answer

- *Vertical jump test, also known as the Sergeant jump test.*
- *Adjust vertical board so that stretched arms and fingertips touch edge end of scale, whilst feet are flat on the floor.*
- *Jumper prepares for take-off by flexing knees.*
- *And then jumps as high as possible.*
- *Touching a calibrated scale.*
- *Measure distance between standing two arm reach and highest single hand jump reached.*

d) Identify **two** skill-related / motor fitness components that are considered important for high jumpers.

2 marks

Answer

- *Agility.*
- *Balance.*
- *Reaction Time.*
- *Co-ordination.*

4) Briefly describe an outline for a week's exercise programme that would be suitable for overweight and ageing adult. In your answer identify the major fitness components to be stressed.

8 marks

Answer

	activity	major fitness component
day 1	45 min slow walk	*stamina*
day 2	15 min stretching (active + passive) working major muscle groups	*flexibility, balance*
day 3	weights circuit at local gym. 30 min light weights, repetition 6–8, 1 set at each of eight different exercises	*muscle strength, local muscle endurance, co-ordination, agility*
day 4	rest day	
day 5	30 min fast walk	*stamina*
day 6	30 min aerobic class	*stamina*
day 7	rest day	

5) There is overwhelming medical evidence that supports the direct relationship between smoking and reduced oxygen transportation. Explain how smoking interferes with oxygen transportation.

4 marks

Answer

- *Smoking scars inner lining of arteries.*
- *Producing a plaque (rigid layer) that clogs the blood vessel.*
- *Thereby reducing vessel elasticity, blood flow and oxygen transport.*
- *One of the toxic gases in cigarette smoking is carbon monoxide.*
- *This gas binds to the haemoglobin sites (the oxygen-carrying component in red blood cells).*
- *Resulting in a reduced oxygen uptake and therefore reduced oxygen carrying capacity.*

6) Lifestyle choices can have a negative effect upon our health and fitness.

a) Identify **three** lifestyle choices that have adverse effects on our future health and fitness.

3 marks

Answer

Select **three** from the following. There could be other acceptable answers.

- *Smoking.*
- *Recreational drugs.*
- *Alcohol.*
- *Diet.*
- *Stress.*

b) Choose **one** of your answers given in part a) and discuss how you could influence an individual to change to healthy lifestyle choices.

3 marks

Smoking:

Discuss the negative effects smoking such as:

- *Reduced life expectancy due to increased risks from diseases such as throat and lung cancer.*
- *Health risks for the passive smoker.*
- *Health risks for the unborn child.*
- *Financial cost of smoking.*

Discuss the positive effects of giving up:

- *Increased life expectancy.*
- *Improved life chances for others.*
- *Financially better off.*

Recreational drugs:

Discuss the harmful effects of drug taking:

- *Damage to bodily organs such as the brain.*
- *Destroys family and social life.*
- *Destroys self-esteem due to drug dependence.*
- *Can lead to criminal behaviour.*

Discuss the positive effects of giving up:

- *Increased life expectancy.*
- *Improved psychological, physiological and social well-being.*

Alcohol:
Discuss the harmful effects of drinking:
- *Alcohol-related diseases such liver cirrhosis and premature death.*
- *Alcohol dependency.*
- *Destroys family and social life.*
- *Destroys self-esteem.*

Discuss the positive effects of giving up:
- *Increased life expectancy.*
- *Psychological, physiological and social well-being.*

Diet:
Discuss the issues of malnutrition - meaning a bad diet:
- *Long-term health problems associated with obesity such as arthritis, coronary heart disease and atherosclerosis.*
- *Long-term health problems associated with anorexia nervosa such as reduced strength and lethargy.*
- *Reduced physical capability and life expectancy.*

Discuss the positive effects of controlling body mass:
- *Increased life expectancy.*
- *Increase lifestyle fitness chances to take part in physical activity.*
- *Improved psychological, physiological and social well-being.*

Stress:
Discuss stress-related issues:
- *Identify the symptoms of stress such as increased heart rate, sweating, nail biting, feeling out of control.*
- *Identify the causes of stress (known as stressors) such as worry, social relationships.*

Discuss the management of stress:
- *Relaxation techniques to control breathing rate, mental activity and muscle tension.*
- *Manage time effectively and think positively.*
- *Keep the body physically active and in good health.*

7) What are the purposes of the three main groups of food?   *3 marks*
Answer

- *Protein - essential for growth, bodybuilding and repair.*
- *Carbohydrate - principal energy giver.*
- *Fat - storage and another source of energy and a carrier of fat-soluble vitamins.*

8) a) Discuss how a balanced diet could be manipulated to increase an athlete's glucose reserves prior to a marathon race.   *6 marks*
Answer

- *Carbo-loading (or glycogen loading) before the event (modern method).*
- *This consists of tapering of training, whilst eating 50% CHO diet.*
- *Partially depletes glycogen stores.*
- *Therefore energy levels are not compromised.*
- *And glycogen synthase activity is increased.*
- *Then, gradually increase CHO intake to 70% of diet, with light training.*
- *Day of rest and 70% CHO diet.*
- *Repletes glycogen stores on day of marathon.*
- *Taking in isotonic fluids during the event will top up blood glucose levels during the event.*

b) Carbohydrates are used as an energy source during both aerobic and anaerobic conditions. It is therefore beneficial that an elite athlete's stores of carbohydrate are at a maximum before competition day. Discuss the advantages and disadvantages of glycogen loading.   *4 marks*
Answer

Advantages:
- *Enhanced glycogen stores in muscle and liver.*
- *Overall effect is for overall times in aerobic activities beyond 90 minutes to improve significantly.*

Disadvantages:
- *Increased body mass due to increased water retention.*
- *Needed for enhanced glycogen storage.*
- *During CHO depletion phase decreased energy levels.*
- *And increased fatigue (if using classic method of carbo-loading).*

c) How can an athlete's diet aid the recovery process?   *2 marks*

Answer

*   *Quick ingestion of carbohydrates after exercise (2 hour window of opportunity) will speed up recovery.*
*   *Eating foods, such as rice and bananas, that have a high glycemic index.*
*   *To raise blood glucose levels quickly and stimulate greater insulin release needed to convert glucose into glycogen.*
*   *Water needed to rehydrate the body.*
*   *Electrolyte replenishment needed to aid the metabolic process.*
*   *Protein needed to aid tissue damage, repair and growth.*

9) You have been asked to provide some nutritional strategies for an elite swimmer competing in seven races in the Regional Championships in a week's time. What can you recommend?   *3 marks*

Answer

*   *Cut back on the swimming training and then rest completely on the last day – this concept is known as tapering.*
*   *This will allow the carbohydrates eaten to be stored as full muscle glycogen stores that will help the swimmer to recover quicker between races.*
*   *Stay with a balanced diet.*
*   *Keep the fat intake low and focus on eating slow-release (low GI) carbohydrates such as lentils and peanuts.*
*   *Continue to eat 2-3 portions of protein a day.*
*   *Keep drinking water – taking care not to be dehydrated during the week before the gala.*
*   *Check colour of urine – it should be pale yellow or almost clear.*
*   *Aim to drink 2 litres of fluids per day, and more in hot weather.*

10) Provide recommendations for carbohydrate, fat and protein intake for a cross-country skier and a ski jumper. Give reasons for your recommendations.   6 marks

Answer

*   *Ski jumper is a power athlete who will need additional protein when compared with cross-country skier who is an endurance-based athlete.*
*   *The difference in protein intake is because after heavy resistance training, the rate of protein breakdown and resynthesis (building – muscle hypertrophy) for the strength / power athlete is greater when compared with the needs of the endurance athlete.*
*   *Fat intake should be restricted for both cross-country skier and ski jumper, since if it is not used an an energy source, fat will be stored as adipose tissue under the skin and in the body cavity.*

Reasons for recommendations:

*   *The cross-country skier will require a higher CHO diet when compared with the ski jumper.*
*   *This is because there are greater demands on replenishing depleted of glycogen stores stressed more in endurance vents such as cross-country skiing.*
*   *Both endurance and power athletes need a balanced diet with the dietary composition adjusted as described above.*

11) What are the effects of obesity on health and what are its causes based on energy considerations?   *4 marks*

Answer

Physical effects are:

*   *The cardio-respiratory system has to work much harder.*
*   *Inability to remove waste heat due to fat layer insulation.*
*   *More likely to suffer from cardiovascular and other diseases.*
*   *Mechanical injury to the body.*
*   *Greater surgical risks.*

Psychological effects of obesity on health:

*   *Embarrassment and fear of ridicule about poor physical condition.*
*   *The major cause for most people is a positive energy balance and lack of exercise.*

12) Describe the most effective way of reducing body weight.   *4 marks*

Answer

*   *Devise a weight loss plan that is personal, specific, realistic and measurable.*
*   *Reduce kilojoule intake and / or increase energy expenditure.*
*   *This can be achieved by continuing to eat a balanced but reduced diet.*
*   *Along with a corresponding increase of energy expenditure (by undertaking exercise) to create a negative energy balance.*
*   *One of the effects of aerobic exercise is to increase the metabolic rate of the body and as a result the obese person can substantially burn off body fat.*
*   *Also he / she would begin to utilise fat as a fuel food since this takes longer to initiate within a given exercise situation than in carbohydrate / glycogen utilisation.*

13) What is body mass index? What is its significance?   *3 marks*

Answer

*   *Body mass index (BMI) determines a person's BMI by dividing body mass in kilograms by the square of the body height in metres.*
*   *BMI values are divided into five categories: underweight, normal weight, overweight, obesity and extreme obesity*
*   *These 5 categories provide boundaries that separate each category and therefore give the individual a picture of the individual's body composition.*

PULMONARY FUNCTION, TRANSPORT OF BLOOD GASES, CARDIAC & VASCULAR FUNCTION

1) a) A hockey player has a match in one hour's time. Describe how inspiration occurs during this resting period.   *4 marks*

Answer

- *External intercostal muscles and diaphragm contract.*
- *Internal intercostal muscles relax.*
- *The action of these contracting muscles is to increase the volume of the thoracic cavity.*
- *As pleural and pulmonary pressures are reduced (air pressure within the lungs is reduced as their volume expands).*
- *Air in the lungs is at lower pressure than the air in the atmosphere outside.*
- *Since air moves from areas of high pressure to areas of low pressure.*
- *Air rushes into the lungs.*

b) During the hockey match, the player must increase the volume of gas exchanged in the lungs and muscles. Explain the changes in the mechanics of breathing (inspiration and expiration) which facilitate this increase.   *6 marks*

Answer

During inspiration:

- *Additional respiratory muscles contract.*
- *Namely sternocleidomastoid, scalenes and pectoralis minor.*
- *Effect diaphragm contracts and flattens (moves downward away from the lungs) with more force.*
- *Increased lifting of sternum.*
- *Which gives increased thoracic cavity volume.*
- *Decreased pleural and pulmonary pressures (within the lungs).*
- *Lower pulmonary air pressure.*
- *So the pressure of air outside is still bigger than inside.*
- *More air rushes into the lungs.*

During expiration:

- *Active respiratory muscles contract.*
- *Namely internal intercostal and rectus abdominus.*
- *The diaphragm relaxes and domes upward thereby compressing the lungs.*
- *The ribs and sternum are pulled in and down with more force.*
- *This decreases the size of the thoracic cavity volume.*
- *Gives increased pleural and pulmonary pressures (the pressure of the air inside the lungs is increased).*
- *So the sir inside the lungs is at a higher pressure than the atmospheric air outside.*
- *More air is forced out of the lungs.*

2) a) The diagram in figure A.48 represents the lung volume changes based on a number of spirometer readings during various breathing actions. With reference to the trace, briefly explain resting tidal volume (TV), expiratory reserve volume (ERV), vital capacity (VC), and residual volume (RV).   *4 marks*

Answer

Definitions:

- *Resting tidal volume is that volume of air that is breathed in **or** out during one breath at rest.*
- *Expiratory reserve volume is that volume of air that can be forcibly expired over and above resting tidal volume.*
- *Vital capacity is the maximal volume of air that can be forcibly expired after maximal inspiration in one breath.*
- *Residual volume is that volume of air remaining in the lungs after maximal expiration.*

b) Using the information in the spirometer trace, state what happens to the following volumes during the exercise period: residual volume, inspiratory volume (IRV), and expiratory volume (ERV).   *3 marks*

Answer

- *Residual volume remains the same.*
- *IRV decreases.*
- *ERV decreases.*

c) Why does tidal volume change by only a small amount during the exercise period?   *3 marks*

Answer

- *Major respiratory regulator is carbon dioxide.*
- *Which controls rate of breathing (f).*
- *And depth (TV) of breathing.*
- *Effect of exercise is to increase pCO_2.*
- *And stimulate a bigger increase in breathing rate when compared with tidal volume.*
- *So that the increased levels of CO_2 are removed quickly from the body.*

d) Identify **two** effects of regular aerobic training on lung volumes and capacities.   *2 marks*

Two effects from the following:
Answer
- *Improved strength of respiratory muscles.*
- *Increase in TV, VC at expense of RV.*
- *At submaximal workloads slight decrease in frequency of breaths.*
- *During maximal workloads big increase in frequency of breaths, hence big increase in minute ventilation.*
- *Hence increased gaseous exchange and $\dot{V}O_{2max}$.*
- *At submaximal workloads $\dot{V}O_{2max}$ will be less because of greater efficiency of O_2 uptake.*

e) A student measured the volume of air that he / she ventilated at rest and during submaximal exercise. The results are shown in table 9 below.
Define what is meant by the term 'minute ventilation volume' and calculate the values for **A** and **B**, clearly showing the method used.   *4 marks*
Answer
- *Minute ventilation volume is the volume of air inspired **or** expired in one minute - notated as $\dot{V}E$.*
- *It is a combination of tidal or inhalation volume (TV) and breathing rate (f).*

	$\dot{V}E$	= TV (inhalation volume) x f (breathing rate).
At rest:	$\dot{V}E$	= 500 x 10.
		= 5,000 ml min^{-1} or 5 dm^3 min^{-1} or 5 litres min^{-1}.
During submaximal exercise:	$\dot{V}E$	= 800 x 30.
		= 24,000 ml min^{-1} or 24 dm^3 min^{-1} or 24 litres min^{-1}.

3) a) Describe how pulmonary ventilation is regulated during quiet breathing.   *6 marks*
Answer
- *Pulmonary ventilation is regulated by the respiratory control centre (RCC), located within the medulla oblongata of the brain.*
- *The RCC consists of two parts: the inspiratory and expiratory centres.*
- *The inspiratory centre is responsible for the basic rhythm of ventilation.*
- *At rest impulses are sent via the phrenic and intercostal nerves to the external intercostal muscles and diaphragm.*
- *Causing these muscles to contract to bring about inspiration.*
- *When stimulation ceases these muscles relax causing expiration.*
- *The expiratory centre is inactive during quiet breathing.*
- *The apneustic centre controls the intensity of breathing. It does this by prolonging the firing of the inspiratory neurones, thereby increasing lung volumes.*
- *The pneumotaxic centre does the opposite of the apneustic centre, resulting in the fine-tuning of the breathing rate.*

b) Identify the **three** chemical stimuli that control the rate and depth of breathing. How do these chemical stimuli control respiration during exercise?   *6 marks*

Answer
- *Partial pressure of carbon dioxide (pCO_2) is the major regulator of respiration.*
- *Partial pressure of oxygen (pO_2).*
- *Acidity (pH).*
How do these chemical stimuli control respiration during exercise?
- *Effect of exercise is to increase the production of CO_2, and H^+, and decrease O_2 and pH.*
- *An increase in pCO_2 or a decrease in pH stimulates the peripheral and central chemoreceptors.*
- *Which send nerve impulses into the inspiratory control centre in the medulla.*
- *Then out via the phrenic and intercostal nerves to the respiratory muscles.*
- *Which contract more forcefully (increased lung volumes) and more frequently (increased f – frequency of breathing).*
- *The response is to decrease pCO_2, levels and increase pH and pO_2.*

4) The breathing characteristics of individuals vary during physical activity. Table 10 shows the proportion of oxygen and carbon dioxide breathed during exercise compared with resting values.

a) Use the information in table 10 to describe the effects of exercise on gaseous exchange in the lungs. Explain why these changes occur.   *4 marks*
Answer
The effects of exercise on gaseous exchange:
- *Exhaled oxygen decreases from 17% to 15%.*
- *Exhaled carbon dioxide increases from 3% to 6%.*
Explain why these changes occur:
- *This is because increased amounts of oxygen are required by skeletal muscle during aerobic tissue respiration.*
- *With a corresponding amount of carbon dioxide being produced as a waste product.*

b) How does the blood transport oxygen? *2 marks*

Answer

- $Hb + 4O_2 \rightarrow HbO_8$.
- Or transported as oxyhaemoglobin.
- 3% of oxygen is dissolved in blood plasma.

c) Explain how oxygen is exchanged **between** the blood and active muscle tissues. *3 marks*

Answer

- Gas molecules, such as oxygen, diffuse from high to low pressure - called a diffusion gradient.
- Arriving oxygen partial pressure (pO_2) in arterial blood is greater than oxygen partial presure in tissue.
- Myoglobin in the tissue cells has a greater affinity for O_2 than haemoglobin in the arriving blood.
- Therefore O_2 detaches itself from the haemoglobin in the blood and is released into active muscle cells.
- Myoglobin transports O_2 to the mitochondria for aerobic energy production.

d) Identify the **three** ways CO_2 is transported by the blood.
   How does increased CO_2 production stimulate further release of O_2 for tissue cell respiration? *5 marks*

Answer

- Carbonic acid (dissociated into H^+ and HCO_3^- ions) (73%).
- Carbaminohaemoglobin (23%).
- Dissolved in plasma (7%).

Method 1:

- CO_2 combines with H_2O to form $H_2CO_3^-$.
- This acid is unstable and so releases H^+ to form a bicarbonate ion (HCO_3^-).
- The freed H^+ reacts with HbO_2 to form haemoglobinic acid.
- Which triggers off the release of more oxygen for tissue cell respiration.
- $H^+ + HbO_2 \rightarrow HHb + O_2$

Method 2:

- CO_2 combines with haemoglobin to form carbaminohaemoglobin.
- Which triggers off the release of more oxygen for tissue cell respiration.
- $CO_2 + HbO_2 \rightarrow HbCO_2 + O_2$

5) The binding of oxygen to haemoglobin depends on pO_2 in the blood and the affinity of haemoglobin with oxygen. The curves in figure A.49 show how different concentrations of carbon dioxide affect the saturation of haemoglobin at varying partial pressures of oxygen.

a) Explain what is meant by partial pressure of oxygen (pO_2). *1 mark*

Answer

- The pressure that oxygen (pO_2) exerts within a mixture of gases.

b) What are the values of percentage saturation of haemoglobin on the three curves when the partial pressure of oxygen is 5.0 kPa? *3 marks*

Answer

- Curve **A** - haemoglobin is fully saturated with oxygen – 100%.
- Curve **B** - haemoglobin is 68% saturated with oxygen.
- Curve C – haemoglobin is 55% saturated with oxygen.

c) What are the implications of the carbon dioxide values for curves **B** and **C** for an athlete? *2 marks*

Answer

- The greater pCO_2 the less % of HbO_2 saturation.
- This is because as more energy is released by respiring muscle cells.
- More CO_2 is produced as a waste product.
- Diffusing across into the blood capillaries.
- Therefore the more CO_2 in the blood and surrounding the red blood cells (and hence the haemoglobin in the red blood cells), the less oxygen can be carried by the haemoglobin.
- This means that the difference (in the case of curve **B** at 5.0 kPa – this is 100–68 = 32% of the oxygen carried).
- Detaches itself from the haemoglobin and diffuses into the muscle cells where it is available for respiration.
- When more CO_2 is present (during violent exercise) as in the case of curve C at pCO_2 = 9.3 kPa, at the same pO_2 (5.0 kPa) haemoglobin releases 100–55 = 45% of the oxygen carried.
- So the more exercise, the more oxygen released and made available for more exercise.

d) Why is the partial pressure of oxygen (pO_2) important to the process of gaseous exchange?   *3 marks*

Answer

- *The increased loading of CO_2 causes more unloading of O_2 from haemoglobin,*
- *And so more O_2 is released for tissue cell respiration to sustain the physical activity undertaken.*

Importance of pO_2 in gaseous exchange in the alveoli:

- *The pO_2 in the lung alveoli must be higher than the pO_2 in the pulmonary blood.*
- *In order for oxygen to diffuse into the bloodstream.*

Importance of pO_2 in gaseous exchange at tissue cell sites:

- *Similarly, the arterial pO_2 must be greater at the tissue site than in the tissue cells.*
- *In order for oxygen to diffuse into tissue cells.*

6) Figure A.50 shows a diagrammatic picture of the cardiac impulse. Using the information in this diagram, describe the flow of blood during the specific stages of the cardiac cycle, in relation to the cardiac impulse. In your answer explain how the heart valves help control the direction of blood flow.   *8 marks*

Answer

Atrial and ventricular diastole:

- *During atrial and ventricular diastole there is no electrical impulse from the SA node.*
- *And so relaxed heart muscle chambers (atria and ventricles) fill with blood.*
- *From the venae cavae (on the right hand side of the heart).*
- *And the pulmonary veins (on the left hand side of the heart).*
- *As the cuspid valves open and the semi-lunar valves close.*

Diastole is followed by systole consisting of two distinct phases:

Atrial systole:

- *The SA node creates an electrical impulse.*
- *This causes a wave-like contraction over the atria myocardium.*
- *Forcing the remaining blood from the atrial chambers.*
- *Past the cuspid valves*
- *Into the ventricles.*

Ventricular systole:

- *The impulse reaches the AV node.*
- *The cuspid valves close during ventricular systole.*
- *The impulse travels down the bundle of His to the Purkinje fibres.*
- *Across ventricular myocardium.*
- *Which then contracts as the semi-lunar valves open.*
- *Blood is forced out of the ventricles.*
- *Into the aorta (left hand side).*
- *And the pulmonary arteries (right hand side).*
- *Myocardial contractions, during systole, are said to be myogenic or under involuntary nervous control.*

7) $\dot{Q} = SV \times HR$. Explain the meaning of this equation and give typical resting values that you would expect in an endurance-based athlete.   *6 marks*

Answer

- *$\dot{Q}$ represents cardiac output – is defined the volume of blood pumped by the left ventricle in one minute.*
- *And is a combination of SV – stroke volume is defined as the volume of blood pumped by the left ventricle of the heart per beat.*
- *$\times$ HR – heart rate is defined as the number of beats of the heart per minute (bpm).*
- *Typical resting values for an endurance-based athlete:*

$$\dot{Q} \qquad = SV \times HR$$
$$5.6\ litres = 110ml \times 51\ (or\ same\ values\ in\ dm^3\ min^{-1}).$$

8) A fit 18 year old female student performs a 400m time trial in one minute.

a) Sketch and label a graph to show a typical heart rate response from a point 5 minutes before the start of the run, during the time trial, and over the 20 minute recovery period.
4 marks

Answer

See graph in figure Q.1.

- *a Anticipatory rise just before start of exercise.*
- *b Initial rapid increase in HR.*
- *c To reach HR_{max} at end of time trial.*
- *d Recovery initially rapid.*
- *e Tapering off slowly towards resting values.*

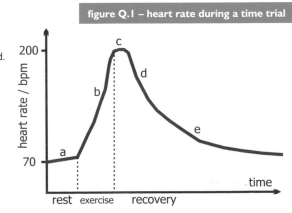

figure Q.1 – heart rate during a time trial

b) Explain why heart rate takes some time to return to its resting value following the exercise period. *2 marks*

Answer

- *There is a raised O_2 demand of active muscle tissue.*
- *There are raised levels of CO_2.*
- *And a build up of lactic acid during high intensity work which takes time to clear.*
- *Body organs such as the heart, need additional O_2 above resting O_2 consumption.*
- *This reflects the size of EPOC or oxygen debt.*
- *Hence HR values stay elevated above resting values until the oxygen debt is purged.*

c) Identify a hormone that is responsible for heart rate increases prior to and during an exercise period. *1 marks*

Answer

- *Adrenaline or noradrenaline.*

d) Heart rate is regulated by neural, hormonal and intrinsic factors. How does the nervous system detect and respond to changes in heart rate during an exercise period? *4 marks*

Answer

- *The cardiac control centre (CCC) responds to neural information.*
- *This is supplied by proprioceptors and other reflexes.*
- *Such as the baroreceptor reflex, sensitive to changes in blood pressure.*
- *And the chemoreceptor reflex, sensitive to changes in CO_2 and pH levels.*
- *For example, a decrease in pH and an increase in CO_2 levels increase the action of the sympathetic nervous system (SNS), via the accelerator nerve.*
- *To increase stimulation of the SA node.*
- *Thereby increasing heart rate.*

9) Running a marathon in hot conditions sets up a competition between the active muscles and the skin for limited blood supply. How does the human body respond to meet the needs of supplying oxygen to exercising muscle and how can the athlete control this response? *3 marks*

Answer

- *Sympathetic nervous system stimulates increase in heart rate.*
- *To compensate for reduced blood volume (due to sweating).*
- *And decreased stroke volume as blood pools in the periphery.*
- *Known as the cardiovascular drift.*
- *Need to take regular drinks during run to keep the body rehydrated.*

10) Jodie Swallow is a top class female British Triathlete, and has a resting heart rate of 36 bpm. Give reasons why such an athlete might have a low resting heart rate. *4 marks*

Answer

- *Due to bradycardia or slow heart beat.*
- *Effects of an aerobic endurance-based triathlete training programme is to produce cardiac hypertrophy i.e. heart becomes bigger and stronger (mainly left ventricle).*
- *Producing an increase in stroke volume (SV).*
- *And decrease in resting heart rate (HR_{rest}).*
- *A reduced resting heart rate allows for an increase in diastolic filling time.*
- *The net effect is that the heart does not have to pump as frequently for the same given resting oxygen consumption.*

11) Table 11 shows the rate of blood flow (in cm³ per minute) to different parts of the body in a trained male athlete, at rest and while exercising at maximum effort on a cycle ergometer. Study the data carefully before answering the following questions.

a) The rate of blood flow to the 'entire body' increases significantly during exercise. Explain briefly how the heart achieves this. *2 marks*

Answer

- *Increased heart rate.*
- *Increased stroke volume.*
- *Therefore increased cardiac output.*

b) What percentage of the total blood flow is directed to the skeletal muscle at rest and during maximum effort? Show your calculations. *3 marks*

Answer

The percentage of total blood flow directed to skeletal muscle at rest is:

- $\dfrac{1000 \times 100}{5000} = 20\%$.

The percentage of total blood flow directed to skeletal muscle during maximal effort is:

- $\dfrac{264000 \times 100}{30000} = 88\%$.

c) How is blood flow to various regions of the body controlled? *4 marks*

Answer

- *Achieved through vasomotor control.*
- *Which creates the vascular shunt.*
- *This is vasodilation, which is the expansion of arteries and arterioles, and relaxation of pre-capillary sphincters to increase blood flow to active muscle tissue.*
- *This is in response to a cessation of neural signals to the smooth muscle walls of these blood vessels.*
- *Also vasoconstriction, which is the restriction of arteries and arterioles, and contraction of pre-capillary sphincters to decrease blood flow to non-active tissue.*
- *This is a response to increased neural signals from baroreceptors which detect changes in cardiac output.*
- *These neural signals go to the smooth muscle walls of these particular blood vessels.*

12) a) What is meant by the concept venous return mechanism? *2 marks*

Answer

- *Venous return is the transport of blood from the capillaries, through venules, veins and venae cavae to the right atrium of the heart.*

b) Describe how it is aided during physical activity when a person is exercising in an upright position. *3 marks*

Answer

- *Venous return is aided by exercise due to increased actions of skeletal muscle and respiratory and cardiac pumps and limited action of venoconstriction of veins.*
- *Increased activity in skeletal muscle results from contracting and relaxing squeezing sections of veins.*
- *Therefore causing increased blood flow back towards the heart.*
- *Blood cannot flow the opposite way because of pocket valves placed every so often in each vein.*

c) Explain the importance of the skeletal muscle pump mechanism during an active cool-down. *2 marks*

Answer

- *Skeletal muscles continue to contract to squeeze vein walls, forcing blood back towards the heart.*
- *Thereby preventing blood pooling / sudden drop in blood pressure.*
- *And removing of waste products such as carbon dioxide and lactic acid.*

d) What effect does enhanced venous return have upon cardiac output and stroke volume? *3 marks*

Answer

- *Stroke volume is dependent on the amount of venous return.*
- *Up to 70% of the total volume of blood is contained in the veins at rest.*
- *Increased venous return will cause myocardial tissue to be stretched even further.*
- *And so contract more forcibly.*
- *To increase stroke volume (Starling's Law of the heart).*
- *Cardiac output is a combination of SV and HR.*
- *Therefore an increased stroke volume will create an increased cardiac output.*

13) a) How is oxygen transported by the blood? *2 marks*

Answer

O_2 transport:

- *Via attachment with haemoglobin $Hb + 4O_2 \rightarrow HbO_8$.*
- *Transported as oxyhaemoglobin (97%).*
- *Dissolved in plasma (3%).*

b) Identify the **main** method whereby carbon dioxide is transported in venous blood. *1 mark*

Answer

CO_2 main transporter:

- *Carbonic acid – 73% (which dissociates into H^+ and HCO_3^-).*

c) Explain how increased levels of carbon dioxide levels affect performance during physical activity. *3 marks*

Answer

- *Chemoreceptors are sensitive to changes in carbon dioxide levels.*
- *When carbon dioxide levels increase the cardiac control centre (CCC in medulla oblongata) is alerted.*
- *CCC sends neural impulses to pacemaker.*
- *To increase heart rate, stroke volume and hence cardiac output.*
- *And increase rate and depth of breathing (f and TV) and hence minute ventilation (VE),*
- *And stimulating redistribution of blood – blood shunting mechanism.*
- *To transport more oxygenated blood to active tissues.*
- *At tissue cell site increased carbon dioxide production causes more unloading of oxygen from haemoglobin (Böhr effect).*

14) A simple calculation for the calculation of blood pressure can be written as:

Blood Pressure = Cardiac Output x Resistance to blood flow

a) Identify **one** factor that affects resistance to the flow of blood within systemic blood vessels. *1 mark*

Answer

One from the following list:

- *Friction between moving blood and the walls of blood vessels.*
- *Length of blood vessels.*
- *Diameter / lumen width of blood vessels.*
- *Viscosity of blood.*

b) Blood pressure is quoted as two numbers. An example would be resting values of 120/80 mmHg. Explain what each of these numbers refer to.

2 marks

Answer

- *The first number (120 mmHg) refers to systolic blood pressure or blood pressure when heart (ventricles) is (are) contracting.*
- *The second number (80 mmHg) refers to diastolic blood pressure or blood pressure when heart (ventricles) is (are) relaxing.*

c) How would these blood pressure values change during a game of football and a rugby scrum lasting 6 seconds? Give a reason for each of your answers.

3 marks

Answer

- *During dynamic exercise such as a football game, an active player's systolic blood pressure would rise.*
- *As a result of increased cardiac output.*
- *And diastolic blood pressure would remain at the same resting value.*
- *A 6 second isometric maximal exertion rugby scrum raises both systolic and diastolic blood pressures to force blood into the capillary bed.*

A reason for each of your answers:

- *Because this isometric position reduces the actions of the skeletal muscle and respiratory pumps.*
- *Which in turn reduces venous return, cardiac output, blood pressure and capillary blood flow.*
- *Therefore both systolic and diastolic pressures increase to force more blood through the capillaries of working muscles.*

15) Table 12 identifies differences in total blood volume, plasma volume, blood cell volume between untrained and highly trained endurance males (same age, height and body mass). Comment on the data that is presented in table 12 and suggest how the trained athlete would benefit from these increased volumes.

4 marks

Answer

- *One of the effects of endurance training is to increase blood volume, resulting primarily from an increase in plasma volume, but there is also a small increase in red blood cells as observed in the figures in table 12.*

Benefits:

- *A bigger plasma volume reduces blood viscosity and improves circulation and oxygen availability.*
- *A bigger red blood cell count, with increased levels of haemoglobin, is available in blood for increased oxygen transport and hence an increase in $\dot{V}O_{2max}$.*

ANALYSIS OF MOVEMENT

Sample questions

Warm-up question 1)
Hockey involves movement at many joints in the body. Identify which bones articulate at each of the following joints: shoulder, elbow, radio-ulnar, hip, knee, and ankle.   6 marks
Answer

- *Shoulder:*   *humerus and scapula.*
- *Elbow:*   *humerus, radius and ulna.*
- *Radio-ulna:*   *radius and ulna.*
- *Hip:*   *femur and pelvis (acetabulum).*
- *Knee:*   *femur and tibia.*
- *Ankle:*   *talus, tibia and fibula.*

Warm-up question 2)
Complete the missing gaps in table 23 by naming the **main** agonist and antagonist muscles, body plane and body axis for each of the actions identified.
Answer

Table 23 – **actions at various joints**

action	main agonist	main antagonist	body plane	body axis
elevating the shoulders	levator scapulae	pectoralis major	frontal plane	frontal axis
extending the elbow joint	triceps brachii	biceps brachii	sagittal plane	transverse axis
flexing the hip joint	iliopsoas	gluteus maximus	sagittal plane	transverse axis
flexing the knee joint	hamstring group: biceps femoris, semitendinosus, semimembranosus	quadriceps group: vastus medialis, vastus intermedius, vastus lateralis, rectus femoris	sagittal plane	transverse axis
dorsiflexing the ankle joint	tibialis anterior	tibialis posterior	sagittal plane	transverse axis
flexing the trunk	rectus abdominus	erector spinae group	sagittal plane	transverse axis

Warm up question 3)
Describe the following movement terminology, and give a physical activity for each movement: abduction, circumduction, rotation and plantarflexion. In which plane(s) does each movement pattern occur?   12 marks
Answer
Abduction:

- *A movement pattern in which a body segment moves away from the midline of the body.*
- *Example: leg action going into a cartwheel.*
- *Frontal (or coronal) plane.*

Circumduction:

- *A body movement which consists of flexion, abduction, extension and adduction to create a cone shape in space.*
- *Example: a small circular hand dance gesture.*
- *Sagittal and frontal planes.*

Rotation:

- *A limb movement around the axis down the centre of a long bone.*
- *Example: delivery phase of a discus throw.*
- *Transverse (or horizontal) plane.*

Plantarflexion:

- *A movement of the foot that results in the toe being pointed downwards.*
- *Example: diving off a springboard.*
- *Sagittal (or median) plane.*

4) Figure A.71 a to c shows the final stride, take-off and flight phase of a long jump. Use these three pictures to help you complete the following joint analysis.

a) Name the type of muscle contraction occurring in the leg whose foot is in contact with the ground in figure A.71a, name the **main** agonist muscle responsible for this muscle contraction and explain why you have selected this muscle.   *3 marks*

Answer

- *Type of muscle contraction: isotonic, eccentric muscle contraction.*

- *Main agonist muscle: quadriceps group: rectus femoris, vastus medialis, vastus intermedius, vastus lateralis.*

- *Explanation: on this final stride prior to take-off, the hips and take-off leg sink into the board, during which time muscles of the quadriceps muscle group are lengthening under tension.*

b) Complete the following joint analysis below in table 24 for figure A.71b: *9 marks*

Answer

Table 24 – **answer to question in table 24**

Joint	joint type	articulating bones	agonist muscles
left ankle	synovial hinge	talus, tibia, fibula	tibialis posterior, gastrocnemius, soleus
left knee	synovial hinge	tibia, femur	quadriceps group: rectus femoris, vastus lateralis, vastus medialis, vastus intermedius
left hip	synovial ball and socket	femur, acetabulum of pelvis	gluteus maximus, hamstring group: biceps femoris, semimembranosus, semitendinosus

c) Describe the changes in movement patterns in the left ankle, knee, hip and trunk from figures A.71 b to c.   *4 marks*

Answer

- *Left ankle changes from plantarflexion to dorsiflexion.*

- *Left knee changes from extension to flexion.*

- *Left hip changes from extension to flexion.*

- *Trunk changes from extension to flexion.*

d) Suggest **two** factors that affect the range of movement at the hip joint.   *2 marks*

Answer

- *Shape of ball and socket joint / shape of bones.*

- *Extensibility of attached muscles / muscle tendons.*

- *Elasticity of attached ligaments.*

- *Length of muscle / bulk of muscle.*

5) Figure A.72 shows a tennis player completing a forehand drive. Use the figure to help you complete the following joint analysis.

a) For the shoulder joint during horizontal adduction, the type of joint, the articulating bones, the **main** agonist muscle and the type of contraction for the agonist.   *4 marks*

Answer

- *Type of joint: synovial, ball and socket.*

- *Articulating bones: scapula, humerus.*

- *Main agonist muscle: pectoralis major.*

- *Type of contraction at agonist: isotonic, concentric.*

b) Using the muscles that create elbow flexion during the forehand drive, explain what is meant by antagonistic muscle action.   *4 marks*

Answer

- *Muscles work in pairs to create movement across a joint - called antagonistic muscle action.*

- *Whilst one muscle is contracting (agonist muscle) the opposing muscle is relaxing (antagonist muscle).*

- *When the elbow flexes the biceps brachii (agonist muscle) contracts.*

- *And the triceps brachii (antagonist muscle) relaxes.*

c) The movement pattern produced on the right hand side of the trunk and the **main** agonist creating this movement.

2 marks

Answer

- *Movement pattern: lateral flexion.*
- *Main agonist muscle: external / internal abdominal obliques.*

d) In which body plane and around which axis does the tennis forehand occur at the flexed right elbow position shown in figure A.72?

Answer

- *Sagittal plane.*
- *Transverse axis.*

6) The athlete in figure A.73 is holding a plank bridge position. Use the photograph to help you complete the following joint analysis.

a) Identify the joint type, articulating bones, the **main** agonist (prime mover) and type of muscle contraction at the hip joint.

4 marks

Answer

- *Type of joint: synovial, ball and socket.*
- *Articulating bones: femur, acetabulum of pelvis.*
- *Main agonist muscle: iliopsoas.*
- *Type of contraction at agonist: isometric muscle contraction.*

b) Explain why the muscle contraction is of this type.

1 mark

Answer

- *Since the muscle length does not change during the exercise.*

c) Explain the role of core muscles in relation to the plank bridge position.

2 marks

Answer

- *Core muscles are responsible for **stabilisation** of the trunk region to hold the plank bridge position.*
- *For example, transverse abdominus and multifidus muscle are acting as core stabilisers within the trunk region.*

d) There are four rotator cuff muscles that are inserted around the cuff or cap over the proximal humerus. Name **one** of these muscles and explain how these muscles provide range of movement and yet collectively protect the shoulder joint.

2 marks

Answer

One from the following muscles:

- *Teres minor.*
- *Infraspinatus.*
- *Supraspinatus.*
- *Subsacpularis.*

Explanation:

- *The function of the cuff rotators (depending on their position) is to enable to shoulder joint to operate as a multiaxial joint i.e. 3 axes of movement.*
- *All these four muscles have their insertions on the bony protrusions (called tubercles) at the proximal head of the humerus.*
- *And therefore stabilise and protect the shallow rounded socket of the scapula from possible dislocation.*
- *By pulling the humerus bone into the scapula socket.*

7) Figure A.74 a – c shows an elite sprinter completing a full running stride.

a) Analyse the action of the hip joint from the strike position of the left leg to the completion of a full running stride.

3 marks

Answer

- *Figure a - hip – extending beyond the straight line position.*
- *Figure b - hip - flexing.*
- *Figure c - hip – extending.*

b) Identify the **main** agonist muscles responsible for these movement patterns in figures a and b only.

2 marks

Answer

- *Figure a, main agonist muscle: gluteus maximus.*
- *Figure b, main agonist muscle: iliopsoas.*

c) At the completion of the full stride focus on the left foot plant. Identify the bones that form the ankle joint, the joint action and the **main** agonist responsible for this movement pattern.

4 marks

Answer

2 marks

- *Ankle joint bones: talus, tibia and fibula.*
- *Joint action: dorsiflexion.*
- *Main agonist muscle: tibialis anterior.*

d) Figure c shows the right knee in the recovery position. Identify the joint type, **main** agonist muscle group, its antagonist muscle group and the type of muscle contraction occurring at this joint. *4 marks*

Answer

- *Joint type: synovial, hinge joint.*
- *Main agonist muscle group: hamstring group.*
- *Main antagonist muscle group: quadriceps group.*
- *Type of muscle contraction: isotonic, concentric.*

e) Explain the term 'body plane'. *2 marks*

Answer

- *An imaginary flat surface / line.*
- *Running through the centre of gravity of the body.*

f) In which plane and around which axis does the sequence of movements of the sprint leg action take place? *2 marks*

Answer

- *Sagittal (or median) plane.*
- *Transverse axis.*

8) Differentiate and give examples of concentric, static and eccentric work. *6 marks*

Answer

- *Concentric work: muscle shortens whilst developing tension.*
  For example biceps muscle during an arm flexion movement. Known as a positive contraction.
- *Static work (isometric contraction): develops muscle tension without changing length.*
  For example rugby scrum.
- *Eccentric work: muscle lengthens whilst developing tension.*
  For example, biceps muscle during arm extension movement. Known as a negative contraction.

LEVERS

1) Sketch the lever system which would represent the action of the biceps muscle in flexing the arm. Show on your diagram the resistance arm of the lever. *3 marks*

Answer

- *See figure Q.2.*
- *E is the effort force in the biceps muscle.*
- *L is the load force applied at the hand.*
- *The triangle is the pivot or fulcrum of the lever.*
- *The resistance arm is the structure (forearm) between hand (load) and elbow (fulcrum).*

2) In figure A.81 of a jumper taking off, name, sketch and label the lever system operating at knee **B** during this action. *3 marks*

Answer

- *See figures Q.3 and Q.4.*
- *This is a class 3 lever (effort between pivot and load).*
- *Note that the effort (figure Q.3) is transmitted to the tibia via the patella tendon, which passes over the knee and inserts below the joint (figure Q.4).*

figure Q.2 – the elbow and forearm lever

E = effort

fulcrum (pivot)

L = load

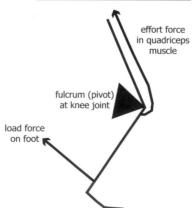

figure Q.3 – jumper's knee 1

effort force in quadriceps muscle

fulcrum (pivot) at knee joint

load force on foot

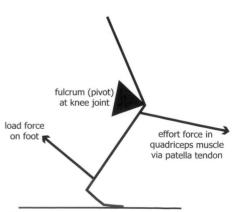

figure Q.4 – jumper's knee 2

fulcrum (pivot) at knee joint

load force on foot

effort force in quadriceps muscle via patella tendon

3) In softball, what order (class) of lever is shown in the hitting action in figure A.82?
State **one** disadvantage and **one** advantage of reducing the bat length for a beginner.

3 marks

Answer

- *This is a class 1 lever.*

Advantage of shortening bat length is:

- *Learning the skill involved may be easier - since the strike point is nearer the hand.*

Disadvantage of shortening the bat would be:

- *Less force can be applied as a load for a given effort, hence the strike on the ball would impart less speed to the ball.*

4) Name, sketch and label the lever system which is operating at the ankle of leg **C** when doing the sprint set action illustrated in figure A.83. *3 marks*

Answer

- *See figure Q.5.*
- *This is a class 2 lever.*
- *Note that the load force is a combination of the weight of the athlete acting downwards through the tibia / fibula on the ankle joint, and the reaction to the accelerating force driving the sprinter forwards.*

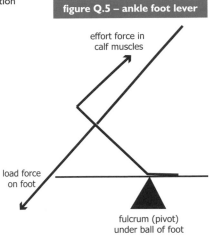

figure Q.5 – ankle foot lever

effort force in calf muscles

load force on foot

fulcrum (pivot) under ball of foot

5) a) Figure A.84 shows an elbow joint A of a person performing an exercise.
Draw a simplified sketch to show the lever system, indicating the various forces operating.
4 marks

Answer

- Figure Q.6 – this is a 2nd class lever.
- Normally the triceps elbow system is a 1st class lever, but here, the pivot is at the hand as shown, which forces the system into 2nd class lever shape.

b) On your diagram draw and label the effort and resistance arm.
3 marks

Answer

- *Resistance arm lies between pivot and weight force (the lever arm is at right angles to the force).*
- *Effort arm lies between point of elbow and pivot.*

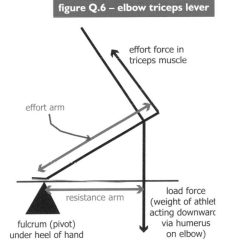

figure Q.6 – elbow triceps lever

effort force in triceps muscle

effort arm

resistance arm

fulcrum (pivot) under heel of hand

load force (weight of athlet acting downward via humerus on elbow)

6) During physical activity the performer uses a combination of levers to produce movement. Explain why the length of the lever will affect performance.
3 marks

Answer

- *The longer the lever (usually length of limb - the resistance arm) the greater the speed at the load (end of limb).*
- *The longer the lever the less effort required.*
- *Shorter levers generate more force (compare compact small gymnasts / weight lifters with taller performers).*
- *1st class levers are used to generate speed.*
- *2nd class levers are more efficient because the effort is further away from the pivot (example - the ankle joint with calf muscles).*

APPLICATION OF THEORETICAL KNOWLEDGE FOR EFFECTIVE PERFORMANCE

See page 86 for a description of the Question Layout.

UNIT 2 – APPLIED EXERCISE PHYSIOLOGY IN PRACTICAL SITUATIONS

1) b) Explain why you would use the principles of training when developing a training programme to improve the fitness of 16+ physical education students.
Answer

- *Specificity*
- *The need to make movements and energy system demands the same as the activity.*
- *For example, hockey players would benefit from back-to-back stick shuttle sprints (stressing the fitness components speed and agility and developing anaerobic lactic acid energy system).*
- *This skill is sport specific because the players are replicating the movement patterns they use in their hockey game.*

- *Progression*
- *Involves the gradual application of the overload principle in order to improve fitness.*
- *The example below shows how progression is achieved by increasing the number of shuttle runs from session one to session three:*
- *Week one - session one:*   *2 sets of 4 back–to-back shuttle sprints with 6 minutes recovery between sets.*
- *Week two - session two:*   *3 sets of 4 back–to-back shuttle sprints 5 minutes recovery between sets.*
- *Week three - session three:*   *3 sets of 5 back–to-back shuttle sprints with 4 minutes recovery between sets.*

- **Overload**
- *Describes training activities which get harder / more intense / longer.*
- *Overload is achieved by increasing the intensity and / or **t**ime or duration of training – these two overload principles form part of what is commonly referred to as the* **FITT principles**.
- *In the example above, progression made from session one to session three demonstrates the increase in anaerobic exercise as shuttle reps increase and recovery between sets decreases (intensity) and duration (**t**ime) of the exercise period increases.*

- *Reversibility*
- *'Use it or lose it' which means that if the training stimulus is not maintained, gains previously made from training are lost.*
- *This means that our hockey players will need to maintain or even continue the increase the volume of work stressing the anaerobic lactic acid energy system, otherwise anaerobic adaptations will reverse.*

- *Tedium*
- *Refers to training that lacks variety and causes boredom.*
- *If our hockey players continue to do the same training session (with the same outcomes and feelings) week in and week out, they may become de-motivated as the feelings of mastery of the activity are reduced.*
- *This can be overcome by setting goals for sessions which vary (even though the activity itself may be the same), or completely change the activity while retaining the same goals (for example goals to improve strength or endurance).*
- *Changing activities in training with the specific aim of reducing tedium is called **variance**, and is a crucial feature of a successful training programme.*

2) b) A group of students wish to create an aerobic weight training programme. Suggest how they could calculate working intensities that would give them optimal strength endurance gains. Illustrate your answer with examples.
Answer

- *1RM*
- *Working intensities can be measured as a proportion of a performer's one repetition maximum or 1RM.*
- *1RM represents the highest successful lift*
  - *that can be achieved for one complete repetition of an exercise*
  - *having failed at the final lift.*

- *Once the 1RM's values are known the students then calculates a percentage of the 1RM in order to create an aerobic weight's training programme.*
- *In this case, training done at less than 50% of 1RM with high repetitions would **stress** the aerobic energy system.*
- *For example a student achieves a 1RM of 50 kg on bench press. This 1RM value can then be used to calculate a working intensity for optimal strength endurance gain chosen at 40% of 1RM.*
- *Bench press session: 3 sets (20 kg x 20 repetitons) short recovery of 60 seconds between sets.*
- *This method can be used to create an interval weight training programme for a variety of exercises that would aerobically stress major muscle groups.*
- *With strength gains achieved as a result of regular systematic training, it is important to retest 1RM values at regular intervals (say once a month) so that percentage training values can be adjusted accordingly.*

3) b) Explain why fitness testing is necessary for both the coach and the athlete?

Answer

- *Provide objective measures about the individual's current state of fitness / health.*
- *Highlights strengths and weaknesses.*
- *Evaluates effects of a training programme.*
- *Motivates individual to reach optimal test scores.*
- *Adds variety to training programme.*

4) b) The aim of Cooper's 12-minute run / walk test is to run as far as possible in 12 minutes.
What aspect of physical fitness does the 12-minute run / walk measure?
Briefly outline the strengths and limitations of this maximal test as a test for aerobic capacity, and identify some of the external variables that could influence the validity and reliability of this test if it test was performed outdoors on a school field.

Answer

Cardio-respiratory endurance: ($\dot{V}O_{2max}$) or stamina.
Strengths:

- *Easy to administer and can involve many participants.*
- *Cheap to administer – only needs tape measure to mark out running surface, a stopwatch to time the 12 minutes and a table to convert distance achieved to a predicted $\dot{V}O_{2max}$ value.*

Limitations:

- *Difficulty in ensuring the subject is exerting maximum effort.*
- *Dependent on level of motivation (arousal levels).*

External variables which may affect the results of the test:

- *Effect of audience / peers.*
- *Footwear - running spikes would give a better grip than flat training shoes.*
- *Clothing - excess weight might be carried during the 12 minute run.*
- *Weather conditions - a major variable which could affect motivation / pace. Wind and rain can be big demotivators.*

5) b) Identify **two** valid and reliable submaximal tests that measure endurance or stamina. Why are submaximal tests often favoured over maximal tests?

Tests:

- *PWC-170 test.*
- *Queen's College Step test.*
- *Harvard Step test.*

Submaximal tests are often favoured over maximal tests because:

- *There is less stress on the performer.*
- *Greater reliability of results.*

6) b) Explain, using examples, why the Illinois agility run test may be of more value to a games player than a 30 metre sprint test.

Answer

- *The Illinois agility run test is a flat-out sprint during which the performer has to weave around a series of cones.*
- *This action requires change of direction and position very similar to the agility required in many games such as rugby and hockey when dodging a player or creating a dummy move is an important agility skill.*
- *On the other hand a 30 metre sprint is a linear flat out sprint test that is less sport specific.*

7) b) From a physiological standpoint, explain why warm-up and cool-down are important within an exercise programme.

Answer

Warm-up:

- *Raises body temperature, increases metabolic rate, raises energy release, reduces response times.*
- *This temperature increase reduces blood viscosity, and therefore increases blood flow to working muscles.*
- *Slightly increased demand for oxygen will increase heart rate and breathing volume, which makes more oxygen available to working tissue.*
- *Blood supply is redistributed to working tissue (**vascular shunt**).*
- *A warm-up also prepares the body for skill demands of the activity - reducing the risk of injury.*

Cool-down:

- *Continued low level exercise and stretching keeps the capillary beds open within active (muscle) tissue.*
- *This enables the flushing out of waste products from the metabolic processes, such as lactic acid.*
- *Enables the body's systems to gradually return to its resting state.*
- *Which limits muscle soreness.*
- *And enhances recovery from the exercise period.*
- *Stretching during cool-down can increase flexibility of joints because the body is still very warm after full effort exercise.*

8) b) You have been asked to prepare a mobility training session for a group of A-level Physical Education students who wish to improve their flexibility for their chosen individual activity.

Explain, with examples, how you would use static, active, passive and ballistic stretching to create a session in the context of safe practice.

Answer

- All stretching should be preceded by a light jog or similar activity to warm-up the body prior to stretching.

Static stretching:

- Should be used at the start of the mobility session.
- These stretches are slow, relaxed, gradual and sustained, achieved without assistance and where an end point position can be held for a few seconds (hence static stretch).
- For example, the sit and reach stretch stretching the hamstring muscle group.
- This is a very safe form of stretching.

Active stretching:

- Is a form of stretching, involves using only the strength of the opposing muscles (antagonist) to generate a held stretch within the agonist.
- For example: stand on one leg, lift the free leg at right angles to the hip and hold the leg straight out for between 10-15 seconds (again a static stretch).
- Active stretching is a very effective form of conditioning.

Passive stretching:

- Is a more aggressive form of slow / static stretching.
- Useful in helping to attain a greater range of movement.
- This is because an external resistance, such as partner or apparatus, aids this type of stretch.
- For example, it is possible to increase the range of motion for the sit and reach stretch. A partner places their hands on the performer's middle back region and gently pushes forward to increase the range of movement.
- When using a partner it is imperative that no jerky or bouncing force is applied to the stretched muscle.
- The stretch is held at the increased end point for a few seconds.
- The stretch must feel comfortable and so must stop if the muscle is stretched to a point of pain.

Ballistic stretching:

- Involves vigorous / rapid / bouncing / swinging movements during which the contraction of the agonist forces the antagonist to relax.
- Is recommended towards the end of the mobility session because of its vigorous nature and risk of muscle tear injury.
- Fails to allow the stretched muscle time to adapt to the stretched position and instead may cause the muscle to tighten up by repeatedly triggering the stretch reflex.

When using all forms of stretching it is important to:

- Stretch both agonists and antagonists to maintain muscle equilibrium.
- Select a range of stretches that stretch all joints and associated muscles, tendons and ligaments.
- Breathe slowly and easily while stretching.

9) b) Your PE group has been asked to devise a running training schedule for an elite 1500m runner. Using your knowledge of both intermittent and continuous training methods show how you could use this information to produce both aerobic and anaerobic adaptations.

Answer

Intermittent training:

- Is also known as **interval** training and can be manipulated by using the following variables:
- Duration of the exercise period.
- Intensity of the exercise period.
- Number of repetitions (reps) within a set.
- Number of sets within a session.
- Duration of the rest interval (rest relief) or recovery.

Our 1500 m athlete would benefit from the following track interval sessions:

- **Lactate acid intervals** increase lactate tolerance.
- Working between medium to high intensity effort i.e. 60-80% of maximum effort).
- Lasting between 30-90 seconds.
- For example, 3 sets x (8 reps x 200m) with 30 seconds rest relief between reps and 5 minutes rest relief between sets.
- Frequency of sessions at least 3 times per week to benefit from anaerobic adaptations.

- **Aerobic intervals** increase aerobic capacity or $\dot{V}O_{2max}$.
- Working at low intensity effort i.e. below 50% of maximum effort.
- For example, 6 reps x 2000m with 3 minutes recovery.

Continuous training:

- Involves continuous activity in which there is no rest or break.
- Is normally associated with developing aerobic capacity ($\dot{V}O_{2max}$).
- Recommended intensity should be between 60-75% of maximum heart (HR_{max}).
- For example, **session 1**: 45 minute steady run at 65% of HR_{max}, **session 2**: 3 km run – 1st km steady at 60% of HR_{max}, 2nd km 70% HR_{max} and 3rd km 75% HR_{max}.
- Frequency of sessions at least 3 times per week to benefit from aerobic adaptations.

10 b) Justify the content of your training programme for an elite 1500m runner, with regard to the expected respiratory adaptations.

Answer

Expected respiratory adaptations resulting from the interval and continuous sessions would be:

- *Improved strengthening of respiratory muscles would enable athlete to train for longer.*
- *Increased pulmonary blood flow, particularly to upper lobes of lungs, and hence greater utilisation of alveoli would increase gaseous exchange and $\dot{V}O_{2max}$.*

The major training adaptations noted during maximal or high intensity sessions are:

- *During a maximal training session, such as during the lactate interval session, long-term adaptations would result from increased breathing rates and increased gaseous exchange.*
- *Resulting in a large increase in minute ventilation.*
- *These adaptations would enable the athlete to increase intensity of training session by delaying the onset of blood lactate accumulation (OBLA) because more oxygen would be available for tissue site respiration.*

- *During submaximal workloads, such as during the 45 minute run, breathing rate and $\dot{V}O_{2max}$ would be less because of greater efficiency of respiratory musculature.*
- *Greater O_2 uptake and increase in lung volumes such as tidal volume.*

- *The $a\text{-}\bar{v}O_{2diff}$ would increase with training, reflecting greater oxygen extraction by the tissues and more effective blood distribution to the active tissues.*
- *Frequency of training sessions would ensure that the respiratory system was stressed sufficiently to ensure that the above adaptations occurred.*

UNIT 1 – SKILLS AND ABILITIES

1) If you were watching a number of performers in sport, what characteristics would you expect the movements of a skilled performer to have?

4 marks

Answer

- *Movement seems effortless.*
- *There are many correct movements consistently performed.*
- *The movement follows a technical model.*
- *The movement is aesthetically pleasing.*
- *The movement is controlled and well co-ordinated.*

2) By using examples from sport, explain what is meant by fundamental psychomotor skills and why they are so important.

4 marks

Answer

- *Jumping, catching, throwing etc.*
- *Basis for the development of other skills.*
- *Learned through early experiences usually via play.*
- *Important because can draw on them for lifetime sports / healthy lifestyles.*
- *Helps personal development / self-esteem.*

3) a) Why is the shot putt often regarded as a closed skill?

2 marks

Answer

- *Tends to be an habitual response.*
- *Little reference to the environment.*
- *There is a definite beginning and end.*
- *More self-paced than externally-paced.*

b) Using passing skills in a team game, explain what is meant by an open skill.

4 marks

Answer

- *When passing a soccer ball you need to take into account any challenge from your opponents.*
- *You need to refer to where your team mate is when passing a netball.*
- *You need to process a great deal of information regarding speed of passing the ball in hockey and the direction of the pass.*
- *When passing the ball in rugby the speed at which you pass is often dictated by how quickly you are being closed-down.*

c) Give one example from sport of each of the following and state why you have chosen your example: continuous skills, serial skills, discrete skills.

3 marks

Answer

- *Continuous skill: cycling - because the subroutines of the pedalling action are not easily separated.*
- *Serial skill: triple jump - because there are a number of discrete elements linked together to make up the whole skill.*
- *Discrete skill: forward roll - because there is a definite beginning and a definite end to the skill.*

4) The diagram in figure B.9 shows a profile for the racing start in swimming scaled across four different continua representing the skill characteristics of the movement.

a) Referring to the profile, describe the swim racing start in terms of each of the four characteristics shown.

4 marks

Answer

- *Continuity: the start is shown as being discrete, it has a distinct beginning and end.*
- *Muscular involvement: the start is shown as having gross muscle actions using large muscle groups violently with little fine control.*
- *Pacing: the start is shown as being externally paced, the swimmer has to react to the external stimulus of the gun or hooter.*
- *Environmental conditions: the start is shown as a closed skill, although the swimmer reacts to an external signal, no interpretation of that stimulus is required, and only the one response (movement from the start box) relevant.*

b) Using this same profile chart, sketch a profile which would describe the characteristics of a table tennis serve.

3 marks

Answer

- *See figure Q.7*

c) Explain why you have chosen your particular characteristic for muscular involvement and environmental conditions. *4 marks*

Answer

Muscular involvement:

- *The table tennis serve is a very delicate movement requiring very fine control of the small muscles in the hands and forearms.*

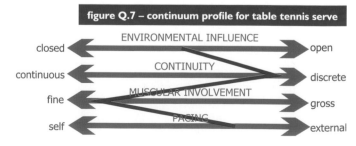

figure Q.7 – continuum profile for table tennis serve

ENVIRONMENTAL INFLUENCE
closed — open

CONTINUITY
continuous — discrete

MUSCULAR INVOLVEMENT
fine — gross

PACING
self — external

Environmental conditions:

- *The serve is a fairly closed skill, then player uses a well-learned technique.*
- *However, a player must be able to use more than one movement pattern in order to be able to respond to the opponent variation in positioning, and / or his / her strength at returning different types of serve, and hence choose appropriately.*
- *And to vary the spin and direction of the ball.*
- *So, each variation of serve will be a closed skill and be part of a well-learned repertoire of serves.*

d) Explain how your profile for the table tennis serve might assist a coach in planning practices for players learning this skill.   *5 marks*

Answer

- *The coach should look at the position of the skill in each continuum to see if it will tell him / her something about how to organise the practices.*

Continuity:

- *Because the skill is discrete, it can be practised in isolation from other aspects of the game.*
- *It should be practised sufficiently to enable accuracy / consistency to develop.*

Pacing:

- *Because the skill is internally paced, the coach should encourage beginners to take their own time in executing the skill.*
- *And to adopt a set routine / mental set for the technique.*

Environmental influence:

- *Although the serve is relatively 'closed', it can be affected by temperature of the playing hall, and pressure of the standing of the event.*
- *Which means that the player should be exposed to practice in this variety of environmental conditions in order to be best prepared for them in the competitive situation.*

5) a) You are observing a number of tennis players being coached. There is a mixture of abilities. Explain what is meant by ability, and give examples of motor abilities and perceptual abilities.   *4 marks*

Answer

- *Ability is a trait / innate / you are born with certain abilities.*
- *Ability is enduring, it tends to last for a long time (all your life?).*
- *Motor ability is concerned with proficiency of movement patterns.*
- *Gross motor ability is an ability to use muscles simply.*
  For example, running or riding a bike or swimming or walking.
- *Perceptual ability is related to processing spatial information.*
  For example, having quick reactions to a stimulus, the reaction of a tennis player to an opponent's stroke.

b) Give **two** types of abilities that are important to play tennis effectively.
Why is it wrong to assume that there is such a thing as natural ability?   *4 marks*

Answer

Types of abilities:

- *Good reactions to stimuli.*
- *Speed of movement.*
- *Explosive strength*
- *Good body balance.*
- *Good timing for hitting the ball and moving into position.*
- *Good degree of body suppleness / flexibility.*

On natural ability:

- *Abilities are not all-encompassing, they are specific.*
- *Specific movements / skills require different abilities.*

INFORMATION PROCESSING

1) Improvement in performance of a skill can be better understood by reference to the processes involved. Figure B.24 shows Whiting's information processing model.

a) Explain the meanings of the terms: **perceptual mechanisms**, **translatory mechanisms**, and **effector mechanisms**, and relate these terms to stages in the Whiting model.

5 marks

Answer

- *Perceptual mechanisms: the part of the brain which makes sense of the surroundings.*
- *And gives this information meaning.*
- *Translatory mechanisms: the part of the brain whose purpose is to select relevant information.*
- *From the total information received via the senses from the surroundings.*
- *Effector mechanisms: the part of the brain whose purpose is to set in motion the appropriate neuromuscular sequences to activate the skill.*
- *They send messages to the limbs and muscles ready to perform the skill.*

b) The diagram also shows five arrows entering the perceptual mechanism and only one leaving. What is the name given to this process and why is it necessary?

4 marks

Answer

- *Selective attention.*
- *The purpose of this mechanism is to filter out unnecessary information.*
- *Many items of information are received by the perceptual mechanisms of sight, hearing, touch - only some of these are relevant to the learning situation.*
- *This process is that of focusing on relevant information.*
- *It is necessary to filter out irrelevant information because there is too much information arriving for the limited capacity of the translatory mechanism.*

c) Identify **three** factors which might help a performer with his / her perceptual mechanisms.

3 marks

Answer

- *High quality of instruction.*
- *Expectation of certain stimuli.*
- *Vividness or intensity of relevant stimulus.*
- *Unusual or contrasting stimulus.*
- *Arousal or alertness of performer.*

2) Identify the **three** main receptor systems used by a performer in sport.
Where is the filtering mechanism found in an information processing model? Explain what happens with information as it passes through this mechanism.

5 marks

Answer

- *Visual - sight.*
- *Auditory - hearing.*
- *Proprioceptors - touch or feeling about body position.*

The filtering mechanism is found:

- *In the short-term sensory store (STSS).*
- *Helps with selective attention.*
- *Makes irrelevant information redundant.*
- *Helps to concentrate effort on information that is important.*

3) Using figure B.25 representing the human motor control mechanism, explain what is meant by short-term memory and long-term memory.   *2 marks*

Answer

- *Long-term and short-term memories are part of the multi-store model of memory.*
- *All information passes through STM.*
- *STM uses information immediately if presented within about 1 minute.*
- *LTM has almost limitless capacity.*
- *LTM stores information over a long period of time.*
- *LTM stores are used if information is over 1 minute old.*

b) How can information be retained in the long-term memory?

4 marks

Answer

- *Through repetition of the stimulus / practice / overlearning.*
- *Through having meaning / relevance to the performer.*
- *Information is novel / unusual / unique.*

- *Stored here if **associated** with another piece of stored information / **chunking** / organise information in groups.*
- *Link information to **past experiences**.*
- *If stimuli are **emotionally** intense / **exciting** / **enjoyable** / **interesting**.*
- *If information is perceived to be **important**.*
- ***Reward** / **reinforce** success.*

4) a) Using the example of a table tennis player receiving a serve what information would be held in the short-term sensory store, and for how long?

4 marks

Answer

- *Information held would be local and temporary.*
- *Pertaining to the immediate surroundings of the player and his / her opponent.*
- *This would be retained for up to 1/4 seconds or sooner if the display changes.*
- *And new more relevant information replaces it.*
- *Examples would be from: position of the ball, placement of opponents hands / bat, placement of opponent relative to table.*

b) Name and describe the purpose of the process by which information is transferred from the short-term sensory store to the short-term memory.

4 marks

Answer

- *The process is called **selective attention**.*
- *And is caused by the individual selecting from the many (thousands) of bits of information which flow through the short-term sensory store each second.*
- *Those items which are relevant.*
- *And avoiding items which would distract the player (such as the crowd, other movements behind the ball).*
- *An example could be the retaining of the ready position of the opponent once the serve has begun.*

5) a) Explain the difference between reaction time, movement time and response time? What advice would you give to a sprinter to cut down on reaction time at the start of a race?

4 marks

Answer

- ***Reaction time*** *= time between onset of stimulus and the initiation of the response.*
- ***Movement time*** *= time it takes to complete the movement required by the stimulus.*
- ***Response time*** *is reaction time plus movement time / it is the time between the onset of the stimulus and the completion of the response.*

Advice given:

- *Coach **concentration** / focusing.*
- *Teach **mental rehearsal**.*
- *Lower **arousal** level of athlete via cognitive / somatic strategies.*
- *Ignore external stimuli other than the starting gun / selective attention.*
- *Teach strategies of driving from the blocks / **practise responding** to the gun.*

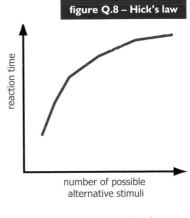

figure Q.8 – Hick's law

reaction time

number of possible alternative stimuli

b) Sketch and label a graph to illustrate Hick's Law.
How does the number of choices available to a performer affect his / her performance?

4 marks

Answer

- *See the figure Q.8.*
- *As the number of choices increases, the time taken to respond increases.*
- *The more choices available, the longer it takes to decide between them which is relevant.*
- *Before reaction can occur.*

c) When taking part in a badminton game, the shuttle occasionally hits the netcord during a rally, and the receiver has to adjust his / her return shot. This causes a delay before the final response can be made. What is this delay called and explain why it occurs?

4 marks

Answer

- *The delay is called the **psychological refractory period**.*
- *This slows down the processing of the response because the first stream of information (speed and direction of shuttle) is interrupted.*
- *A second stream of information is then begun (new speed and direction of shuttle after the netcord).*
- *The process of reaction is then started again - hence a delay in response.*

d) What factors could affect response time in any game or sport?　　　　　　　　*4 marks*

Answer

- *Number of choices to be made during the response process.*
- *Whether the skill is open / complex / externally paced.*
- *Whether there are a number of sequential (one after the other) stimuli / the psychological refractory period.*
- *Distractions / ability to selectively attend or focus on the stimulus.*
- *Spectator distractions / social inhibition / presence of significant others.*
- *Age / gender.*
- *Level of personal fitness / health / body type or shape (somatotype) / length of neural pathways (whether the athlete is tall or short for example).*
- *Past experience / presence of motor programmes / level of skill / level of ability.*
- *Environmental factors such as weather / state of playing surface or court / state of personal kit or shoes.*

6)　a) Explain what is meant by a motor programme and give an example.
　　How can a programme become a subroutine?　　　　　　　　*4 marks*

Answer

- *A motor programme is a set of movements stored in the long-term memory.*
- *Movements are so well-learned they are almost automatic.*
- *One decision can stimulate the onset of a programme.*
- *Examples: a basketball dribble, throwing a ball, cycling.*

How can a programme become a subroutine?

- *The programme is so well-learned / habitual / overlearned.*
- *That it becomes part (subroutine) of a more complex movement.*
- *For example, a basketball dribble becomes a subroutine of the lay-up shot.*

b)　How is closed loop control used to make a movement more skilful?
　　Explain the contribution of the use of subroutines to open loop control and the autonomous phase of learning.　　　　　　　　*5 marks*

Answer

Closed loop control contributes via:

- *Proprioception / intrinsic feedback gives information about errors and / or correct movements.*
- *This information can then be used to correct errors or reinforce correct movement.*
- *Information is sent via the command mechanism / effector mechanism for muscular control.*
- *There has to be little conscious attention during closed loop control.*

Explanation of use of subroutines to open loop control:

- *Well-learned subroutines linked together to produce a finely balanced skill.*
- *Contribute to the autonomous phase of learning due to the fact that the skill is well-learned.*
- *And little intervention is required from a coach.*
- *Little feedback is required (except for final knowledge of results / performance) because the skill is performed automatically.*
- *Hence open loop control, and the motor command to perform the skill produces the movement with very little feedback during the movement itself.*

7) a) Looking at the figure B.26, list **six** major subroutines of the executive programme for throwing.　　　　　　　　*6 marks*

Answer

List six from the following:

- *Grip on implement.*
- *Initial body / arm / feet / head position.*
- *Action of right leg (right handed thrower).*
- *Action of trunk during throw.*
- *Action of right arm during throw.*
- *Sequence of legs - trunk - arm during throw.*
- *Position and action of left side / leg / arm before delivery.*
- *Position of head / eyes (view) during delivery.*

b) Briefly explain how the analysis of skills will influence a coach in organising training for javelin throwing as compared with basketball free throw.

4 marks

Answer

- *The breaking down of the skill into subroutines will enable the coach to analyse the movements objectively.*
- *And thereby set a programme for practice of the individual subroutines.*
- *As drills or individual skill practices which are made separately.*
- *Which would then be incorporated into the motor programme as a whole.*

LEARNING AND PERFORMANCE

1) Figure B.50 shows the improvement in performance of a gymnast over a period of time. Name the stages **A**, **B** and **C** shown on this chart and explain their significance to the gymnast.   *6 marks*

Answer

- *A - Cognitive stage.*
- *For example, a beginner watching a demonstration.*
- *He / she is able to perform simple routines without much technical complexity.*
- *B - Associative stage.*
- *For example, the gymnast has learnt a number of simple routines which he / she can now put together into a more complex sequence.*
- *Trial and error and complex advice from the coach now lead to more rapid progress.*
- *C - Autonomous stage.*
- *For example, the gymnast is able to perform complex skills without much cognitive effort.*
- *His / her routines are now technically excellent and can be performed without the constant intervention of a coach.*
- *The coach's role is now to choreograph and advise on the shapes and sequences of movement rather than the techniques involved.*

b) Identify the characteristics of a performer in phase **C**.   *4 marks*

Answer

- *Almost automatic in movements.*
- *Seems confident / has predetermined goals.*
- *More likely to complete complex movements.*
- *Is successful consistently.*
- *Less likely to lose concentration / is focused.*
- *Advanced performers will only stay in this phase if they keep referring back to the associative phase / keep practising.*

c) How might the type of mental practice change in the last phase of learning?   *4 marks*

Answer

- *Concentrating on only very few stimuli / very selective in attention.*
- *Less about skill performance, more on keeping calm and controlling arousal.*
- *Utilising imagery of the sequences as part of the warm-up.*
- *Visualising success more than other phases.*
- *Thinking more about tactics / strategies.*

2) According to Fitts and Posner, learning passes through three stages. Use an example from one of your practical activities to describe the key characteristics of each of these stages.   *5 marks*

Answer

Select your practical activity.

Stage 1: *cognitive*

- *Learner is using trial and error learning*
- *Getting an idea of the skill.*
- *Many mistakes made.*
- *Movement is inconsistent.*
- *Movement lacks fluency*
- *Performer concentrates on every aspect of the movement.*

Stage 2: *associative*

- *Movement is smoother.*
- *Subroutines linked.*
- *Performer can use kinaesthetic feedback.*
- *Motor programmes are formed.*
- *Practice required / awareness of mistakes.*

Stage 3: *autonomous*

- *Movements are automatic.*
- *No conscious thought or attention required,*
- *Tactics and strategies can be focused on.*
- *Reaction time is reduced.*
- *Detailed external feedback can be used.*
- *Errors can be detected and corrected without help.*
- *Must practice to remain in this stage.*
- *Fluent, flowing.*

3) a) Describe what is meant by the term feedback, and briefly describe **three** functions of feedback. *5 marks*

Answer

- *Feedback is any kind of information received by a learner as a result of a particular response or act.*
- *This information would be available during and after the movement had been completed.*
- *And would be brought into the system both during the course of the movement and after the movement had been completed.*

Functions of feedback are:

- *Motivational: success or failure, clear goals, inspires the performer to continue striving for perfection.*
- *Reinforcing: increases the chance of the performer repeating the performance.*
- *Informational: the outcome of the performance, is it correct or incorrect?*

b) Where possible explain the kinds of feedback available to a performer which would be classified as:
  i) Intrinsic and internal.
  ii) Extrinsic and internal.

4 marks

Answer

- *Intrinsic and internal feedback represents feedback that is perceived by the performer.*
- *By proprioception, the feeling of muscle tension.*
- *And the performer is able to relate this to feelings of success or failure.*
- *Extrinsic and internal feedback represents feedback that might be due to a crowd noise reacting to a game situation.*
- *Which leads to a feeling of well being or success.*
- *Or seeing other performers reactions to your performance which leads to the same feelings.*

4) Explain how feedback differs through the associative and autonomous stages of learning as a performer makes progress. *4 marks*

Answer

- *In the associative stage, the performer begins to monitor his / her own feedback.*
- *He / she still needs feedback from the coach which is more technically exact than for the novice (cognitive phase) performer.*
- *Feedback will be more extrinsic then intrinsic.*
- *In the autonomous stage, the performer would be less reliant on knowledge of results.*
- *He / she would be able to detect his / her own errors and use kinaesthetic feedback to do this.*
- *He / she would be able to correct his / her own performance without coach intervention.*

5) A pole vaulter makes rapid progress when first learning the event, but then reaches a plateau of performance.
a) Explain what the plateau is and why it might occur. *4 marks*

Answer

A plateau:

- *A plateau is when the performance stops improving / levels out.*

The plateau occurs because:

- *The person has limited ability and has reached the limits of possible performance.*
- *The training tasks are too difficult for the performer.*
- *The person has reached the limits of the cognitive stage of learning, and is ready to move to the associative stage – with different ways of learning and guidance.*
- *There is a transitional period before development of a more complex skill.*
- *The person is injured or overtrained.*
- *The person becomes bored with the skill learning process.*
- *The person is fatigued.*
- *Coaching has reached the limit of the coach's ability.*
- *Once a certain level of performance is reached, the person is less well-motivated to learn or train.*
- *Once a certain level has been reached, the skill or power level required to improve further requires much more time and intensity of focus.*

b) What strategies could be used to improve from the plateau level? *4 marks*

Answer

- *Give new goals that can be reached.*
- *Give praise that is deserved.*
- *Give new responsibility (team captain?).*
- *Ensure that there are regular rest intervals.*
- *Maintain motivation and employ positive cognitive techniques.*
- *Explain what the plateau is, and why progress will be made in the future.*
- *Provide appropriate feedback.*
- *Vary types and methods in training.*
- *Re-establish physical fitness.*
- *Look at technical development for possible variations or improvements.*

- *Improve coaching knowledge.*
- *Change the way in which a skill is taught, with whole-part-whole practice.*

6) a) What sort of motivation methods would you use to motivate a beginner in gymnastics?   *4 marks*
Answer
- *Give achievable goals / give success.*
- *Reinforce through praise or success.*
- *Only praise when it is deserved.*
- *Verbal encouragement.*
- *Vicarious processes / give models of similar ability.*
- *Introduce a small element of competition.*
- *But keep competition to a minimum.*
- *Emphasise personal progress.*
- *Raise status of the activity.*

b) How would the motivation methods used for a skilled performer differ from those used for a beginner?   *3 marks*
Answer
- *Give more demanding goals / just beyond reach.*
- *Emphasise results.*
- *Comparisons play a bigger part.*
- *Larger extrinsic rewards.*
- *Use of audience / presence of others.*
- *Reinforce success.*
- *Reinforce tactical aspects.*
- *Attribute success to internal factors.*

7) a) Explain how you would use operant conditioning to teach a sports skill of your choice.   *5 marks*
Answer
- *Operant conditioning is shaping behaviour by reinforcement.*
- *The sportsperson has a go at the sport, and the correct effort is reinforced, and the incorrect effort negatively reinforced.*
- *This is done by the teacher praising success, and hence giving the sportsperson a feeling of well-being when success is achieved.*
- *When an incorrect effort is achieved, praise is withdrawn or not given.*
- *So the sportsperson learns to associate (connect) praise (and well-being – the stimulus) with a correct effort (the response).*
- *This is called the stimulus-response bond.*
- *The sportsperson is learning by trial and error.*
- *Eventually, incorrect responses will disappear, because the person wants to feel good.*
- *This process can be extended by showing the sportsperson how to perform the activity, this is called shaping, then the correct shape is reinforced (rather than just the shuttle going over the net as in badminton).*
- *For example, to teach a high long serve in badminton.*
- *Give demonstration (shaping)*
- *Get opponent to stand in service box opposite with racket held high (shaping)*
- *Give targets to aim for (shaping) – aim to get the shuttle over the opponent's head.*
- *Give knowledge of results (reinforcement) – did the shuttle pass over the opponent's head and land inside the baseline?*
- *Give feedback about performance (reinforcement) – was the shot performed with the correct wrist movement?*
- *Give praise (reinforcement).*

b) Describe what is meant by reinforcement and give examples of different types.   *4 marks*
Answer
- *Reinforcement is the manipulation of a stimulus to ensure that a response reoccurs.*
- *For example, positive reinforcement - giving praise when a swimmer wins a race.*
- *For example, negative reinforcement - taking away the praise if the swimmer subsequently loses*
- *For example, punishment - telling the swimmer off for not trying very hard if he / she loses the race.*

8) a) Using examples from sport explain what is meant by the S-R bond. *4 marks*
Answer

- *A certain response is connected to a certain stimulus. For example, a forehand is hit by a right-handed player because the ball appears on the right hand side of the player's body.*
- *The stimulus acts as a cue to be associated with a response. For example, in volleyball a player will jump to block a ball being smashed across the net by the opposition.*
- *The response is almost automatic because the bond is so great between stimulus and response.*
- *For example, a 'reflex' save by a goalkeeper to a shot on goal.*
- *Or a sprinter driving out of the blocks when the gun goes.*
- *The bond (link) is strengthened by reinforcing correct responses – giving praise for correct responses, and withdrawing praise or giving punishment for incorrect responses.*

b) Explain how a coach in a sport could ensure that a correct response follows a particular stimulus. *5 marks*
Answer

- *Give praise / positive reinforcement.*
- *Give feedback / give direct knowledge about what to do.*
- *Give satisfaction if movement is correct (Thorndike's Law of Effect).*
- *Give negative reinforcement (withdraw praise) if movement is incorrect.*
- *Give punishment if movement is incorrect.*
- *Repeat the correct movement to establish a motor programme.*

9) a) In racquet sports, coaches give demonstrations to aid skill development. Identify the stages of Bandura's model of observational learning, giving an appropriate example of each stage to illustrate your understanding. *4 marks*

Answer

- *Attention - key areas of the skill are highlighted.*
- *Retention - the performer must remember information in order to reproduce it.*
- *Motor reproduction - the performer must be physically capable of reproducing the skill.*
- *Motivation - the performer must be motivated to perform the skill, by intrinsic or extrinsic means.*

b) Explain the cognitive theory of learning as proposed by Gestaltists and apply this to a practical situation. *4 marks*
Answer

- *Gestalt means 'whole' - the learner must look at the problem associated with learning a skill in its entirety.*
- *Concerned with understanding and insight.*
- *A racquet player will understand the necessity for performing a particular shot.*
- *In respect of the tactics of the game, and the exploitation of an opponent's weakness.*

10) Stimulus-response bonding has been used to explain how a physical skill can be learned. What is a stimulus-response bond and how can a Physical Education teacher ensure that it is strengthened when teaching swimming or athletics? *6 marks*

Answer
Definition of S-R bond:
  - *Performer learns to link a particular response to a particular stimulus.*
  - *For example, the starter's gun in swimming (stimulus) triggers the swimmer's movement (response) from the blocks / poolside.*
Strengthening the S-R bond:
  - *Must use swimming / athletics example.*
  - *Use reinforcement / praise / punishment / to ensure that the person is made to feel good about the correct response, and bad about an incorrect response.*
- *Thorndikes - Law of Readiness:*
  - *A performer must be mentally and physically able to do the task.*
  - *For example, a learner swimmer must want to and be physically capable of trying butterfly if she is to master the stroke.*
  - *For example, an 11 year old boy will be physically incapable of performing a slam dunk in basketball.*
- *Thorndikes - Law of Exercise:*
  - *Practice of the task will strengthen the S-R connections.*
  - *For example, the athlete has frequent attempts at the sprint start.*
- *Thorndikes - Law of Effect:*
  - *If the response is followed by satisfaction / positive feedback (a 'satisfier'), the bond is strengthened.*
  - *If the response is followed by a intense emotional feeling (of well-being) the bond is strengthened.*
  - *For example, the swimmer who feels pride after doing 25m for the first time.*
  - *If the response is followed by an 'annoyer' / negative feedback the bond is weakened.*
  - *For example, a young high jumper who repeatedly knocks the bar off because the bar is too high.*
- *Positive reinforcement / Reward / Praise:*
  - *Operant conditioning / shaping / increases the chance of the behaviour occurring again.*
  - *For example, the swimmer gains a badge for completing 25m.*

- *Negative reinforcement:*
  - *The behaviour is likely to be repeated when a stimulus is withdrawn.*
  - *For example, no-one makes fun of the pupil who usually comes last when he / she achieves a better placing.*
- *Punishment:*
  - *The stimulus given prevents a particular response occurring.*
  - *For example, a pupil is made to perform an extra lap of the track for unsafe behaviour in the javelin lesson.*

11) a) Using examples from sport, identify **four** items of information stored as schema.　　　　　*4 marks*

Answer

- *Knowledge of the environment, for example, knowing how far away you are from the basket before you shoot in basketball.*
- *Response specifications, for example, knowing what you have to do to score.*
- *Sensory consequences, for example, what the movement feels like as you are shooting.*
- *Response outcomes, for example, the end result which would be either success or failure.*

b) Comparing the skills of throwing the javelin and taking a free throw at basketball, explain how the skills are related using schema theory.　　*4 marks*

Answer

- *Knowledge of initial conditions (of the environment) - awareness of the foul line and the need to complete the throw behind it (javelin), awareness of side line again with the need to complete the throw outside the court proper (basketball).*
- *Knowledge of response specifications - knowing that you have to throw as far as possible into the field (javelin), knowing that you have to throw to a colleague on the court (basketball).*
- *Knowledge of sensory consequences - the feeling of the movement of throwing (both).*
- *Knowledge of response outcomes - distance thrown (javelin), correct receipt of the ball by colleague (basketball).*

12) How could a teacher of Physical Education use his / her knowledge of schema theory when planning a practice session for a named activity?　　*5 marks*

Answer

- *Information in LTM used to modify:*
  - *motor programmes*
  - *a set of rules that determine the performance of a skill*
  - *a scheme that provides the basis for a decision.*
  - *for example, teacher tells group that they are going to learn reverse stick dribble in hockey by using the information already stored.*
- *Variability of practice:*
  - *building up a set of 'rules' through different variations*
  - *practice takes into account all the possibilities.*
  - *for example, practising throwing different lengths / speeds / directions / angles.*
- *Errors can be included in practice to develop the schema.*
  - *for example, the defender can only learn to block an opponent by having a go.*
- *Recall schema starts:*
  - *the movement*
  - *initial conditions*
  - *body position*
  - *details concerning the environment contained in recall schema*
  - *for example, the distance between players for specific passes in an invasion game.*
- *Response specifications:*
  - *what is required to do the skill.*
  - *for example, the players need to know how fast to move to get free.*
- *Recognition schema:*
  - *controls the movement*
  - *information required to evaluate the movement.*
  - *for example, sportspeople need to know what to do to improve.*
- *Sensory consequences:*
  - *information based on kinaesthetic or proprioceptive feedback*
  - *information using all the sensory systems.*
  - *for example, remind the players of how the skill felt last time.*
- *Response outcomes:*
  - *use of knowledge of results*
  - *comparison between actual and intended outcome*
  - *refer to past experiences.*
  - *for example, was the shot at goal successful?*

13) Explain **four** different types of transfer of learning.   *4 marks*

Answer

Any four from:

- *Positive transfer is one skill helping the learning / performance of another.*
- *Negative transfer is one skill hindering the learning / performance of another skill.*
- *Bi-lateral transfer is the transfer of learning / performance from limb to limb.*
- *Retroactive transfer is the influence of a skill being learned on a previously learned skill.*
- *Proactive transfer is the influence of a skill being learned on future skills, a skill learned in the past has an influence on a present skill.*

14) a) Using a practical example, explain what is meant by the term transfer in skill learning.
How can transfer be detrimental to performance? Give a practical example.   *5 marks*

Answer

Transfer in skill learning:

- *The influence of the learning or performance of one skill on the learning / performance of another skill.*
- *If you perform one skill and then perform another, the second may well be affected by the first.*
- *For example, you perform a push pass in hockey and then you perform a flick, the actions of the first skill may help that of the second (positive transfer).*

Detrimental to performance:

- *The performance of one skill may well hinder the performance of another.*
- *Because there may well be inappropriate movements / information processing which could confuse the performer.*
- *For example, a badminton player may play tennis immediately after playing badminton and the forehand in tennis may be far too 'wristy' because of the confusion in the response.*

b) How can a teacher or a coach ensure that as much positive transfer takes place as possible in a training session?   *5 marks*

Answer

- *The coach uses as many different practices as possible in training – drills are varied.*
- *Emphasise the transferable elements of the skills.*
- *Tell performers about transfer to heighten awareness.*
- *To ensure the building of schema.*
- *Make sure training is relevant to the 'real' game.*
- *Environmental conditions need to be similar.*
- *Tactics / strategies / information processing elements need to be similar.*
- *Avoid confusing practises to avoid negative transfer.*
- *Ensure that skills are thoroughly learned before moving on to other skills.*
- *Give distributed practice sessions / rest intervals for mental assimilation.*
- *Positive previous experiences or values assist transfer.*

15) A coach reinforces good performances in training with praise. Why does this reinforcement work rather than punishing poor performance? Explain what is meant by reinforcement and punishment in this case.   *5 marks*

Answer

- *Reinforcement works because the praise (giving a pleasant experience) to the performer will enhance and give motivation to the performer to repeat the good performance.*
- *The S-R bond is enhanced.*
- *Punishment of a poor performance (giving an unpleasant experience) has the chance that the person could be demotivated by the activity.*
- *And good performances never attained.*

What is meant by reinforcement?

- *Reinforcement is the giving of pleasant experiences for good performances to attempt to enhance the S-R bond and stimulate the correct response.*

What is meant by punishment?

- *Punishment is the giving of unpleasant experiences for poor responses / performances.*
- *This is an attempt to make a performer reject an undesirable response.*
- *And hence try harder to attain a correct response.*

16) a) Explain the difference between massed and distributed practice. 2 marks

Answer

- *Massed - no rest intervals / practice conditions of long duration.*
- *Distributed - rest intervals at regular periods of time during a session.*

b) Justify the choice of practice conditions for a training session of a sport of your choice. 6 marks

Answer

Massed:

- *To ensure motor programmes are learned / for overlearning.*
- *To encourage an habitual response.*
- *To cut down on response / reaction time.*
- *Good for learning discrete skills.*
- *Good for skills performed over a short duration, for example, basketball shots.*
- *But can lead to fatigue / boredom / demotivation.*

Distributed:

- *To give physical rest / recuperation.*
- *To give mental rest / gather thoughts.*
- *To relieve stress.*
- *Provides safety for dangerous activities.*

c) Name **two** characteristics of the task, and **two** attributes of the learner which might lead you to decide which method (massed or distributed) of practice to use. 4 marks

Answer

Two characteristics of a task from the following:

- *Whether the skill was complex and lengthy or short and discrete.*
- *Whether the task required great fitness levels.*
- *Whether the task was dangerous or not.*

Two attributes of the learner:

- *The motivation levels of the learner.*
- *The personality of the learner (whether or not he / she would be prepared to persist in the learning task).*

17) a) What are the **main** positive effects of setting goals in sport? 2 marks

Answer

- *Raising motivation levels.*
- *Controlling anxiety or stress.*

b) Show what is meant by short-term goals and long-term goals by using examples from sport. 4 marks

Answer

- *Short-term goals - process oriented goals.*
- *Which affect aspects of performance.*
- *For example, the goal of following through into court after a serve in tennis.*
- *Long-term goals - product oriented.*
- *Which affect the result or future aim.*
- *For example, to beat your personal best in athletics or to win the league at soccer.*

c) As a coach how would you ensure that your goal setting was as effective as possible? 6 marks

Answer

- *Goals must be attainable / within your reach.*
- *Goals which are challenging are more motivating.*
- *Set goals which are positive rather than negative.*
- *Goals should involve individual as well as team targets.*
- *Goals should be measurable.*
- *Target dates are important so that the performer is accountable.*
- *Goals should be negotiable.*
- *Goals should have shared ownership.*
- *Goals should be a mixture of process and product.*

UNIT 2 – SKILL ACQUISITION IN PRACTICAL SITUATIONS

1) a) Figure 2B.13 shows Mosston's spectrum of teaching styles in terms of decision making in the learning process. Identify the teaching style at A, and explain its consequences for teaching method.
What are the advantages and disadvantages of this teaching style in teaching a sport or sport skill?

Answer

Teaching style at A:

- *Command / autocratic / authoritarian style.*
- *Teacher makes most of the decisions.*
- *Learner takes little or no responsibility for the progress of the learning process.*

Advantages:

- *More control / discipline.*
- *Good if time is short / efficient.*
- *Good for dangerous situations.*
- *Effective for large groups / teams.*

Disadvantages:

- *No individual feedback.*
- *No participation in decision making.*
- *No social interaction.*
- *Creativity of performer not taken into account.*

2) a) What is meant by the reciprocal teaching style and what are its drawbacks?
What are the **main** advantages of the discovery method of teaching?

Answer

- *Reciprocal style = teacher develops pupils as teachers.*

Drawbacks are:

- *Lack of control.*
- *May be false information passed on.*
- *Lack of credibility of teacher-pupils.*
- *If communication skills poor, then teaching ineffective.*

Main advantages of discovery method of teaching are:

- *Facilitates creativity.*
- *Sense of ownership over your own learning.*
- *Great deal of satisfaction if success is experienced.*
- *Work can be undertaken at the learner's own pace.*
- *Many experiences can build a large store of schema.*
- *Learning is more long-lasting / more meaningful.*

3) a) Generally a skill should be taught as a whole as far as possible. Give reasons for this.
Some skills need to be split up into parts to be taught effectively. What are the advantages and disadvantages of this type of skill presentation?

Answer

Teaching skill as a whole:

- *The performer can appreciate skill in its entirety.*
- *Has overall kinaesthetic sense of the skill.*
- *The flow of the skill is not interfered with.*
- *Much more efficient in skill learning / quicker to learn.*
- *Can help understanding / cognitive development of the performer.*

Splitting into parts:

Advantages:

- *Useful if skill is dangerous / to lower fear level.*
- *Good for complex / difficult skills.*
- *Good for serial skills.*
- *Gives success at each stage / less likely to fail overall skill.*
- *Helps confidence and motivation.*

Disadvantages:

- *Transfer of movements from the part skill to the whole may not work.*
- *Some skills cannot be split up into subroutines very easily.*
- *Loses the overall kinaesthetic sense.*
- *Loses the flow of the skill.*
- *Takes up too much time.*

4) a) Explain the difference between massed and distributed practice.
   Justify the choice of practice conditions for a training session of a sport / game of your choice.
   Name **two** characteristics of the task, and **two** attributes of the learner which might lead you to decide which method (massed or distributed) of practice to use.

Answer

- *Massed - no rest intervals / practice conditions of long duration.*
- *Distributed - rest intervals at regular periods of time during a session.*

Massed:

- *To ensure motor programmes are learned / for overlearning.*
- *To encourage an habitual response.*
- *To cut down on response / reaction time.*
- *Good for learning discrete skills.*
- *Good for skills performed over a short duration, for example, basketball shots.*
- *But can lead to fatigue / boredom / demotivation.*

Distributed:

- *To give physical rest / recuperation.*
- *To give mental rest / gather thoughts.*
- *To relieve stress.*
- *Provides safety for dangerous activities.*

Two characteristics of the task from the following:

- *Whether the skill was complex and lengthy or short and discrete.*
- *Whether the task required great fitness levels.*
- *Whether the task was dangerous or not*

Two attributes from the learner:

- *The motivation levels of the learner.*
- *The personality of the learner (whether or not he / she would be prepared to persist in the learning task).*

Make sure you use the above answer in relation to a sport / game of your choice.

5) a) Other than visual guidance, what other **main** methods of guidance are there? Give a practical example for each.
   How would you optimise the use of visual guidance in teaching motor skills? What are the drawbacks of this method?

Answer

- *Verbal - for example, instructions to an athlete before a race.*
- *Manual - for example, supporting a gymnast doing a handspring.*
- *Mechanical - for example, a child using stabilisers on a bicycle.*

Visual guidance:

- *The coach or teacher would use an accurate demonstration.*
- *Cueing the performer to important elements.*
- *Use immediately before performance.*
- *If visual guidance is used as feedback, it must be used immediately after the performance.*
- *Make sure it is supplemented with verbal guidance.*
- *If models / videos are used, ensure relevance to the learner.*
- *Make sure the model presented is attainable.*

Drawbacks:

- *Confusion if too much visual guidance is shown at a time.*
- *Model / demonstration may be inaccurate.*
- *If videos are used, these may be boring / demotivating.*
- *Model seen may be perceived as unattainable.*

6) a) Identify **two** different mechanical items which might assist movement skill learning.
   Give reasons for the use of these mechanical items to help a learner come to grips with a motor skill.

Answer

Any two examples of mechanical aids to learning:

- *Support belt in trampolining.*
- *Stabilisers on bicycle.*
- *Arm bands in swimming.*

Give reasons:

- *Gives confidence to learner.*
- *Provides safety.*
- *Enables success.*
- *Builds up subroutines and enables part-learning.*
- *Gives an idea of the skill with similar kinaesthesis.*

7) a) Explain how feedback in a sports skill learning situation helps the sportsperson improve performance.

Answer

- *Helps with motivation, and increases self-confidence.*
- *Helps with detecting and correcting errors.*
- *Reinforces correct actions / skills, so that the performer knows what to do.*
- *Strengthens the S-R bond in the learning situation, so that the correct movement is perceived by the sportsperson to be the correct thing to do.*
- *Reduces / prevents bad habits.*
- *Helps reduce likelihood of inhibition / drive reduction theory.*

8) a) Define the term feedback, and briefly describe **three** functions of feedback.
   How would you make feedback effective when teaching a motor skill?

Answer

- *Feedback is any kind of information received by a learner as a result of a particular response or act.*
- *This information would be available during and after the movement had been completed.*
- *And would be brought into the system both during the course of the movement and after the movement had been completed.*

Functions of feedback are:

- *Motivational - success or failure, clear goals, inspires the performer to continue striving for perfection.*
- *Reinforcing - increases the chance of the performer repeating the performance.*
- *Informational - the outcome of the performance, is it correct or incorrect?*

Effective feedback:

- *Feedback must be accurate and well-informed.*
- *Knowledge of results is important.*
- *Be specific and selective with information / not too much information at a time.*
- *Make the feedback interesting to hold attention and aid retention.*
- *Information should be understood by the performer.*
- *Feedback should be given straight after the performance.*
- *Encourage intrinsic feedback / the feel of the movement / kinaesthesis.*

UNIT I – I: INTRODUCTION TO CONCEPTS

1) Identify possible physical objectives of a major game, swimming or athletics as part of your Physical Education programme.　　*3 marks*

Answer

The objective of improving:

- *Health / improved heart rate.*
- *Fitness / getting stronger / increased mobility / endurance.*
- *Skills / skilfulness / prowess.*
- *Techniques and strategies.*
- *Physical competition / effort.*
- *Enjoyable / physical feel-good factor.*

2) What are the **main** educational qualities of outdoor education? Illustrate your answer using a specific outdoor activity.　　*3 marks*

Answer

Select a specific outdoor activity and relate it to the following qualities:

- *Leadership skills.*
- *Problem solving.*
- *Strategy building.*
- *Thrilling / exciting emotional experiences.*
- *Appreciation of the natural world / environment.*
- *Social / group awareness (having fun with friends, learning how to co-operate with group).*

3) Identify **four** characteristics of sport using a game to illustrate each of them.　　*4 marks*

Answer

Select your game to illustrate four characteristics from:

- *Vigorous physical exertion.*
- *Complex physical skills.*
- *Institutionalised.*
- *Highly competitive.*
- *Involves team / opposition.*
- *Fair play / sportsmanship.*
- *Retains the characteristics of play.*
- *Can be in one's free time.*
- *Involves personal choices.*
- *Pleasurable and rewarding.*

4) Discuss the **main** similarities and differences between physical recreation and sport.　　*4 marks*

Answer

Similarities between physical recreation and sport:

- *They can be similar activities.*
- *They both tend include a physical component.*
- *Both have social values.*
- *Individuals choose to take part in both.*
- *Both identify enjoyment as important.*

Differences between physical recreation and sport:

- *Sport is highly competitive – recreation can be fun and done for its own sake.*
- *Sport is highly organised – recreation can be spur of the moment with its own rules and boundaries.*
- *Sport tends to be at a higher standard – recreation can be at whatever standard people want.*
- *Sport has more stringent rules / regulated – recreation has its own time and space with rules wanted by the participants.*
- *Sport tends to require more time / commitment – recreation can be as short or as long as wanted – usuually no commitment except to the present activity.*

5) a) In the UK and Europe people participate in sport, leisure and recreation. Define and outline the differences between these three forms of activity.　　*3 marks*

Answer

- *Sport is a competitive physical activity between opponents.*
- *Sport is highly organised with formal rules.*
- *It has set times and space (venue).*
- *It is codified.*

- *Leisure is free time or / time not at work.*
- *Leisure can be used for many activities.*
- *And can be passive or active.*
- *Recreation is non-competitive and is usually less serious than sport.*
- *Recreation is less organised and more flexible.*
- *Recreation has intrinsic value to the performer.*

b) How can a school provide opportunities to participate in both sport and recreation?   *3 marks*

Answer

- *Sport is provided as extra-curricular activity.*
- *Schools make provision for sports teams and fixtures.*
- *Schools set up sport education programmes.*
- *Recreational sport takes place in lunchtimes or sports clubs in breaks or after school.*
- *Schools provide visits and taster sessions at local sports centres.*
- *Schools open up their facilities on weekends and holidays.*
- *Schools offer a wider range of activities including outdoor recreation.*

c) Outline the basic requirements needed to undertake sport or recreation.   *3 marks*

Answer

Sport and Recreation require:

- *Time - free time or leisure time.*
- *Money - disposable income.*
- *Transport / mobility to get to a facility.*
- *Access to a sport / recreation facility*
- *Access to a space to play (local sports centre).*
- *Resources (kit / clothing / equipment).*
- *Fitness at a basic level.*
- *Some activities require good health (GP check up sometimes advisable).*
- *Ability and a certain skill level.*
- *Knowledge of the game / sport.*
- *Enthusiasm for the sport.*

6) a) Leisure is time in which there is the opportunity for choice. Use an example of a leisure activity to explain this statement.   *4 marks*

Answer

- *Free time is a fundamental feature of leisure.*
- *Opportunity - although leisure facilities may exist it must be available for you.*
- *Choices - your right whether to engage or not :*
    - *your choice of activity*
    - *your choice of where and when.*

Application to a suitable leisure activity. Choose your own example:

- *For example, hill walking requires the time (days at a time), the opportunity (how near you are to suitable hills, or have you the transport to get there), and the choice (I would rather sit in front of the TV and watch the rugby).*

b) Explain the changes which occur as the concept of leisure is narrowed to reflect a 'Sport for All' campaign.   *4 marks*

Answer

- *Time - your time commitment is increasingly controlled.*
- *Space - specialised areas are increasingly required.*
- *Spontaneous - increasingly rule based / controlled by officials.*
- *Enjoyment - continues, but includes more extreme emotions, such as joy on the one hand and pain on the other.*
- *Intrinsic - continues, but increasingly with extrinsic influences.*
- *Non-serious - increasingly serious / increasingly productive.*

7 a) Select a children's play activity and use figure C.29 to explain the characteristics of play which should be evident while they participate in this activity.   *4 marks*

Answer

Choose a play activity (tag, hopscotch, chase, skipping etc):

- *Time - there are limited constraints on how long / when they play the activity.*
- *Space - there are very few constraints on where the activity can be played.*
- *Enjoyment - played with a fun element.*
- *Spontaneous - played with minimal rules.*

b) Explain why it is thought that when children play they increase mastery over reality whereas adults at play tend to be escaping from reality.

4 marks

Answer

Children increase mastery because :

- *Practice - repetition of skills.*
- *Pretend - learn through make-believe.*
- *Rehearse - play is often rehearsing activity in real life.*

Adults escape from reality because :

- *Obligations - takes them away from work.*
- *Stress relief - escape from anxieties.*
- *Relaxing - relief from effort based activity.*
- *Fun - release from serious emotions.*

8) Briefly discuss the view that play is more than an activity, but also a valuable experience.

5 marks

Answer

- *As an activity play allows the child to be free to choose to participate.*
- *To choose how long to play / where to play / freedom of time / space.*
- *They are having fun / emotionally enjoyable / non-serious activity.*
- *As an experience, there is skill learning going on.*
- *Relationships and friendships are being forged.*
- *They are learning more about themselves / developing a self-concept.*
- *Mastering reality through the experience of play.*

9) Outdoor education is a means of approaching educational objectives through adventurous activities in the natural environment.
a) Select an outdoor adventurous activity and explain it in terms of four levels of adventure.

5 marks

Answer

Level one:

- *A process of discovery in a new environment which is exciting but safe*
- *For example, canoeing on a canal or calm lake or river or swimming baths.*

Level two:

- *An element of adventure where skills and confidence will be tested but where risks will be minimal.*
- *For example, canoeing down a white water river with flattened rapids and elements of endurance.*

Level three:

- *Adventure at the upper level of the performer's ability, testing prowess and temperament, but with full safety procedures in place.*
- *For example, white water canoeing on graded water involving difficult rapids and falls.*

Level four:

- *Misadventure, where the performer finds themselves in real risk, facing hazards which are beyond their ability.*
- *For example, inexperienced canoeists tackling water without safety procedures in place and in adverse conditions.*

b) Use Figure C.30 to explain values associated with an outdoor adventurous activity of your choice.

5 marks

Answer

Excitement hinges on:

- *The unpredictability of the situation in a natural environment.*

Challenge involves:

- *Coping with the elements and new skills in this environment.*

Discovery concerns:

- *Dealing with the unexpected / finding out more about yourself.*

Risk exists in the form of:

- *Perceived risk by the performer and the possibility of unpredicted real risk in a hostile environment.*

One mark would be given for using an application (a recognised outdoor adventurous activity).

UNIT I – 3: THE ROLE OF SCHOOLS AND NATIONAL GOVERNING BODIES IN CREATING OPPORTUNITIES FOR INCREASING PARTICIPATION

1) What were the **main** components of the 1902 Model Course? *3 marks*

Answer

- *Military / Army style drill.*
- *Direct teaching method.*
- *Taught by NCO's.*
- *Involves marching.*
- *Compulsory for boys and girls.*
- *Exercises with dumb bells and staves / simulating weapon.*

2) What were the **major** changes which reflected post-Second World War attitudes to movement in physical education lessons in schools? *5 marks*

Answer

- *Children made central – from the idealism of winning the war.*
- *Lessons were intended to use the discovery method, with a desire to encourage independent thinking.*
- *There was innovative apparatus which had to be learned from commando tactics and training, or the result of rebuilding programme after the bomb destruction.*
- *There were no more formal tables, with a desire for individual freedom.*
- *Learning is fun / play, developed from mother's and primary influence during the war.*
- *Skilfulness and skill central, from a desire to develop sporting links.*
- *Lots of child inspired games, as a result of a war which rated decision-making, and experiences in prisoner-of-war camps.*
- *Significance of fresh air, developed from limited travel during the war, reflecting freedom / what we fought for / experiences by evacuees.*
- *Awareness of individual differences which was learnt from rehabilitation of those injured during the war.*
- *Partner and group developments, developed from lessons learnt about sharing and caring / expression of a new post-war world.*
- *Swimming and dance were central experiences, giving children lots of choices which the war years had not allowed.*

3) Describe the basic organisational framework of Sport in the UK. *4 marks*

Answer

- *Mixed administrative pattern of state / private and voluntary status / decentralised structure.*
- *Raising the Game, 1995.*
- *UKSI / UK Sports Institution to provide Britain's best sportsmen and women with their needs.*
- *Home Country Sports Institutes for Home Countries with same roles.*
- *Sport England accountable to Parliament, with nine regional offices.*
- *Governing Bodies responsible for individual sports.*
- *English Institute of Sport, responsible for network of regional institutes.*
- *Network of centres of excellence or 'hubs' , some at universities. For example, 'hubs' are based at Bath and Loughborough Universities.*
- *The hubs contain expertise for elite performers / world class programme.*
- *Projects, such as Sports Mark to promote school sport.*
- *sports coach UK with coaching programmes in different sports.*
- *CCPR remains as a pressure group to promote sport.*

4) Young people often fail to continue with sport once they have left full-time education. Explain the reasons why this might happen. *3 marks*

Answer

- *Once a person starts work, he / she has less free time.*
- *And the commitment to work may involve work in the evenings or at weekends.*
- *Other interests might compete for time – boyfriends / girlfriends, clubbing, peer pressure.*
- *It now costs money for use of facilities.*
- *People can choose not to take part, whereas it used to be compulsory at school.*
- *Maybe people did not like sport in school.*
- *Some areas have very poor links between school and local clubs.*

5) Explain the advantages of offering activities such as tennis and basketball as part of a physical education programme in year 11 in school.   *4 marks*

Answer

- *Both sports are popular outside school.*
- *Suitable for both sexes.*
- *Based on skill and technique not strength.*
- *Most schools have sports halls or tennis courts with easily adapted equipment.*
- *Alternative to major games (hockey / soccer / rugby / netball).*
- *Can play at recreational level.*
- *Can learn sportsmanship and co-operation in both sports.*

6) Identify the theory behind the sports development pyramid and explain the intentions behind each section.   *6 marks*

Answer

- *A policy with the intention of having a place for all would be participants recognising the different levels they might achieve.*
- *This becomes a pyramid because fewer competitors can reach the highest level.*
- *The bottom level is called the foundation level.*
- *It involves low ability performers to learn basic skills / knowledge and understanding / and is often delivered as part of school PE programmes.*
- *The 2nd level is called the participation level.*
- *It involves the individual in participating in an increased number of recreational / leisure options / and awareness of health-related fitness / often promoted in extra-curricular sport.*
- *The 3rd level is for high performance athletes and is call the performance.*
- *This involves specialist coaching / development at club / regional / national levels.*
- *The top of the pyramid, excellence level, involves performers reaching national standards / with public recognition.*

7) Discuss the changing attitude to sport in the elite 19th century Public Schools and its affect on the emergence of amateur sport in the UK.   *5 marks*

Answer

- *Phase one was the initial stage of boys bringing in mob activities.*
- *These activities were pursued in the boys' free time.*
- *They were often cruel and violent / including mob games, fighting and blood sports.*
- *Phase two marked attempts by teachers to make the games socially acceptable.*
- *They allowed periods of time to play and fixed rules / produced a sports calendar.*
- *Major games specific to the school emerged / rowing developed / cross country was encouraged / fighting was stopped and boxing begun.*
- *Phase three was full athleticism, when a tradition was build up in the school with facilities and timetabling.*
- *Based on Muscular Christianity / code of honour and sportsmanship / and social control.*
- *Written rules and diverse programme / interschool games established / old students very active.*
- *Emergence of games in Girls High Schools and Old Girl's organisations.*

8) Discuss the role of Sports Colleges in the development of School Sport Partnerships (SSPs).   *4 marks*

Answer

- *Approximately 475 Sports Colleges (within England) form the centres of the SSP infrastructures.*
- *The central figure is the partnership development manager (PDM) who is normally based in the Sports College.*
- *The PDM develops links (partnerships) with surrounding schools and local facilities, such as clubs and leisure centres.*
- *SSP policy is achieved with the PDM managing a team of support staff, namely up to 8 school sport co-ordinators (SSCos) and between 30-45 primary and special school link teachers (PLTs).*
- *SSCos concentrate on the day-to-day task of improving school sport opportunities across the local family of schools within the SSP structure - including out of hours and intra and inter-school competitions.*
- *PLT's focus on improving the quality and quantity of PE and sport within their own schools.*

9) UK Sport is responsible for managing and distributing a sporting programme. How do the UK Sports Institutes co-ordinate elite sport development within the UK?   *4 marks*

Answer

There are many possible answers to this question. We have highlighted some key points.

- *UK Sport is responsible for managing and distributing public investment and funds (raised by the National Lottery).*
- *UK Sport supports the development and maintenance of facilities and elite athletes.*
- *UK Sport devolves its regional responsibilities into Home Country Sports Councils.*
- *For example English Institute of Sport (EIS) has nine multi-sport high performance centres called 'hubs'.*
- *Hubs provide world class support services, such as an Athlete Medical Scheme supporting elite performers.*
- *Elite performers are encouraged to live and train at these hubs. For example, UK elite cyclists live and train at Sports City, Manchester.*
- *Governing Bodies (within the UK Sports Institutes) organise coaching conferences supporting UK's top coaches with latest / cutting edge information, organise national competitions and pick teams for international competitions.*

UNIT 1 – 4: POTENTIAL BARRIERS TO PARTICIPATION AND POSSIBLE SOLUTIONS FOR VARIOUS TARGET GROUPS

1) Opportunities available to people in society determines their participation in sporting activities.
a) Explain the term 'inclusiveness'.

2 marks

Answer

- *Government policy in recent years has been to include all members of society in whatever the activities are.*
- *This contrasts in the past to the effective exclusion of certain parts of the population from some activities.*
- *Most people would normally expect to be able to do (to be included in) most activities*
- *Today there is a very strong move to engage disabled people in all aspects of society including sport (participation in the Paralympics is an example of this).*
- *Older people are included in all plans for sports facilities – special rates at certain times of the day for example.*
- *This can be productive for health as well as self-esteem and confidence of the people involved.*

b) Explain the term 'stereotyping'.

2 marks

Answer

- *Stereotyping is the presumed inferiority of groups.*
- *Stereotyping concerns the attitudes of parts of the population about the place and capability of other parts of the population.*
- *Usually, this takes the form of assumed inferiority, which may be based on tradition, gender, genetics / ethnicity, wealth, age or even a resistance to change.*
- *An example of stereotyping which presumes superiority in certain activities is that of the attitude of some of the white population to participation of black people in sport.*
- *The stereotype is that black people are more likely to be good at sport, but less likely to be good at academic studies.*
- *The stereotype of women assumes that female sportspeople are less capable at strength / endurance / speed activities.*

c) Explain the term 'prejudice'.

2 marks

Answer

- *Prejudice can be defined as a prejudgement of a person, group, or situation.*
- *Based on inadequate information or inaccurate or biased information which reinforces stereotypes.*
- *Prejudice is the outcome of negative attitudes and stereotyping by one part of the population towards another.*
- *An example of this is that women are often excluded from male dominated sports clubs or events.*
- *It is expected that females will not be interested or want to participate in the sport in question (golf, rugby, boxing).*
- *People prejudiced against female participation usually do not listen to or believe arguments that women should be allowed to participate.*

2) Identify the problems faced by the disabled in the sporting context and outline ways in which some of these problems have been addressed.   *5 marks*

Answer

- *The tradition is that only able-bodied people pursue sport – but there is much more opportunity today.*
- *The attitude by some disabled people is that sport is not for them through lack of self-esteem – but there has been a great deal of publicity and media coverage to show that this should not be the case.*
- *Esteem and therefore take-up is particularly poor where double discrimination exists such as ethnic, female and aged disabled – there are policies to encourage these particular groups and they have special rates of entry to facilities.*
- *A history of little or no organisation for disabled performers – there are now numerous sporting activities which enable different levels of competition.*
- *Limited provision for participation, advancement or coaching opportunities – but there are now specialist coaches and coaching courses available through UK Sport and sports coach UK.*
- *There used to be very limited access for disabled spectators or facilities – there is now a legal obligation for access to be available in all places open to the public.*
- *There used to be very limited performance pyramid development for the disabled – there is now development and media coverage of the Paralympic Games.*

3) Mass participation in sport includes a policy of 'Sport for All'.

Why is the chance to participate desirable, but the policy of 'Sport for All' difficult to implement?

6 marks

Answer

- *The desire to participate is based on the evaluation that physical exercise reflects a healthy lifestyle.*
- *That lifetime sport or lifelong physical activity is a valuable goal, and therefore worth doing.*
- *Inactivity can certainly lead to obesity and possible illnesses and premature death.*
- *Should be part of education and particularly P.E.*
- *Regularly promoted by the media and particularly sports' stars.*
- *Sport for everyone may be an ideal, but not a real possibility.*
- *In a free society, people can say no to physical activity.*
- *There may not be the opportunity to participate.*
- *There certainly isn't the provision for all.*
- *There isn't the belief by sports organisations in their programmes.*
- *There may not be the self-esteem, particularly with minority groups to begin to participate.*
- *Tendency in schools have been to sell sports facilities / focus on SATS.*
- *Though more people are attending gyms, the norm is inactivity over a certain age / affluence and sedentary jobs / careers / leads to obesity.*

4) Discuss the terms opportunity, provision and esteem in the context of female discrimination in sport. *5 marks*

Answer

- *Opportunity to participate reflects the chances women have to participate in sport compared to men.*
- *This is less a problem than in the past as opportunities today as legally gender discrimination is not acceptable.*
- *Provision to allow opportunity has not totally caught up with the law.*
- *There are still facilities, which are unsuitable for women in some sports, which have been historically used by men only, for example toilet and changing provision.*
- *Certain private club traditions have retained limitations for women, e.g. there are very few independent women's rugby clubs / equal rights in many private golf clubs.*
- *Many clubs full with predominance of young men.*
- *Some clubs remain exclusively male or female.*
- *The main problem today lies in women's low esteem regarding context of sport and participation in competitive sport.*
- *Self-conscious in a male environment / as a beginner.*
- *They presume that some sports are not suitable for them, for example boxing.*
- *They feel that their female image is damaged / becoming muscular.*
- *Certain females may be discriminated against on other grounds, such as age, race or disability.*
- *Some lack the free-time to participate, with jobs and dependents.*

5) The National Sports Councils have a role to play of identifying and targeting minority sub-cultures who for various reasons do not fully participate in Active Sport.

a) What are the **main** reasons why young women do not have as high a profile as their male counterparts in sport in the UK? *4 marks*

Answer

Four main reasons from the following:

- *Tradition - historical role of women having low sports profile.*
- *Physical - presumption that women are physically inferior.*
- *Social - present role of women as wives and mothers.*
- *Economic - only male sportspeople are fully professionalised.*
- *Media - biased media coverage towards male sport.*
- *Administration - men dominate administration, coaching and officials in top level sport.*
- *Esteem - large numbers of women do not feel equal in sport.*

b) Suggest **four** reasons why young children should be discouraged from specialising in a particular sport too early. *4 marks*

Answer

Four reasons from the following:

- *Foundation - important that young children should taste a range of different skills.*
- *Play - value of play - freedom and fun.*
- *Growth - stress on under-developed body parts.*
- *Burn-out - physical / psychological.*
- *Adolescence - body changes at puberty.*

c) Suggest reasons why women over 47 years of participate in sport less than any other minority sub-group. *4 marks*

Answer

- *Tradition - older women may not be convinced about modern trends.*
- *Influence - less organised than other groups.*
- *Social - tend to have other preferences / time filled up.*
- *Health - feel they are not fit enough / limited medical advice.*
- *Esteem - sense of embarrassment.*
- *Administration - not adequately catered for.*
- *Preference and availability - perhaps older women would prefer dancing and this is not offered at the local leisure centre.*

d) Explain the contradiction that there are many black professional soccer players, but very few black soccer spectators. *4 marks*

Answer

Black soccer players have:

- *Ability - proved themselves as talented or more talented than white players.*
- *Attitude - are as committed to club and game.*
- *Tradition - have been through this discrimination barrier.*
- *Professional - not drawn from a local community.*

Black spectators have:

- *Tradition - local fan tradition against acceptance.*
- *Racism - racist feelings still existing despite legislation.*
- *Attitudes - emotional / vulgar crowd behaviour is threatening.*
- *Historical - limited affinity with soccer until recently.*
- *Constraint - not worth taking the risk of being subjected to racial abuse or violence.*

6) Suggest reasons why rugby football is still only played by a small proportion of women.

4 marks

Answer

Opportunity:

- *Most girls do not learn the game at school.*
- *There are virtually no women-only rugby clubs.*
- *Still limited number of men's clubs running women's teams.*

Provision:

- *Facilities are not readily available for women.*
- *There are very few female coaches.*
- *The media fails to give the women's game any coverage.*
- *Sponsorship is limited.*

Esteem:

- *It is traditionally a man's game, organised by men.*
- *Women generally regard themselves to be too physically weak to play the game.*
- *They feel to play is to threaten their feminine image.*
- *Rejected as unsuitable by many men.*

7) Explain the popularity of track and field athletics to Afro-Caribbean (A-C) performers.

4 marks

Answer

The popularity of track and field to A-C performers is caused by:

- *A-C role models make it attractive to young A-C performers.*
- *An inexpensive sport, basics are taught in all schools.*
- *Top A-C performers and coaches give time and encouragement to help the next generation.*
- *A dream of making a break out, financially and socially.*
- *Natural athletic interest and potential.*
- *Popular for young males and females.*
- *Colourful and sponsored activity.*

F

G

INDEX